# OPERATION GOMORRAH

## The Hamburg Firestorm Raids

# HAMBURG—THE GOMORRAH ATTACKS

# OPERATION GOMORRAH

## The Hamburg Firestorm Raids

Gordon Musgrove

JANE'S
LONDON · NEW YORK · SYDNEY

First published in the United Kingdom in 1981 by
Jane's Publishing Company Limited
238 City Road, London EC1V 2PU

ISBN 0 7106 0079 8

Published in the United States of America by
Jane's Publishing Incorporated
730 Fifth Avenue
New York
NY 10019

ISBN 0 531 03727 4



Printed in Great Britain by
Hartnoll Print Ltd,
Bodmin, Cornwall

# CONTENTS

# FOREWORD

27 May 1943
Operations Order No. 173

## INFORMATION

1. The importance of Hamburg, the second largest city in Germany with a population of 1½ millions, is well known and needs no further emphasis. The total destruction of this city would achieve immeasurable results in reducing the industrial capacity of the enemy's war machine. This, together with the effect on German morale, which would be felt throughout the country, would play a very important part in shortening and in winning the war.
2. The 'Battle of Hamburg' cannot be won in a single night. It is estimated that at least 10,000 tons of bombs will have to be dropped to complete the process of elimination. To achieve the maximum effect of air bombardment this city should be subjected to sustained attack.

### Forces to be Employed.

3. Bomber Command forces will consist of all available heavies in operational squadrons until sufficient hours of darkness enable the medium bombers to take part. It is hoped that the night attacks will be preceded and/or followed by heavy daylight attacks by the United States VIIIth Bomber Command.

## INTENTION

4. To destroy Hamburg.

## EXECUTION

### Issue of Orders.

5. Detailed instructions for each individual attack will be issued from this Headquarters on Form 'A' in the normal way.
6. The initial attacks are to be made with the maximum force of heavy bombers available in operational squadrons. The opening waves are to be made by one third of the crews from each Group. These crews are to be the most experienced available. The timing of these and subsequent waves will be notified on Form 'A' on the day on which each operation is ordered.

Pathfinder Force.

7. The Pathfinder Force are to mark the aiming point selected and are to keep this point marked for the duration of each attack by the most suitable means available.

Bomb Loads.

8. On the first attack a large number of incendiaries are to be carried in order to saturate the Fire Service. The proportion of high explosive bombs to be carried may be increased on subsequent attacks after widespread fire damage has been achieved.
9. For the first attacks the bomb loads are to be as follows:–
   (a) All Lancasters are to carry maximum economic incendiary loads except G.S.Lancasters and 50% Lancaster II's which are to carry 8,000 lb. H.C. bombs.
   (b) Stirlings and Halifaxes are to carry 2/3rds incendiary and 1/3rd H.E. bomb loads.

Types of Bombs to be carried.

10. (a) Incendiary Bombs.

50% of incendiary containers are to be filled with 30 lb. incendiary bombs and the remaining 50% are to be filled with 4 lb. I.B's, 15% of which are to be X I.B's.

(b) High Explosive Bombs.

High Explosive bomb loads should as far as possible be made up with large H.C. bombs fused instantaneous and M.C. bombs fused T.D. .025. Where G.P. bombs have to be carried 50% of these are to be fused T.D. .025 and 50% long delay with 845 fuse and No. 37 pistol.

Routing.

11. 12. 13. (2 Routes given)

Date of Operation.

14. Attacks of this nature will be notified to Groups by a code name to be issued separately. On the morning of the operation details will be passed as outlined in paragraph 5 above.

Security.

15. It is of the utmost importance that knowledge of these operations is confined to as few individuals as possible. At present this knowledge is to be confined to A.Os-C and their S.A.S.O's only.

(Source: Public Record Office AIR 24/257)

# ACKNOWLEDGEMENTS

The author gratefully acknowledges permission from Her Majesty's Stationery Office, the Public Record Office, the Imperial War Museum and Hamburg Staatsarchiv to reproduce material and photographs. Transcripts of Crown-copyright records in the Public Record Office appear by permission of the Controller of Her Majesty's Stationery Office. The author is also indebted to the Meteorological Office at Bracknell, the Fire Research Centre (Borehamwood) and the German Weather Service (Hamburg) for their information and assistance. In addition, I should like to thank the USAF Photographic Section and Records Office for their help and willing co-operation.

Perhaps the most gratifying part of my research was the time I spent in Hamburg. In Hans Brunswig I found a man passionately keen to have the history of those ten days recorded from both sides of the North Sea, so much so that he allowed me to use material and photographs from his private source. My thanks are also due to Ben Witter, who gave me a vivid account of life in Hamburg during and after the *Gomorrah* attacks. He also introduced me to Joanne Runkel, who unstintingly gave her time to act as interpreter during interviews and to translate German documents.

I wish also to express my gratitude to Air Chief Marshal Sir Arthur Harris and Air Vice-Marshal D.C.T. Bennett for their help in clarifying controversial points; to Air Commodore John Searby for the account of his *contretemps*; to Ron Alfrey for his assistance and co-operation with maps and diagrams; to Peter Lowe for reading, correcting and criticising the manuscript; and finally to Joan, my wife, who once again did all the onerous and dull tasks without which this book would never have been completed.

# ABBREVIATIONS

| | |
|---|---|
| AA | Anti-aircraft |
| ABC | *Airborne Cigar* |
| AFCE | Automatic flight control equipment |
| AI | Air interception |
| AOC | Air Officer Commanding |
| AP | Aiming point |
| AP | Anti-personnel (bomb) |
| ASI | Airspeed indicator |
| ASV | Air-to-Surface Vessel (radar device) |
| AVM | Air Vice-Marshal |
| BCHQ | Bomber Command Headquarters |
| CAS | Chief of the Air Staff |
| Do | Dornier |
| DR | Dead reckoning (navigation) |
| ETA | Estimated time of arrival (navigation) |
| FLAK | *Flieger-Abwehr-Kanone*, German anti-aircraft force; came to mean anti-aircraft shells. |
| F/Lt | Flight Lieutenant |
| F/O | Flying Officer |
| Fw | Focke-Wulf |
| G/Capt | Group Captain |
| GCI | Ground-controlled interception |
| GP | General-purpose (bomb) |
| GPI | Ground position indicator |
| HC | High-capacity (bomb) |
| HE | High-explosive (bomb) |
| He | Heinkel |
| HQ | Headquarters |
| H2S | An aid to navigation |
| IAS | Indicated airspeed |
| IB | Incendiary bomb |
| IFF | Identification friend or foe |
| IP | Initial point |
| Ju | Junkers |
| LBTI | Long-burning target indicator |
| LD | Long-delay (bomb) |
| LNSF | Light Night Striking Force |
| MAN | *Maschinen Fabrik Augsburg-Nürnberg* |
| MC | Medium-capacity (bomb) |
| Me | Messerschmitt |
| Met | Meteorological |
| MPI | Mean point of impact |
| MT | Motor transport |
| NJG | *Nachtjagdgeschwader*, German night fighter group |
| ORB | Operations Record Book |
| ORS | Operational Research Section |
| OTU | Operational training unit |
| PFF | Pathfinder Force |
| PFFHQ | Pathfinder Force Headquarters |
| P/O | Pilot Officer |
| PoW | Prisoner of war |
| PPI | Plan position indicator |
| PRU | Photographic reconnaissance unit |
| QDM | Magnetic bearing to base |
| RAAF | Royal Australian Air Force |
| RAF | Royal Air Force |
| RCAF | Royal Canadian Air Force |
| RNZAF | Royal New Zealand Air Force |
| SAAF | South African Air Force |
| S/Ldr | Squadron Leader |
| TI | Target indicator |
| TOT | Time on target |
| TRE | Telecommunications Research Establishment |
| USAAF | United States Army Air Force |

| | |
|---|---|
| USSBS | United States Strategic Bombing Survey |
| UXB | Unexploded bomb |
| VHF | Very high-frequency (radio) |
| VLBTI | Very long-burning target indicator |
| WAAF | Commonly called Waaf, member of Women's Auxiliary Air Force |
| W/Cdr | Wing Commander |
| W/O | Warrant Officer |
| W/T | Wireless telegraphy |

# GLOSSARY

| | |
|---|---|
| Big City | Berlin. |
| Boffins | Technical scientists, "back-room boys". |
| *Boozer* | Detected enemy radar illumination of the bomber. |
| Butt Report | Collated information on the accuracy of British bombing under various weather conditions, states of the moon and types of target. Its conclusion that only one in five aircraft got within 75 miles of the target contributed to a lowering of crew morale. |
| *Carpet* | Jammer which was introduced to supplement *Window*, helping Pathfinders and stragglers who did not reap the full benefit of *Window*. |
| Cat's-Eyes fighters | See *Wild Boars*. |
| Chop rate | Average loss of aircraft on operations. |
| *Cigar* (ground) | Jammed German VHF telephonic communications. ABC was airborne *Cigar*. |
| Coned | Caught and held by searchlights |
| Cookie | 4,000lb bomb. |
| Cope | Successful *Oboe* sortie. |
| Corkscrew | Dive and climb manoeuvre in which the bomber's path resembled a corkscrew. The most successful of the evasive techniques. |
| *Corona* | Spurious, contradictory orders to German fighters. |
| Creepback | Drift of bomb impacts further and further back along the line of approach to the target. |
| Christmas trees | German name for TIs. |
| *Dartboard* | Designed to jam the Stuttgart radio transmitter broadcasting directions to German night fighters. |
| Ditching | Forced landing of an aircraft on water. |
| *Drumstick* | Was to W/T what *Corona* was to R/T. With the R/T jammed the German ground controllers resorted to W/T, although this method was slower. The confusing messages were sent out by high-powered transmitter from England. |
| *Düppel* | German name for *Window*, after small town near Berlin where it was first tried by the Germans. |
| *Fidget* | Introduced to prevent the Germans from using Main Force beacons to direct their fighters into the bomber stream. |
| *Fishpond* | Tail-warning device using H2S equipment. |

| | |
|---|---|
| Flash-over | Spontaneous combustion. |
| Gaggle | Loose formation formed by British bombers on daylight operations. |
| *Gardening* | Minelaying in enemy waters. The mines were called *Vegetables*; the areas were given terms like *Forget-me-not* and *Artichoke*. |
| *Gee* | Radar aid to navigation employing at least three ground stations. See Appendix II. |
| *Goodwood* | Maximum effort. |
| Graviner | Fire extinguisher placed near the aircraft engines. Three methods of detonation: either automatically by thermostatic control or manually by button or switch. |
| *Grocer* | Temporary ground-controlled jamming of German AI equipment. |
| Happy Valley | The Ruhr Valley. |
| *Hauptbahnhof* | German, main railway station. |
| H2S | Radar aid to navigation and target identification. See Appendix III. |
| J beams | Radio signals beamed onto points in Germany as an aid to navigation. First used in an effort to keep *Gee* a secret until enough sets had been manufactured to equip the Main Force. |
| *Jostle* | Device for jamming German radar, especially AA barrage. |
| *Knickebein* | German navigation and bombing aid. |
| *Korfu* | Device used by German submarines to give an early warning of the approach of British aircraft; forerunner of *Naxos*. |
| Lapse rate | The rate of change in the temperature of the atmosphere with height; approximately 3°F per 1,000 feet. |
| *Little Screws* | German ground-controlled night fighters orbited these ground beacons until called to make an interception, and returned to them afterwards. |
| *Luftschutzleiter* | German, air protection leader. |
| *Luftschutzwart* | German, air-raid warden. |
| *Mandrel* | Radio swamping of the German early-warning system. |
| Marking techniques | *Newhaven*, *Parramatta* and *Wanganui*. See Appendix IV. |
| *Monica* | Tail-warning device emitting a series of pips which increased in tempo as the two aircraft drew nearer; range could be preset. |
| *Musical* | The adjective Musical was added to *Parramatta* and *Wanganui* when *Oboe* aircraft dropped the primary markers. |
| *Naxos* | German radar device enabling fighters to home onto transmissions from British bombers using H2S, *Fishpond* and *Monica*. |
| *Newhaven* | Visual ground marking. See Appendix IV. |
| *Oboe* | Blind-bombing radar device. |
| *Pampa* | Code name for meteorological operation. |
| Pan | Concrete dispersal point for aircraft, usually circular. |
| *Parramatta* | Blind ground marking using radar. See Appendix IV. |
| *Pinetrees* | Code name for USAAF HQ. |

| | |
|---|---|
| Purple Heart | US military decoration awarded to any member of the armed forces wounded in action. |
| Purple Heart Corner | The name given to the low group in an Eighth Air Force formation because it was the most vulnerable. A system of rotation between groups was instituted. |
| Random error | The MPI of all bombs aimed at a target. |
| *Sampson* | Blind *Gee* bombing attack. |
| Scrambler | Telecommunications device which made conversation garbled to an eavesdropper. |
| Scrub | RAF slang for cancellation. |
| *Shaker* | Method of illuminating and marking a target with the aid of *Gee*-equipped aircraft. |
| Spoof | Subsidiary attack designed to draw the fighters away from the Main Force. |
| *Splasher* beacons | British MF beacons situated at intervals over the East Anglian countryside. |
| *Strasse* | German, street; usually written as one word with the name of the street. |
| Systematic error | When crews were ordered to bomb target indicators and not attempt to identify the target for themselves the random error decreased dramatically but a new error was introduced: "the displacement of the markers from the aiming point". This was known as the systematic error. |
| Tour | Time spent on an operational squadron. |
| *Wanganui* | Blind skymarking. See Appendix IV. |
| *Wehrmacht* | German armed forces. |
| *Wild Boars* | "Freelance" German night fighters, also known as Cat's-Eyes fighters. |
| *Tinsel* | Code name for British airborne jamming of telephonic communication between German night fighters and ground controllers. |
| "Y" aircraft | Aircraft equipped with H2S. |
| "Y" Service | British-based monitoring of communications between German ground controllers and night fighters. |
| *Zephyrs* | Averaged winds from selected crews, broadcast to all bombers. |
| Zero hour | Scheduled time for the attack to open; sometimes referred to as H hour; Z−3 means 3 minutes before zero hour, Z+3 means 3 minutes after. |

# Chapter I

# A Raid is Planned

THE SCENE opens at Bomber Command Headquarters, High Wycombe; the date, July 24, 1943; the time, 0900 hours. Through the door leading into the underground bunker, Bomber Command's operations room, stepped the Commander-in-Chief, Air Chief Marshal Sir Arthur T. Harris, followed closely by the Deputy C-in-C, Air Marshal Sir Robert Saundby. Harris walked purposefully towards the centre of the room, where a table and chair were set for this daily routine. The sound of the door opening was a signal for the many acolytes, who had been assembling for the past 30 minutes or more, to gather in a semicircle round the table. On the wall behind them was a huge board which recorded the availability of crews and aircraft by squadrons; along the bottom was a total by Groups and also a grand total. At 1800 hours the previous day each Group had sent in a Form G giving the availability figures for the following day (**Fig 1**). Since these figures were compiled at this fixed time, often before the bombers had taken off for their target, revised figures had to be phoned in to HQ when losses and damage had been assessed after an operation. As aircraft became serviceable, when crews returned from leave and the sick and injured became fit for duty, the figures were updated. The board was referred to as the "Tote" because of the constant changes in the odds. To their right, on the wall at the end of the room, was a map of the British Isles with all the RAF stations plotted on it. Each station had two small bulbs – one red, one green – to denote its state of serviceability. On the opposite wall on their left was a large map of Europe on which the route would later be marked in red tape.

As soon as the C-in-C sat down, Mr Magnus Spence, Command Meteorological Officer,[1] stepped forward and placed the weather chart on the table in front of him, where there was already a map of Europe. Saundby stood motionless behind his chief's chair, almost daring anyone to move. Harris discussed the weather prospects with his met chief, studied the synoptic chart and then scratched his lapel, his unique way of indicating that he had finished with it. Spence stepped forward and took it from the table. The Air Chief Marshal looked over the map as if trying to locate the target and then he said three words: "Hamburg, *Goodwood*,[2] late[3]". He then rose from the chair, looked casually round the semicircle and retreated through the door by which he had entered minutes earlier.[4]

---

1. Spence had already discussed the met situation with the Group met officers as daily routine, and with the Meteorological Office at Dunstable.
2. Maximum effort.
3. Zero hour to be after midnight.
4. There are other accounts describing the proceedings at Bomber Command HQ and undoubtedly Harris may have behaved differently from time to time. When Bomber Command was operating both day and night in 1944 and when the Army phoned for help, the procedure would be different, but certainly in 1943 he had done his homework before he came to the bunker. Harris himself showed me the well-known

*(Continued on next page)*

**Figure 1: Consolidated Form G, 1800 hours, August 2, 1943**

| | | AIRCRAFT | | | OPERATIONALL | | |
|---|---|---|---|---|---|---|---|
| (A) Group | (B) Type of aircraft | Aircraft establishment | Aircraft strength (operational squadrons) | (C) Aircraft fit | (D) Operationally fit | (H) Leave | (J) Non-effective |
| 1 | Lancaster | 120 | 120 | 122 | 143 | 34 | 14 |
| 3 | Stirling | 136 | 126 | 116 | 113 | 19 | 22 |
| 3 | Lancaster | 16 | 16 | 18 | 17 | 3 | 3 |
| 4 | Halifax | 168 | 168 | 159 | 171 | 41 | 25 |
| 5 | Lancaster | 176 | 171 | 153 | 197 | 50 | 22 |
| 6 | Halifax | 64 | 64 | 66 | 76 | 11 | 12 |
| 6 | Lancaster | — | — | — | — | — | — |
| 8 | Lancaster | 88 | 88 | 76 | 73/14 | 16/1 | 3/1 |
| 8 | Halifax | 40 | 40 | 42 | 26/16 | 8 | 1 |
| | HEAVIES | 808 | 793 | 752 | 846 | 183 | 103 |
| 1 | Wellington | 40 | 40 | 42 | 44 | 10 | 7 |
| 4 | Wellington | 16 | 16 | 16 | 19 | 2 | 3 |
| 6 | Wellington | 32 | 32 | 28 | 27 | 8 | 8 |
| | MEDIUM | 88 | 88 | 86 | 90 | 20 | 18 |
| 8 | Mosquito | 40 | 39 | 40 | 47/1 | 6 | 3 |
| | LIGHT | 40 | 39 | 40 | 48 | 6 | 3 |
| | GRAND TOTAL | 936 | 920* | 878 | 984 | 209 | 124 |

* As at 1800 hours, August 1, 1943. (Source: Public Record Office AIR 24/257)

The remainder of this chapter describes the activities of the various Bomber Command units and the involvement of the many thousands of people concerned with the "target for tonight," and takes the reader up to the moment when the first route markers fell at 53°43N 08°36E, some 60 miles to the north-west of Hamburg. The target was no real surprise – Hamburg had been "on the menu" for two days – but bad weather had caused its cancellation previously, and Operation *Gomorrah*[5] was of the highest priority.

At Pathfinder Headquarters in Huntingdon, Air Vice-Marshal D.C.T. Bennett and his team were assembled to await the call from High Wycombe. The Pathfinder Force, which had been functioning for almost a year, had by now become the focal point of all Bomber Command attacks – Main Force crews were briefed to bomb on PFF markers –

*(Continued from page 1)*

painting of his briefing, which showed Saundby to be the only one behind his chair. He pointed out other people in the group and mentioned particularly the liaison officers, whose backgrounds he knew, and explained why they were there. I am equally certain that the weather was the only factor that concerned him at that time, and he has repeatedly said this. When he entered the briefing room he knew where the force was going – weather permitting – and also the alternative targets. Occasionally he did ask his Air 1 a question but it would be on a technical point and in no way influenced his decision. Like any good leader he left the details to his Air Staff, and Saundby was so efficient that only rarely was Harris called upon to make further decisions, except to cancel an operation.

5. Code name for this series of attacks on Hamburg.

| T CREWS | | CREWS IN CONVERSION UNITS AND NON-OPERATIONAL SQUADRONS | | | | | |
|---|---|---|---|---|---|---|---|
| tablishment, perational squadrons | Total in columns D, H, J | (G) Squadrons re-equipping, forming and training | (L) Under training in conversion units | (M) Converting in squadrons | Establishment, conversion units and non-operational sqns | Total in columns G, L, M | Aircraft with crews |
| 165 | 191 | — | 141 | 2 | 108 | 143 | 122 |
| 187 | 154 | 18 | 117 | 30 | 163 | 165 | 106 |
| 22 | 23 | — | 9 | — | 6 | 9 | 17 |
| 231 | 237 | — | 153 | 28 | 108 | 181 | 156 |
| 242 | 269 | 16 | 165 | 29 | 130 | 210 | 152 |
| 88 | 99 | 45 | 53 | 5 | 134 | 103 | 65 |
| — | — | 29 | 4 | — | 34 | 33 | — |
| 121 | 108 | — | — | 18/1 | — | 19 | 73 |
| 55 | 51 | — | — | 5 | — | 5 | 40 |
| 1111 | 1132 | 108 | 642 | 118 | 683 | 868 | 731 |
| 55 | 61 | — | — | 3 | — | 3 | 42 |
| 22 | 24 | — | — | 1 | — | 1 | 16 |
| 44 | 43 | — | — | — | — | — | 26 |
| 121 | 128 | — | — | 4 | — | 4 | 84 |
| 50 | 57 | — | 28 | 11 | 42 | 39 | 35 |
| 50 | 57 | — | 28 | 11 | 42 | 39 | 35 |
| 1282 | 1317 | 108 | 670 | 133 | 725 | 911 | 850 |

and somewhere along the line the responsibility for planning the routes had been transferred to Bennett.[6]

Saundby, who had not retreated with his chief, now took command, and his first job was to phone Bennett. "Can you scramble?"[7] Bennett and Saundby repeated aloud what each said to the other so that both their staffs knew precisely what was discussed, ensuring that no details were overlooked. The target usually came first. Immediately this was announced, Bennett's navigation officer – who was already standing in front of the large map of Europe, which took up the whole of the wall at one end of the PFF ops room – stuck a red pin in the town and began planning the routes. On this Saturday morning the usual procedure was unnecessary because they had been planned on the Thursday, when the target was first proposed. Next, Saundby announced the size of the force, the bomb load, including the percentage of incendiary bombs (IBs), and the zero hour (time on target). On the 24th *Window*[8] would be used for the first time and there was to be some *Gardening*[9] by 6 Group in the Elbe estuary.

6. No one seems to know precisely when this happened, but as Bennett selected the method of marking the target he was obviously best able to say how the Main Force should approach the aiming point.
7. A telecommunications device which made conversation garbled to any eavesdropper.
8. A radar countermeasure. See Appendix I and Glossary.
9. Code name for laying mines (*Vegetables*). Mines were dropped along the whole of the North European seaboard from Denmark to Bordeaux, in the river estuaries and the sea lanes.

Then followed the discussions. The route would be the one planned previously. The duration of the attack, the type of marking and the size of the marking force required to keep a good supply of target indicators (TIs) burning in the target area throughout the attack were the main items. To try to prevent creepback some Pathfinder crews (Recenterers) were to re-mark the aiming point at intervals throughout the attack. In addition, selected PFF crews would pass their latest winds to 8 Group HQ, where they would be averaged to produce *Zephyrs* and relayed to other Group HQs, which in turn relayed them to the bombers. It was hoped that in this manner crews would bomb more accurately. Finally, Saundby wanted to know how Bennett proposed to use his Mosquito force.

The Main Force usually attacked in waves. The first wave was drawn from all Groups and invariably comprised only senior crews who could be relied upon not to bomb before the TIs were dropped. As the marking was to be *Newhaven* (visual ground marking) it was essential that no IBs were dropped before the TIs went down; although light was needed to help identification, the incendiaries were so bright that they tended to blind the bomb-aimers and obscure ground detail. If this first wave started a significant fire the attack was invariably a success. With six Groups converging on one position – in this instance 54°45N 07°00E – from different areas in England, and because the four types of bombers flew at different heights, a sequence of waves had to be worked out to prevent collisions.

At the same time as Bennett and Saundby were having their discussion other members of the HQ team were passing information by phone to the five bomber Groups (1, 3, 4, 5 and 6): target, bomb loads and crew requirements were the chief items. In addition, the information was passed to the USAAF, the Royal Navy HQ, Fighter Command, Coastal Command, Training Command and Army HQ. The Navy, which had two liaison officers permanently at Bomber Command HQ, was interested in mining operations, and all Commands needed to know each other's movements. The Navy and convoys were naturally apprehensive of approaching aircraft, and "Shoot first, apologise later" was a reasonable policy from their point of view. Fighter Command had to be told, since the normal hazards to the bombers were more than enough without being chased all over East Anglia by friendly fighters.[10] Fighter Command sent aircraft to patrol night fighter airfields and harass the enemy. Training Groups had to be put in the picture to prevent crews from OTUs (operational training units) from being in the vicinity of Main Force aerodromes during the times of take-off and landing. Coastal Command was in charge of the Air/Sea Rescue launches which were on alert during all operations, both night and day, ready to go to the aid of any unfortunate crew who had to ditch in the sea. The Army, in charge of ground defence, also had to know the plans: far too many RAF aircraft were used for target practice,[11] particularly near the coast.

Group Commanders were allowed to select their own met officers, and each considered his the best. In this Bennett was no exception. Immediately he had put down his phone Senior Met Officer Mr M.J. Thomas placed his synoptic chart in front of the CO and gave his interpretation of the weather situation. The method of marking, *Newhaven*,

10. In spite of these precautions it still happened, though only rarely.
11. Not necessarily always due to slackness on the Army's part, for bomber crews sometimes forgot to switch on their IFF (Identification friend or foe).

was finalised, the position of the route markers decided, the colours of the TIs selected and the route confirmed. Then Bennett departed and left the details to Air Commodore C.D.C. Boyce, his Senior Air Staff Officer (SASO).

Flying personnel were required to clock in at the flight commander's office by 0900 hours, unless they had been operating the previous night, when they did not report until 1400 hours. On a table just inside the door there were three boxes of vitamin AD, B and C pills; they were there to be taken but were not compulsory. A fourth box contained "wakey-wakey pills" (benzedrine), which were principally for the gunners; they did not consume these until shortly before take-off. By 1000 hours the stations had received the target and the crew requirements. The Squadron Commander called in his Flight Commanders and the crews were selected for the battle order. Next, the captains (usually the pilots) were informed and they passed the word to their crews.

Only the Station Commanders, the Squadron Commanders and the Intelligence Officers were supposed to know the target, and it was the rule[12] that immediately the target was known outgoing calls of a private nature were forbidden. Most stations had somewhere where this target information could be obtained; at Leconfield it was the cookhouse, where a favourite few would be told. Speaking personally, my second visit was to the met office, where the met man was always ready to discuss the local weather and conditions on the Continent. Although he would be at briefing, the information he gave then was controlled by Group Met.

So far all the information from High Wycombe and the Groups had been given by telephone. The first teleprinter communication was the A Form (**Fig 2**), which was sent out by Command to all Groups to confirm the verbal orders; it contained each Group's commitment, together with the target. Then came the Notes; there were seven on the 24th. Those of immediate concern were the route, the bomb load and the "H" (zero) hour. By lunchtime all the stations had received the route, which would be put on the map in the station briefing room and covered from prying eyes.

In the summer briefing was usually around 1700 hours, and before then the time seemed to go all too slowly. Most crews checked their flying equipment. Navigators made sure they had plenty of sharp pencils, two pairs of dividers, a protractor, a ruler and an ICAN computer, and they also checked their sextants; even in the days of *Gee*[13] it could be a lifesaver. Bomb-aimers would check their maps, and the rest of the crew did anything to fill in the time until lunch. Everything possible was done to prevent tension later in the day.

When the Squadron Commanders had selected their crews the full crew list was passed back to Group. Each Group's ops room had a crew board on which the captain's name and his aircraft letter were chalked up, usually by squadrons.

It might appear that so far only the administrative staff had been working, but that would be far from the truth. The stations' ground staff had been at work on the bombers since 0800 hours, and although on the 24th their charges had been ready for ops for the past two days, there were still the daily chores and everything had to be checked. By 0900 hours the technical Flight Sergeant had his "state of readiness" (number of serviceable aircraft) for his Flight Commander. If there were problems he could report

12. Not necessarily the practice.
13. See Appendix.

**Figure 2: Order of battle, August 2/3, 1943 (signal from Bomber Command HQ to Groups)**

| Group | Number of aircraft | Primary target |
|---|---|---|
| 1 | 118 | Operation on Hamburg |
| | 32 | Operation on Hamburg |
| | 6 | Minelaying, Heligoland Approach |
| 3 | 95 | Operation on Hamburg |
| | 16 | Operation on Hamburg |
| 4 | 146 | Operation on Hamburg |
| | 12 | Operation on Hamburg |
| 5 | 140 | Operation on Hamburg |
| 6 | 56 | Operation on Hamburg |
| | 21 | Operation on Hamburg |
| 8 | 32 | Markers on Hamburg |
| | 52 | Markers on Hamburg |
| | 27 | Operation on Hamburg |
| | 10 | 5 on Hamburg, 5 on Duisburg |

**Note 1**

| | |
|---|---|
| 1st wave: | 55 Lancasters of 1 Group and 54 Lancasters of 5 Group, Z plus 2m to Z plus 10m |
| 2nd wave: | 16 Lancasters of 3 Group, 37 Halifax of 4 Group and 56 Halifax of 6 Group, Z plus 10m to Z plus 18m |
| 3rd wave: | 95 Stirlings of 3 Group, Z plus 18m to Z plus 25m |
| 4th wave: | 32 Wellingtons of 1 Group, 40 Halifax and 12 Wellingtons of 5 Group, and 21 Wellingtons of 6 Group, Z plus 25m to Z plus 33m |
| 5th wave: | 69 Halifax of 4 Group and 40 Lancasters of 5 Group, Z plus 33m to Z plus 41m |
| 6th wave: | 63 Lancasters of 1 Group and 46 Lancasters of 5 Group, Z plus 41m to Z plus 49m |

**Note 2**
Bomb load: "ARSON" except that Lancasters IIs are to carry maximum number of 8,000lb bombs.

**Note 3**
Route: BASE — 54.20N 07.00E — 53.45N 08.32E — 53.00N 10.00E — TARGET — 54.00N 10.00E — 54.30N 07.00E — BASE.

**Note 4**
Zero hour: 2000 hours, but Groups are to be prepared for an early start.

**Note 5**
The method of marking the target will be broadcast by AOC PFF.

**Note 6**
"WINDOW" is to be used in accordance with BC Operation Instruction No 70. Rate of discharge — RATE "C". On the return flight aircraft are to continue to discharge "WINDOW" until west of 06.00E.

**Note 7**
Aiming points: First 4 waves — 4,000 yards, 3° from HAMBURG "D". 5th and 6th waves — 1,050 yards, 341° from G.S. 151. All crews are to be specially warned at briefing that the A/P is changed after the first 4 waves have attacked.

(Source: Public Record Office AIR 24/257)

on the chances of any aircraft in doubt being ready in time for take-off. From this report the Flight Commander decided which aircraft needed an air test (the NFT, night flying test), and usually the crew who were to take it on the operation carried out the test during the morning.

Engineers, fitters, radio and instruments mechanics were all at work checking and re-checking for faults. The Flight Sergeant in charge of these men had a small office in a hut situated conveniently within reach of the dispersal pans[14] which housed the aircraft under his care. The Form 700 was technically the most important document in his charge, and each aircraft had its own. It was tabulated, and across the top was a list of all the items which had to be checked daily, with the dates going down the left-hand side. Special checks were made before a sortie and the person who carried out the check initialled the Form 700 in the appropriate column. The checks were very comprehensive: for example, each engine had its own column, in which its serviceability was vouched for. When the Flight Sergeant was satisfied that the inspection had been carried out efficiently and all the columns were initialled he put his own signature on the document. The aircraft was then ready to fly. Other important data entered on the form were time of take-off and time of landing for every flight, providing a running total of the number of hours the aircraft had flown. The aim was to keep the aircraft constantly airworthy, but even more thorough inspections were advised from time to time.

Flight mechanics A & E (airframes and engines), electricians and armourers (guns) were attached to only one aircraft. Ground crews took an inordinate pride in their charges. Aircrew might have been the "glamour boys," but an aircraft represented its ground crew on the sortie. If it came back damaged they tended its wounds more conscientiously than any doctor or nurse looked after a patient. Other sections worked on groups of aircraft, the numbers varying according to the establishment. There were no hard and fast rules because when ground crew became sick or went on leave the Flight Sergeant could deploy his men as the situation demanded.

The work of the sections overlapped: many of the instruments could only be tested when a particular engine was running; the electricians had to co-operate with both armourers (bombs) and the instrument section; the bomber had very little spare space inside, and it was impossible to pass someone without touching. The navigator's and wireless operator's compartments were full of equipment of one type or another; there was always competition for these niches. The compass, *Gee*, air position indicator (API) over the navigator's table, his light, oxygen point and intercom, and H2S (if fitted) were all serviced by different people. The wireless operator was even more hemmed in, particularly if he was using special equipment. The armourers (guns) were probably less subject to interference than many of the others – their work was done at the nose, tail or halfway down the fuselage – but without some co-operation they could hold up or be held up by someone testing the intercom or the oxygen. All the oxygen points had to be tested and the spare bottles checked.

The Photographic Section suffered from chronic undermanning (if this is the right word for a unit which comprised many female personnel). Initially, when only a small percentage of aircraft carried cameras, they may not have been overworked, but by July

14. Circular concrete areas scattered in groups outside the perimeter track, often on the far side of the airfield and away from the main buildings, to guard against a large number of aircraft being destroyed by a hit-and-run raider.

1943 cameras were carried in most Bomber Command aircraft and certainly in all of 8 Group's. S/Ldr H.W. Lees, 8 Group's photographic leader, remarked that it was no mean feat for a Waaf[15] to fit a heavy F24 camera into a Lancaster. They worked long hours: Chapter III finds them hard at work once again after the aircraft had landed, since the Group Commander required a set of prints on his desk by early morning. Photographs were the crews' proof that they had dropped the bombs in the right place, and ORS (Operational Research Section) used them to make a bomb plot of the attack.

However, all the other sections might have claimed with some justification to be understaffed. Perhaps the Air Ministry did not realise the strain imposed on ground crews, who worked against time for long hours, in all weathers, in wet clothing when it rained, freezing cold in the winter and sweltering hot in the summer. In addition, they were often blamed unfairly by aircrew if a piece of equipment did not function perfectly, and by the officer in charge of their section if it caused an early return.

The petrol load varied with each trip and each type of aircraft; the amount to be carried was stated in the B Form. While the final decision did rest with the stations, some very good reason would have to be given if the Group figure[16] was not strictly adhered to.

At 1155 hours details of the bomb loads were received at the stations. An Air Staff Armaments Officer attended the 9 o'clock conference and he would go back to his office and ring all the Group Armament Officers to discuss loads and types, though only in general terms. Much thought and careful planning by armament staff went into the preparation of basic loads which could be held in readiness in the bomb dump. Next to flying personnel, armourer (bombs) was the most dangerous occupation in Bomber Command. The war establishment allowed only two teams per flight of 10 aircraft and, on average, it took one team an hour to fuse the bombs in the loading shed and bomb-up one aircraft. So for a maximum effort, usually 10 aircraft from each flight, and allowing for the inevitable delays, which admittedly would include a mug of tea and a wad, bombing-up took the best part of six hours.

Fusing mixed loads was always a hazardous task. Although the following incident took place on July 25, 1943, it serves to show the daily risks run by anyone working in the bomb dump, where a mistake usually cost the lives of everyone in the vicinity. At 1810 hours, during a fusing operation in the Graveley bomb dump, a 1,000lb general-purpose bomb exploded, killing seven people. The armourers were under pressure and, although it was against the rules to use the No 37 arming pistol near a mixed load of bombs, the Air Ministry inquiry reached the conclusion that someone took a chance.

Boyce's first task after Bennett had left the PFF ops room was to prepare a notice entitled "Method for Tonight" and send it by teleprinter to the other Groups. From this information and the A Form each Group compiled a B Form, which was transmitted to all the stations within the Group. It contained the other Groups' commitment and its own by squadrons: the target, the routes, the zero hour, the times of each wave, the fuel and bomb loads, the special instructions and the method of marking.

On July 24, 1943, the special instructions included the use of *Window*, the rate at which it was to be dropped, and the latitude and longitude positions for starting and

---

15. Member of Women's Auxiliary Air Force (WAAF), commonly called Waaf.
16. Groups were not equidistant from the target, so the amount of petrol required varied with each Group.

stopping. For *Zephyrs*, the times of broadcast were listed. Then came the Pathfinders' method of marking (Source: Public Record Office AIR 25/156):

1. The Pathfinder method will be NEWHAVEN ground marking.
2. Route-markers T.I. Yellow will be dropped by the aid of special equipment at position A, 54°11N 08°50E as an aid to navigation on the way to the target.
3. The aiming point will be marked with Ground Markers T.I. Red dropped by visual markers, backed up by Ground Markers T.I. Green. Long sticks of flares, White Illuminating and Ground Markers T.I. Yellow may be seen in the target area, but these are for the exclusive benefit of the P.F.F. and are to be strictly ignored by the Main Force.
4. Main Force aircraft should aim their bombs at the T.I. Red if seen, otherwise at the centre of the pattern of T.I. Green.
5. On the way home Route-markers T.I. Yellow will be dropped at position E, 53°43N 08°36E as an aid to navigation.

At first glance it seems complicated, but it proved straightforward if the Intelligence Officer passed the information clearly and concisely and the crews were paying attention. Even new crews had seen a demonstration by PFF while they were still at OTU, and their pilots had also had actual experience over the target.[17] Lastly came the information for navigators, which included the bearings of the "J" beams[18] which were operating that night.

The C Notice (it was not referred to as a Form) was the only other pre-operational form sent out from Bomber Command HQ. If any change in the plans was necessary it was sent in a C Notice. There were none on the 24–25th, but on the 27–28th the change from *Newhaven* to *Parramatta*[19] made it necessary to despatch one.

Briefing in the summer began at 1700 hours on most stations, with the crews assembling in the briefing room from 15 minutes beforehand. In almost every crew there was someone who was superstitious, and the briefing room was the one place where it was unashamedly manifest. It took all sorts of forms: the crew must sit in the third row; the captain must go in first or the rear gunner last; the navigator must sit next to the wireless operator; the bomb-aimer must ask a question. These were but a few of the rituals which most of them would probably refuse to admit to today.

Methods varied from Group to Group and Station to Station, but invariably a senior officer, either the Station or Squadron Commander, would lead and control the briefing, assisted by specialist officers. As he came through the door the room would be called to attention. The first duty was the roll call. In practice the captain was responsible for making sure his crew was present, so to save time only his name was called out and it was accepted that he was answering for his crew. Then the Commanding Officer would uncover the chart which showed the target and routes. If the target was well defended, like Berlin or the Ruhr, the audience would express their feelings with low-pitched murmurings or groans. Italian sorties produced an entirely different

17. Before taking their own crew on ops most captains acted as second pilots on a sortie with an experienced crew.
18. See Glossary.
19. See Appendix IV.

response, since the targets were comparatively easy. It was the length of time that crews were exposed to the danger of fighters or mechanical failure, and the fatigue from being constantly on the alert, that caused concern on these operations.

A description of the route[20] came first, then the zero hour, the time of their wave and the length of the attack, the strength of the attacking force, the bombing height[21] and, in great detail, the method of marking, the colours of the TIs that would be burning in the target area during their wave, and which of them to bomb. The position and the colour of the TI route markers were also impressed on all crews. Then the Met man would take the floor: he began with conditions at base for take-off and then described the weather which the crews would meet en route and at the target. This report would include the height and amount of cloud, the forecast position of any front across their path, and the type of weather they could expect at base on their return. The state of the moon, the time it rose and set, and its declination were part of his briefing.

With one or two exceptions the remainder of the briefing was concerned with the crews' own protection; much of it was repeated at each briefing and was directed at individuals rather than the whole crew. The Armament Officer discussed the bomb load and the fusing, and warned the gunners of new tactics being employed by the night fighters. The Signals Officer would discuss *Monica*, *Boozer*, *Mandrel* and *Tinsel*[22] in general terms and announce the times of Group broadcasts and, in particular on the 24–25th, of *Zephyrs*. Each specialist had to give a serious answer to every question, no matter how trivial it seemed, and, what was more irritating, repeat information he had given minutes earlier if someone had not been paying attention.

The Intelligence Officer probably held the floor longer than anyone else and was perhaps questioned more than the other specialists. The object of the raid and the importance and a general description of the target were his concern. It was he who pointed out the flak and searchlight belts, fighter areas, barrage balloons, dummy fire sites and smoke screens, and gave their location when known. Intelligence Officers were the butt of the crews and somehow they usually managed to say something incautious which produced laughter, jeers or whistles, but they took it all in good grace: "It does mean they are paying attention." One night a squadron detailed to drop mines in the Kiel Canal were informed that it was not defended – loud laughter. Command were sending aircraft ahead of them to shoot up the anti-aircraft guns – cheers and whistles.

On the 24–25th, however, they had three items of information which received everyone's attention. *Zephyrs* were introduced by the Wireless Transmission Officer. The duty of the Recenterers was explained by the Intelligence Officer, who also introduced a new weapon, *Window*. Then followed a description, its purpose and what had to be done to get the maximum benefit from it[23] (**Fig 3**).

Then there were the usual warnings to empty all pockets of anything which might be useful to the enemy, and, if captured, to give name, rank and number only. There was

---

20. Groups varied in this respect, and selected crews had special instructions. In 8 Group individual aircraft had to be on target at a specific time.
21. This varied with the type of aircraft.
22. For all code names see Glossary. For *Mandrel* and *Tinsel* see also Chapter II.
23. Bomber Command considered it such an important innovation that each station was issued with an identical document which had to be read out verbatim (PRO AIR 24/257).

also a reminder that escape aids would be issued if required. Finally, although each specialist had asked "Any questions?", the CO rose and repeated the enquiry. There were usually none by then, so he would say: "Let's synchronise watches." This formality completed, he would announce that specialist briefings followed immediately and took his leave with a "That's all, gentlemen, good luck."

The navigators would go to their special briefing, where they would be given the route; the latitude and longitude of all turning points; the positions for route markers and *Window*; the winds for selected heights at base, en route and over the target; the "J"

**Figure 3**

INSTRUCTIONS TO INTELLIGENCE OFFICERS ON THE USE OF WINDOW

1. Tonight you are going to use a new and simple countermeasure 'WINDOW' to protect yourself against the German defence system. 'WINDOW' consists of dropping packets of metal strips which produce almost the same reaction on RDF equipment as do your aircraft. The German defences will, therefore, become confused and you should stand a good chance of getting through unscathed while their attention is being wasted on the packets of 'WINDOW'.
2. You will already have been told how to drop 'WINDOW'; it has been worked out as carefully as possible to give you maximum protection, but there are two points which I want to emphasise strongly.
3. Firstly, the benefit of 'WINDOW' is a communal one: the 'WINDOW' which protects you is not so much that which you drop yourself as that which is already in the air dropped by an aircraft ahead. To obtain full advantage, it is therefore necessary to fly in a concentrated stream along the ordered route.
4. Secondly, the task of discharging the packets of 'WINDOW' will not be an easy one. You are hampered by your oxygen tube, inter-comm. connections, the darkness and the general difficulties of physical effort at high altitudes.
5. Despite these hardships, it is essential that the correct quantities of 'WINDOW' are discharged at the correct time intervals as you will understand after a moment's thought.
6. So important is this new Hun-baffling device considered, that special semi-automatic machines are being produced to ensure a steady flow from each aircraft and it is up to you to maintain a machine-like regularity until these devices arrive on the Squadron.
7. Intelligence shows that while concentration is maintained on the outward route. there is often a serious spread on the return, giving the enemy nightfighters a better chance to attack. Two thirds of our present losses therefore occur on the way home. 'WINDOW' can only reduce these homeword losses if each of you make a special effort to adhere strictly to the ordered return route.
8. When good concentration is achieved, 'WINDOW' can so devastate an R.D.F. defence system that we ourselves have withheld using it until we could effect improvements in our own defences, and until we could be sure of hitting the enemy harder than he could hit us. The time has now come when, by the aid of 'WINDOW' in conserving your unmatched strength, we shall hit him even harder.

Date. 17 July 1943.

**Author's note** The rate at which the bundles were to be dropped was governed by the number of aircraft on the sortie and was given at briefing as follows:

Rate A 1 bundle per 2 minutes
B 1 bundle per 1½ minutes
C 1 bundle per 1 minute
D 2 bundles per 1 minute
E 3 bundles per 1 minute

beam frequencies; the *Gee* chains which were operating; and the stars which would give the best astro fixes. Each would collect a chart and a log and then sit down to plot the routes and work out a flight plan detailing a course and time for each leg of the route, time of take-off and expected time of arrival back at base. It was the navigator's responsibility to collect the "flimsy", several sheets of rice paper bearing secret information. Each station had an identification beacon which flashed two letters in morse, and these were altered nightly. The flimsy contained a list of stations and the letters they were flashing. Other information included challenge-and-reply letters and the colours of the day; our defences were supposed to stop attacking a bomber when the correct letter was flashed or a Very cartridge of the correct colour was fired. The cartridges were also used as signals over the aerodromes when W/T communications between aircraft and flying control were unserviceable. Most navigators carried the cartridges, possibly because they had the biggest bags.[24] If the bomber was shot down over enemy territory it was the navigator's duty to eat the flimsy to prevent the Germans from obtaining the information; the rice paper dissolved readily enough but the taste of the ink was nauseating.

The bomb-aimers would be given a re-briefing on Pathfinder techniques, what TIs they would see and which to bomb. Target maps would be issued to supplement the half-inch Ordnance Survey maps of the whole of England and the region around the target. A final warning: "Beware of creepback, look out for decoy TIs and fires, don't undershoot: your route takes you through the target and there is no reason to drop early." The bomb-aimer would probably be reminded of the order of the bomb switches and where the photo-flash was wired. The wireless operator would be reminded to listen out for *Zephyrs*, which were to be broadcast in seven-letter groups[25] instead of the normal four, and, if he was carrying special equipment, when and where to operate it. Gradually the operators would all gather in their respective messes for a meal of bacon or sausage and eggs, with tomatoes when in season. Baked beans, peas or anything that tended to make gases in the stomach were not on the menu; colic at height is very painful, and sitting on an Elsan whilst the bomber is being attacked by a fighter is to find oneself too exposed, to say the least.

About an hour and a half before take-off crews would assemble down at the flights to collect their parachutes and don their flying gear, aiming to be at the aircraft an hour before take-off. If aircraft were to take off at minute intervals this was the minimum time required. Each crew member had his own duties to perform: the captain had to sign the Form 700, the bomb-aimer to inspect the bombs and gunners their ammunition, and the gear had to be stowed away neatly. It was the pilot's responsibility to see that the pitot head[26] cover had been removed and stored in the aircraft. Many airmen had small rituals – some to appease the gremlins, others to keep away evil spirits – and all made a point of answering the call of nature before boarding the aircraft.

---

24. Navigators carried their equipment in a large green bag. I made myself responsible for this chore but do not recall being ordered to do so.
25. 1 and 2, height in thousands of feet; 3, 4 and 5, direction in degrees true; 6 and 7, speed in knots.
26. The pitot head supplied the atmospheric pressure and drove the airspeed indicator. The atmospheric pressure was set on the height dial before taking off. Pressure decreases with height, so the aircraft's altitude relative to the take-off point was indicated.

The engines would be started, usually in a customary order. To preserve the aircraft battery an outside accumulator on a trolley, the "trolley ac", was plugged in to start the engines. The starboard inner invariably claimed the honour of being the first because the generator was wired to this engine (it was wired also to the port inner, so the choice was arbitrary[27]) followed by the starboard outer, port inner and port outer. The engines were run up and tested for faults, the commonest being a magneto drop. This trouble had a peculiarity in that it rarely occurred when the engine was running and could develop after the mechanic had done his tests. Each engine had two separate magnetos and they were wired to separate sets of plugs. Thus the engine might start perfectly and the fault would show only when the pilot tested each magneto individually. Everything which could be tested on the ground was tested, from table lamps to hydraulics and turret rotation. Probably the only pieces of mechanism not tested were the gun triggers and the undercarriage lever.[28] Then, about four minutes before take-off time: "Close the bomb doors." "Bomb doors closed." "Chocks away." The flight engineer would then signal to the ground crew, who pulled away the wooden blocks from in front of the wheels. One of them would guide the aircraft onto the perimeter track and the aircraft would wend its way slowly towards the dispatcher's caravan at the end of the runway. F/Lt S. Baker of 7 Squadron, having received a green from the dispatcher's Aldis lamp,[29] took up his position on the runway at Oakington. "Everybody OK?" Then as the pilot opened the throttles the aircraft started to accelerate down the runway. The engineer called out the speeds to the pilot, then the bumping stopped and the aircraft was airborne. Baker's was the first of the 114 PFF crews to take off. His navigator checked the time and made the first entry in his log: "Airborne 2155 hours". "Undercarriage up and locked," from the engineer. "First course, Skipper, 032 degrees," from the navigator, and the crew was on its way.

F/Sgt N.J. Matich of 35 Squadron was the only one to run into trouble on take-off. He and his crew had a very fortunate escape: his Halifax was a bare two feet off the ground when both the outer engines cut. Matich was forced to make a crash landing in a field at the end of the runway, but there were no casualties.

On the 24th most aircraft would climb on track and be at operational height by 54°45N 07°00E.[30] Navigators would be taking *Gee* fixes every six minutes and checking ground speed and ETA at 07°00E. The good ones would not alter course until near this point unless the winds were awry, which they were not. From 07°00E the course was 103° (True)[31] and about ten minutes later, at 54°34N 07°30E, the first bundles of *Window* were being pushed down the flare chute.

---

27. On the Halifax it was wired to all four engines. Most of the essential equipment had alternative sources of power. These, strangely, varied not only between types but also between marks.
28. There was usually one or more spare aircraft in case some unforeseen fault developed.
29. The dispatcher was usually an airman.
30. Stirlings in particular needed a long time to climb to height. If the North Sea crossing was a short one – when going to the Ruhr, for example – they had to gain height over England by climbing over base, although most crews did a triangular cross-country run over England to cut down risk of collision.
31. The course given to the pilot would be different because every compass had its own magnetic variation calculated for each aircraft; each part of the world also varies, there being a difference of 4° between London and Hamburg. These lines of variation change yearly.

# Chapter II

# Prelude to Chaos

WHETHER by day or night, the most efficient way of discouraging any attacking force is to destroy a significant portion of it and make the damage it causes, or the ground it takes, not worth its expenditure of men and material. Against air bombardment this means shooting aircraft out of the sky or damaging them in sufficient numbers.

After the British bombers had received a mauling from the *Luftwaffe* by day – they were both slower and outgunned – the RAF turned to night bombing in the hope that underneath the cloak of darkness they would be able to penetrate German airspace relatively unmolested. They did achieve a measure of success but, perversely, the darkness which hid them from the enemy also hid the target. The navigators had been trained to find their way by pinpointing landmarks on the ground and this was virtually impossible at night from height and with no moon. Astro-navigation was introduced, but while the stars are as predictable as the sun, taking three shots[1] and plotting them was a lengthy process. It needed clear skies above, a knowledge of the heavens, a steady hand and infinite patience. Accurate astro-navigation required a high degree of skill, both in the taking and the plotting. Each crew planned its own route and, within limits, could choose its own TOT.[2] Predictably enough, many got lost. Fortunately the *Luftwaffe* was as unprepared for the switch as the British crews, and in those days Bomber Command losses were due chiefly to damage by flak or running out of petrol.

Cloud over the North Sea, the English Channel and, in particular, the English coast deprived navigators of fixes at a crucial stage in the sortie, when crews were tired and petrol was running low. On November 5, 1940, six Blenheims of 82 Squadron, based at Wyton, were sent to attack Flushing. The aiming point was the docks and all crews reported seeing flashes as their bombs dropped in the target area. P/O F. Metcalf, with Sgt G. Martin (navigator) and Sgt S. Merrett (wireless operator/air gunner), had already attacked the same target on September 26, when the port was partially cloud-covered and positive identification was difficult. On the 5th they were so elated at finding the aiming point so easily that they agreed to hurry back to base and make a second attack. The forecast winds had been so accurate on the outward run that they did not anticipate any trouble, but in the meanwhile the winds had backed and the English coast was covered in cloud. By the time Merrett had obtained some radio bearings and Martin had sorted out the new wind the return journey had taken far too long and a second trip would have been too risky.

On October 13, 1941, F/O F. Thompson and crew took off from Wyton to intercept and attack the *Lutzow*, which had been sighted near the Norwegian coast, but after an

---

1. Operating a sextant to measure the azimuth angle between the aircraft and the selected star. The altitude of the aircraft made no difference because it was infinitesimal compared with the distance to the star.
2. Time on target.

hour's flying they were recalled to base. Back at Wyton they had scarcely finished their meal when they were told that they were operating that night and briefing was at 1700 hours. Their target was the docks at Brest, where the German warships *Scharnhorst* and *Gneisenau* had put in for urgent repairs. Take-off was after midnight and the hope was that all the bombers would be back over England before dawn. The Stirling took off at 0045 hours and P/O L. Millett, the navigator, had no problems on the outward run, obtaining pinpoints on leaving the English coast and later when making landfall over France. Over the target the flak was intense and some aircraft were coned[3] but Thompson had a trouble-free run across the port. However, like Martin, Millett had problems on the return flight, cloud having unexpectedly formed over the English Channel and covered the English coastline. Their route took them over Start Point but the cloud prevented definite identification, and immediately afterwards the Stirling was flying over solid 10/10ths cloud. Millett asked the Wop (wireless operator), Sgt Richardson, to get a radio bearing to check his latitude. To his dismay, though not surprise, the station was jammed with similar requests from other navigators in the same predicament. Meanwhile the flight engineer, Sgt Brown, had announced that, unless the fuel gauges were wrong, the Stirling was running short of fuel. The crew therefore prepared to abandon aircraft as soon as the first engine cut. They donned their parachutes, drank the rest of the coffee and smoked a cigarette.[4] One of the hazards of baling out above cloud was that the aircraft might not crash in open country. Then Richardson announced triumphantly that he had got a bearing, and after Millett had plotted it they decided to head eastwards and make for base since the engines were still giving the lie to the fuel gauges. Thompson had decided to have the front turret manned by Sgt Clare, although by now the sun was well above the horizon and visibility was perfect except when looking downward. Suddenly Clare yelled on the intercom: "There's a hole in the cloud, dead ahead." Thompson eased the Stirling down towards the hole and, to everyone's amazement, what looked like an aerodrome lay directly underneath. The skipper did not hesitate, making a half circuit to choose the best approach line before putting the Stirling down on the grass. The grazing sheep obligingly fled out of the way of the strange monster hurtling towards them. The airfield, RAF Wroughton, was so new that it was not on the latest maps. When eventually a petrol bowser came and refuelled the Stirling it was calculated that the tanks contained only seven gallons of petrol, not even enough for a second circuit.

In the early days, when the first German night-fighter *Gruppe*[5] was formed, the problem of finding another aircraft in the dark appeared to be insuperable, and distinguishing friend from foe proved almost as difficult. In fact I/NJG 1's[6] first "kill" turned out to be one of their own Me110s. At this stage aircraft recognition by both sides at night left much to be desired. Thus, when on July 20, 1940, the *Gruppe* had its first success, *Oberleutnant* Werner Streib had first closed in and flown alongside a Whitley, and he was not satisfied until he saw the RAF roundels on the fuselage. For their part the British crew imagined that Streib's aircraft was another Whitley and were probably envious of its turn of speed. When the tail-gunner awoke from his

3. See Glossary.
4. The Stirling had an all-metal fuselage so smoking was permitted.
5. *Gruppe* = Wing.
6. I/Nachtjagdgeschwader 1 = No 1 Squadron, No 1 Night-fighter Group.

lethargy it was too late; first the starboard and then the port engine were set on fire, with fatal results for the British crew. Once it had been proved that it could be done, others took heart and succeeded too. But the ground defences still claimed sole rights within the city areas and, in contrast with the welcome accorded to the pioneers of 1943,[7] the *Wilde Sau*,[8] it was "enter at your peril" for the night fighters.

The credit for using ground radar, in this instance *Freya*,[9] to help locate the enemy belongs to *Hauptmann* Wolfgang Falck. Its limitations were readily realised, however. In April 1940, just after the occupation of Denmark, British bombers made dawn attacks on Aalborg, where Falck was based at that time. He conceived the idea of pursuing the bombers on their homeward route, and asked a local signals officer in charge of a *Freya* to give him the bombers' track. The pursuers did get a fleeting glimpse of the enemy from time to time and once fired a few rounds at a Hampden before it disappeared into the dark sea mist. Curiously, at night both the bomber and the fighter required the same weather conditions to carry out their missions successfully: moonlight and predominantly clear skies.

In October 1940 Josef Kammhuber was promoted to *Generalleutnant* with the added title of "General of the Night Fighters". Kammhuber's idea was to prepare a line of searchlights, away from the big towns and the AA defences, to spot the bombers for his night fighters. The Germans, like the British, usually gave their operations and

**KAMMHUBER LINE**

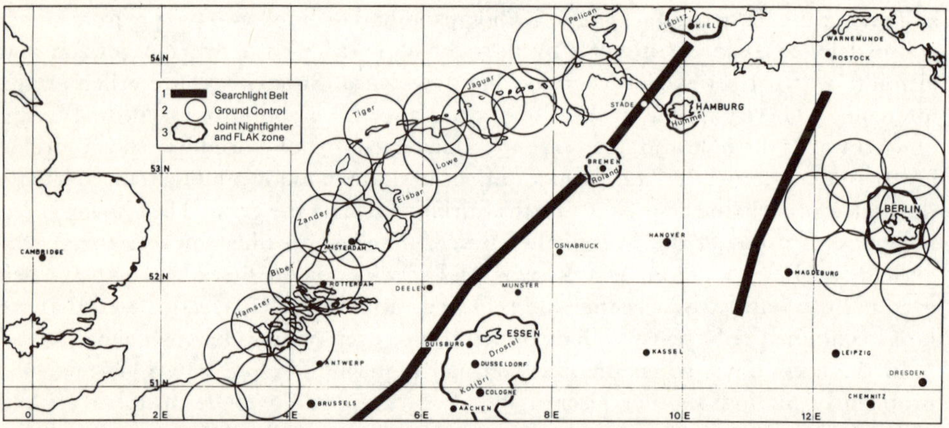


**1** Searchlight belt (*Helle Nachtjagd*) originally built west of Munster to cover the approach to the Ruhr. Later extended northward almost to Kiel. A second belt was built to protect Berlin. Gave way to: **2** Ground-controlled zones where a night fighter was guided to intercept a bomber. **3** Important towns or areas where fighters and ground defences worked in co-operation. Southern towns were not neglected: eg, Frankfurt, Stuttgart and Mannheim were considered important enough to protect. The named zones were well known and boasted a high number of kills, usually more than a hundred.

7. In the target area flak was restricted to a certain height to enable the fighters to operate there in safety.
8. *Wilde Sau* = Wild Boars. See Glossary.
9. German ground-to-air radar.

equipment code names and nicknames, but this was one of the exceptions, being called *Helle Nachtjagd* (Illuminated Night fighting).

Munster seemed to be on the RAF's favourite route to the Ruhr[10] and so the first Kammhuber Line, with its batteries of searchlights and sound detectors, was set up to the west of the town. The obvious tactic for the bombers was to slip by to the north or south, but Kammhuber extended the line[11] until it was more than 20 miles long and roughly six miles in depth, being composed of three rows of batteries three miles apart; along the 20-mile length there was a mere two miles between them. Because at this stage of the war the damage done by Bomber Command was not causing too much concern, the searchlights given to Kammhuber were all transferred from anti-aircraft divisions. Most of the *Würzburg A*[12] radars were being assigned to the FLAK[13] but General of the Night Fighters Kammhuber did get some, and General Martini (head of the NVW, the German signals and communications system) assigned six companies of trained *Würzburg* operators to work them.

As soon as the first warning of an attack was passed to their bases the night fighters took off. *Freya*s positioned along the coast were used for the early warning, and those *in situ* along the Kammhuber Line then monitored subsequent progress. Three fighters were allotted to a particular sector within the belt and each had its own beacon (*Little Screw*) around which it patrolled until the searchlights coned a bomber. Two *Würzburg*s were assigned to each battery, one to control a master searchlight (*Leitscheinwerfer*), the other to search for victims.

The advantages were still with the bomber: it was odds-on that the fighter was in no position to attack, and trying to manoeuvre to approach from the rear proved not to be as easy in the air as it seemed on the ground; the danger of fighter pilots being blinded by the searchlights and losing night vision for minutes was very real; the belt had relatively little depth, so the bomber pilots could minimise their exposure by flying through it at maximum speed; and once a bomber had passed through the searchlight belt the night seemed blacker than before to the fighter pilot. Experience was what counted most, and this was true for both sides. More bomber crews were shot down during their first five sorties than at any other time on a tour.[14] Nor was 30 operations for a tour just a number drawn out of a hat, since the next highest "chop rate"[15] came between 25 and 30. Was it over-confidence or just a matter of luck turning sour? No one seemed to know the answer.

Among the night fighters the young pilots quickly lost patience and asked for a transfer: "I can't see at night, Herr Major," was a common complaint. "Patience, it needs patience, come and see me again in a month if you still feel the same way." Usually they had had some success by then and a second request was rare. Here too the greatest losses were during the early forays. Only a few night fighter pilots became aces, and even some of these did not survive. Again, was it carelessness or overconfidence?

---

10. Within certain limits crews planned their own routes in 1940.
11. In fact it was a belt rather than a line.
12. The *Würzburg* was the first German RDF (Radio Direction-Finding) equipment to meet the exacting requirements of the AA.
13. *Flieger-Abwehr-Kanone*. German anti-aircraft force.
14. The time spent on an operational squadron.
15. See Glossary.

The searchlight belt was later extended northwards as far as Hamburg, with a second belt west of Magdeburg northwards to Rostock as an extra line of defence for Berlin. By the end of 1940 the night fighters had gone well ahead of the ground defences in their tally of bombers destroyed, claiming 42 to 30.

It would be to do Kammhuber an injustice not to mention his intruders. An aircraft is probably most vulnerable when taking off and landing; Kammhuber realised this and sent night fighters to patrol the English bases when Bomber Command was operating against the Reich. Two-thirds of the German night-fighter successes at this time were achieved by these intruders. I/NJG 2 operated Do17s and Ju88s armed with 4lb anti-personnel bombs[16] which burst on contact. In general they did no damage and caused few casualties, although they did create confusion. Stations under attack doused their lights and returning bombers had to be diverted, but if the timing was right the fighter arrived over the station at the same time as the returning bombers, joined the circuit and shot down his unsuspecting prey. What made this tactic particularly effective was the fact that the RAF ground gunners dared not shoot at an intruder for fear of hitting a bomber. July 1941 was the best month for the intruders, which claimed to have shot down seven British aircraft – three Wellingtons, two Hampdens, an Oxford and a Spitfire – in that time. The British claimed to have destroyed four Ju88s that month; one crashed into a Wellington and another crashed while making an attack. September 1941 was the intruders' worst month: in 110 sorties they made only three interceptions and damaged just one bomber. Their best prize came early in October, when they shot down a 3 Group Stirling at Oakington. This was their last success against front-line aircraft, for British records suggest that there were no intruder sorties after October 1941. In fact German records show October 12 as the last date, and by the end of the month they had been posted to Sicily. Bomber Command flew 27,008 sorties during the first ten months of 1941 and in the same period the German intruders flew 1,920. In all they made more than 100 interceptions, destroyed 27 British bombers and damaged a further 29.[17] German losses were less than 2%.

Hitler made what many astute observers consider to be one of the worst blunders of the war by disbanding the intruders. The German people, he averred, wanted to see the "terror bombers" strewn across Germany, brought down beside their damaged houses. Victories in England did nothing to boost civilian morale. So the English bases were mainly left in peace for the rest of the war.[18]

Kammhuber has many critics but most would admit that he was not afraid to experiment and that he possessed the driving power to see things through. In the summer of 1941 he began to replace the Kammhuber Line with a ground-controlled interception (GCI) belt along the Northern European coastline; no searchlights were used in this system. The belt was divided into overlapping circular zones about 20 miles apart, the radius being determined by the range of the equipment, which was approximately 30 miles, increasing later to 45. Each zone had a *Freya* for early warning, two *Würzburg*s and a *Seeburg Tisch* (evaluation screen). Probably because the

---

16. Cajus Bekker, *Luftwaffe War Diaries*, says 100lb AP bombs.
17. In addition they destroyed about 10 non-operational aircraft at a cost of two Ju88s lost in collisions.
18. Intruder flights were resumed from time to time, particularly in 1945, but only one was really successful. On March 3–4, 1945, of a force of 186 bombers 19 were destroyed and 8 were damaged, and 3 crews on training flights were shot down over England.

four units were used in combination to carry out the operation, the system was named *Himmelbett*,[19] and the name soon became applied adjectivally to the zones.

Although the night fighter pilots originally considered themselves pariahs and a posting to an NJG unit a punishment, their successes soon gave them a pride in themselves. However, during this period they believed that they were a forgotten force, and certainly Kammhuber had to fight hard against powerful opposition for every piece of equipment, and only because of his rank was he able to achieve expansion. It was a slow process but he almost doubled night fighter strength in 1941, and as the year drew to a close he could muster 300 aircraft. Moreover, the problems of night fighting had been recognised in high places, and plans to solve them had been well in hand as early as 1940.

The *Freya* was the standard RDF equipment and in general was used for long-range early warning. Its wide beam was a great asset when working near the limits and accuracy was of secondary importance. At between 90 and 100 miles, its range outstripped that of any of its rivals, if indeed it had any in this particular sphere. The echo was displayed on a cathode ray tube, the equipment being rotated laterally until the strongest signal was obtained; the bearing was then read off on a scale. When used in a GCI role it had one big drawback: it had no facility for measuring height. A *Würzburg* would be installed to perform this vital task. The system followed bomber and fighter alternately. After a few minutes the track and speed of the bomber would be calculated and represented on a plotting table by a mechanical device indicating the bomber's progress. The *Freya* was then free to monitor the fighter, which was followed in a similar manner. The controller then vectored the fighter onto the bomber by radio-telephone so that the mechanical "beetles" converged.

*Würzburg* was first tried out in this role by Ernst Udet and Wolfgang Falck over Berlin in 1937. Udet, flying blind and following the instructions of a controller on the ground, had intercepted Falck with monotonous regularity. The groundwork had thus been done, and the refinements followed.

The *Würzburg* performed in a similar manner to the *Freya* but, in addition to measuring range and bearing, it could calculate the height of the approaching aircraft. However, it never superseded the *Freya* because of its limited range, which was in the region of 30 miles. Its big brother, the *Giant Würzburg*, was more accurate and had an increased range of 45 miles, but again was no match for the *Freya*. The whole apparatus could be rotated through 360°, and the dish aerial could also be manoeuvred in the horizontal and vertical planes. The crew of three was housed in a cabin which rotated in harmony with the horizontal movement. The display had three tubes, one each for distance, height and bearing. The distance tube was the only automatic display: the dish had to be elevated to calculate the height and the cabin rotated to obtain the bearing. The beam was narrow compared with that of the *Freya*, which gave it more accuracy but made it more difficult to hold an aircraft.

The *Seeburg Tisch*, which was housed in a T-shaped hut, was a circular glass screen roughly 13ft in diameter and presented a detailed map of the area to 1/25,000th scale. The data from the *Würzburgs*, one each for fighter and bomber, were projected onto the screen in the form of dots, the movements of which across the screen were relative to the

19. Four-poster bed.

movements of the protagonists. Initially both dots were black but if the bomber started weaving it was not uncommon for the controller to become confused, so red and green lights were substituted.

The night fighter carried a transmitter/receiver (FuG 25 or 25a) tuned to the *Würzburg*[20] frequency. When the fighter was held in the beam of the *Würzburg* a red neon light shone in the cockpit,[21] warning the pilot, and the FuG transmitted a code letter so that the ground crew knew they had homed onto the correct fighter. Another piece of special equipment in the aircraft was a radio telephone, the direct link between fighter and controller.[22]

Immediately the *Freya* picked up the approaching bombers, its crew informed the "T" hut. A telephonist contacted HQ and the night fighter crews were alerted. As the zones overlapped and covered the whole length of the coastline the bombers had no choice but to pass through some of the zones, so the night fighters were scrambled, one for each GCI station, with a number of reserves ready to take over if needed. Each GCI site had three *Little Screw* radio and visual beacons. The radio beacon transmitted a letter, and the visual beacon flashed the same letter. The middle beacon, situated close to the "T" hut (roughly four miles), was used by the reserve. The front and rear beacons were about 15 miles from the hut. The fighter took up his position over the front beacon when the bombers were on the outward journey and over the other when they were homeward bound. The pilot orbited the beacon until his controller started to work him, and he returned to it after his *Sieg Heil*[23] or an unsuccessful interception. The visual beacons were switched off during the attempted interception.

Once the fighter was in position over its *Little Screw* the pilot informed the "T" hut and then came under direct command of his controller. The *Würzburg* would swing onto him and in the "T" hut a plotting clerk would project a green light onto the glass map overhead. In the meantime, the second *Würzburg* was searching for the bombers. Each controller had his own idiosyncrasies: some liked to get their fighters into position early, others thought height was more essential. The important thing was to establish a rapport, and the controller's attitude naturally depended on his successes or failures with the airborne crew.

There was usually some small talk between air and ground. Later this was tightened up when the Germans realised that the British were listening in ("Y" Service)[24] and gaining useful and perhaps secret information, with the result that transmissions were prefixed "Order" or "Question". The operator in the night fighter was obliged to answer the controller. If he did not understand him he said "*Ricardus*," meaning repeat. If he understood he said "*Viktor*," message understood. The exception was when he was given a vector; he then repeated the order.[25] The controller usually ordered the fighter to a position at the limit of his *Würzburg*'s range. The moment the second *Würzburg* picked up the signals its crew warned the plotter. There were probably three or four

---

20. Or in the case of the 25a to a *Freya*.
21. Note similarity to *Boozer*. See Glossary.
22. The messages could be sent by wireless but the method was rarely used because immediate compliance with an order was essential.
23. One of the pilot's methods of signifying that he had shot down the bomber.
24. A listening service which monitored German transmissions.
25. For brevity code words were used.

blips on the *Würzburg*'s display panel, and the one selected depended solely on the *Würzburg* operator's whim. Men's lives depended on his choice, which was often a random one.

Whatever the determining factor, as soon as the choice of blip on the *Würzburg* was made the plotter would project a red dot on the *Seeburg*. This was when the controller, usually an officer, earned his wages. He it was who had to manoeuvre the fighter into the best position to intercept the bomber as quickly as possible. He would know the local wind speed and direction and would have converted it into drift for one or more of the headings. He then gave the pilot a course to steer, followed by the track and height of the bomber, and then, as the minutes slipped by, any corrections to the original course, either to speed up the interception or to make it a certainty.

The average time for an interception was 7½ minutes, but this varied with the individual and many took as long as 13 minutes. Again, some controllers could bring their fighters to within 300 yards of the bombers, while others only dreamed of such skill. The whole system depended on teamwork and practice. The limitations were obvious: only one fighter could be controlled at any one time, and beyond the range of the *Würzburg* it became a game of blind-man's-buff. Under the latter conditions it was more profitable to give up the chase and stay within the control limits,[26] since the odds were high that there would be another bomber along in a moment if the controller was adept. One fact became obvious under operational conditions: it was much easier to get two lights to fraternise on a screen than to get a fighter and bomber within shooting distance. Altercations between pilot and controller were not infrequent, particularly when a bomber was getting near the maximum-range circle.

The fighter pilot could only be put in the vicinity of the bomber; he then had to find it visually. At that stage he did have one thing in his favour, in that any aircraft he saw must be the enemy. Clearly, what was needed was an airborne device to bridge the last thousand or so yards. Trials were carried out with infra-red equipment, code-named *Spanner*, but it proved to be more of a liability than an aid. Its beam was narrow, so the vector and height had to be very accurate. The range was short, probably less than was needed for a visual identification on a clear night. In addition, as one operator said: "It is heavy on bulbs and murder on power." It required so much power that nearly everything electrical, including the radio, had to be switched off, and that meant that the pilot had lost contact with his controller at a vital time. The net was cast wider and eventually, on August 9, 1941, night fighter ace *Oberleutnant* Ludwig Becker, piloting an Me110 fitted with a *Lichtenstein*,[27] claimed a success – probably P/O Littlewood, captain of one of 40 Whitleys on their way to Kiel. This was good news for the Germans, because it resulted from the *Lichtenstein*'s first sortie.

Not all the pilots were enthusiastic about the new radar, however. They considered the loss of 20 mph resulting from the installation of a *Lichtenstein* too high a price to pay, and continued using the *Cat's-Eyes*[28] method in unmodified aircraft. Two leading aces, Helmut Lent and Paul Gildner, were of this school of thought, and their acolytes

---

26. Bomber crews were prone to relax after leaving the enemy coast on the homeward journey. After the attack on Wuppertal on May 29, 1943, Me110s of NJG 1 followed the bombers out to sea and literally caught them napping, bringing the tally for the night to 33.
27. Germany's first airborne radar.
28. See Glossary.

followed suit. Kammhuber, nothing daunted, had more than 450 aircraft converted in 1943 and Becker kept totting up his successes, so Lent and Gildner eventually had to come into line. A lighter aerial which cut down the speed only marginally proved a face-saver for them.

It is interesting to compare the development of the *Lichtenstein* with that of H2S.[29] In 1939 Telefunken had demonstrated airborne interception (AI) in a Junkers 52 but the *Luftwaffe* was not interested. Not that this was surprising, since no one expected *Reichsmarschall* Goering to be called upon to eat his hat. So the company, trying to recoup some of their development losses, turned the system into a radar altimeter. When the cry went up for AI all they had to do was turn their altimeter through 90° and the basic equipment was ready-made. In Great Britain the early need was for AI. When the call went out for an unjammable navigational aid British boffins[30] turned the AI equipment 90° in the reverse direction and used it as a prototype H2S. In both cases the technology preceded the requirement.

The aerial was the main reason for the long delay (more than a year) before *Lichtenstein* arrived in the front line. Originally the Germans tried to mount it inside the aircraft. The initial sets had a range of only 2½ miles, but this was no real problem if the controller did his work efficiently.[31] Had Bomber Command pilots known that the *Lichtenstein*'s aerial had a restricted field of view (25°) they might have taken more violent evasive action and so avoided a combat.

In May 1942 Kammhuber received another setback. Behind the scenes the *Gauleiter*s (area commanders) had been pressurising Hitler to bring all the searchlights under the control of the FLAK and to do away with the Kammhuber Line. The *Führer* acceded to their requests and all the important cities were ringed with searchlights to aid the AA.

In general the *Gauleiter*s were nobody's favourites. They jealously guarded their autonomy in their own districts. Albert Speer[32] and his subordinates were always falling foul of them, and even the forces found their interference irksome, but this time they were right. Although in the spring of 1942 the FLAK and night fighters were sharing the honours, only 15% of the fighters' claims were attributable to searchlight assistance, while 80% of FLAK successes came when bombers were coned.

If Kammhuber felt any slight he did not show it. His controlled fighters operated with mounting success and the searchlight belts were spoiling his batting average. He extended his GCI zones inland, put a ring round Berlin and planned to protect the southern cities. Moreover, he put more stations (sometimes as many as three) in each zone, thus cutting down the airspace between each controller. By December 1942 there were five *Geschwader* (Groups) of night fighters containing 18 *Gruppen* (Wings). More zones meant more successes, but there was always the weakness that only one fighter could be controlled in each box.[33] A system for continuing the pursuit beyond box boundaries did not exist, and night fighter kills were confined to narrow belts across a big country. However, provided the RAF entered and left the Continent on a broad front, Kammhuber was confident that he would take his toll.

29. See Glossary.
30. See Glossary.
31. The interception rate was 1 in 5, and the successful combat rate significantly lower.
32. Appointed Armaments Minister in 1942 and second only to Hitler himself as a power on the home front.
33. Name given to sub-division of zone.

It is absorbing to view this development from the other side of the North Sea. It was obvious that at some time the night fighters would become a major threat to Bomber Command. The bomber crews in 1940 were as raw as the Germans in their new role and their aircraft as ill-equipped. For example, the Course Setting Bombsight, designed as it was for daylight, was useless at night. The bombs, filled with amatol,[34] did far less damage pound for pound than their German counterparts and the proportion which did not explode was also higher. Both of these faults persisted for most of the war. The RAF's poor navigation has already been referred to, but in fairness to the navigators it must be pointed out that pilots were not used to steering precise courses or holding steady airspeeds. Trained to map-read themselves, when they saw the next turning point looming up in daylight they would veer off course to "help the navigator get back on track". At night an inaccurate airspeed or course resulted in a spurious wind; both together were a disaster. Such errors are cumulative, and the result of using a spurious wind was to get even further off track. The point can be brought into sharper focus: the Butt Report[35] of August 18, 1941, stated that only 20% of the crews who claimed to have bombed the target dropped their load within 75 square miles of the aiming point. When Harris was pressing for more bombers and crews Prime Minister Churchill replied: "My dear Harris, halving the bombing error would be the equivalent of doubling the force."

I am not denigrating the crews, far from it. Given the equipment of later crews they would have performed just as well. When the "O" (Observer)[36] navigators came back for a second tour, they proved to be better H2S operators than those brought up on the aid; it must also have taken more guts to set off night after night to face the unknown. Nor were their successors necessarily any better: on the last Main Force attack on Berlin on March 24–25, 1944, some crews were more than 60 miles off track; many navigators found the correct wind but it was so far from the forecast one that they did not use it. Thus it was that Bomber Command was unable to capitalise on the *Luftwaffe*'s unpreparedness.

Fortunately for the RAF, however, the improvement in the performance of the German night fighters was being matched within Bomber Command. Four-engined bombers were coming into service: first the Stirling (February 10, 1941), then the Halifax (March 11, 1941) and finally the Lancaster (March 10, 1942). Even more important, *Gee* (see Appendix II), first used operationally in August 1941, was by 1942 being fitted in all front-line aircraft. Navigators could obtain accurate fixes over Germany at least as far as the Ruhr, so much of the anxiety about getting lost was dispelled and, barring other accidents, the prospects of getting back to base were greatly enhanced. Finally, as Harris put it: "The tactical aim of Bomber Command in this period can be described in one word—'concentration'."[37]

The first aim was concentration at the target. The "1,000-bomber" raids on Cologne, Essen and Bremen were to prove not only that a mass attack would produce

---

34. American bombs had greater blast power than British weapons. There were those in the Air Ministry who knew of ways of making British bombs more effective but no serious efforts to improve them were made until 1944.
35. See Glossary.
36. In contrast to navigators "N" they were also trained to drop the bombs and pinpoint the target.
37. Harris Despatch.

more damage than the joint effect of smaller ones, but also that larger numbers of bombers swamped defences, with the result that fewer aircraft were shot down. One interesting point did emerge: if concentration did reduce losses it was because more aircraft got through unscathed. The AA kept up a steady average (as opposed to a percentage) of kills throughout the raids, irrespective of numbers.

With the advent of *Gee* there was, too, some hope that a measure of concentration could be maintained on the route to the target and back. It was reasonable to assume that more aircraft passing through the fighter belt at the same time would cut down the percentage of interceptions. Bomber Command was so confident of this assumption that when *Window* was the main item at a meeting held in November 1942, Harris sent his deputy, who said that Bomber Command did not wish to "press for *Window* at this time". This seems an astonishing decision: although *Monica*, a tail-warning device, was being fitted into Bomber Command aircraft, the losses credited to fighters had for some time been more than those attributed to flak.[38] Moreover, *Monica* did not prevent interception, but merely warned the rear gunner that it was imminent.

A photograph of a *Giant Würzburg* on a building in the Tiergarten which fell into the hands of Allied intelligence confirmed that radar was being used for gunlaying, and *Boozer* was introduced to warn the pilot that his aircraft was held by radar and he could expect some predicted flak, probably already on its way up. Again, this was a defensive measure only.

When crews reported interceptions and combats in a searchlight belt away from towns, Intelligence was called upon to verify the reports and discover the extent of the new developments. Listening stations were set up around the English coast and two sets of signals were found. The instructions from the controller to the night fighter were monitored, and bearings identified the zones. Reconnaissance photographs were taken, often at low level, and secret reports came from China and America, including the snapshot of the *Giant Würzburg* in the Berlin Tiergarten. These were all significant pieces of an enormous jigsaw puzzle.

The next urgent need was for scientific and technical information on *Würzburg*. Fortunately there was some to hand just across the Channel. A combined operation was laid on and, during the night of February 28, 1942, a daring raid on a country villa near Bruneval, a small seaside town 11 miles north-east of Le Havre, was successfully carried out. The equipment captured confirmed all the British suspicions, and added the disturbing fact that the system was in large-scale production. The *Giant Würzburg* in the Tiergarten was probably its big brother.

From crew reports it was apparent that there were two types of interception taking place, one along the coastal area and another inland, involving searchlights, along the Kammhuber Line. Reconnaissance photographs of a site at Nieuwerken, just north of the St Trond aerodrome, which was assumed to be part of the searchlight belt revealed a battery of searchlights and the associated *Freya*, and, surprisingly, a *Giant Würzburg*.

A sortie to Domburg, on Walcheren Island, later in the year confirmed the conclusions of the Intelligence Branch, revealing a *Freya*, two *Giant Würzburgs*, a T-shaped hut and no searchlights. In May another visit was made to the searchlight belt, only to find that it had disappeared. Comparison of the dates of British intelligence reports and

---

38. The acronym for the German AA service had come to mean anti-aircraft shells.

those quoted in German sources reveal an excessive time lag between suspicion and confirmation. This was particularly true of *Lichtenstein*. Though this system was first used in October 1941, it was 15 months before its existence was "confirmed beyond all doubt". Small wonder morale was low among the bomber crews.

To be fair to Harris, even as late as September 1942 most of what was known about the German night fighters and GCI was speculative, and it would have been foolish to play an ace (*Window*) when a lesser card might suffice. Harris knew that two new countermeasures, *Mandrel* and *Tinsel*, would be reaching the squadrons before the end of November, and it probably seemed desirable to test their effectiveness before using *Window*. Since they were launched simultaneously it was impossible to say which caused the defences the greater headache. *Mandrel* sets caused interference on the *Freya*'s frequency band, and so either delayed the scrambling of the night fighters or at least obscured the point of entry over the Continent. Bomber Command used many methods to keep the target a secret as long as possible, including spoof[39] marking, spoof attacks and feints. The *Freya*s provided the Germans with early information, so *Mandrel* played an important role in the guessing game which continued until the end of the war. It was so important in the overall strategy that, in addition to the airborne sets, ground stations in England also radiated signals. Aircraft carrying *Mandrel* could, as well as jamming coastal *Freya*s, jam inland installations and so prevent early tracking of the bombers even after they had crossed the enemy coast. Although losses of aircraft carrying *Mandrel* were no higher than in the rest of the Main Force, it emitted signals which made it possible for the Germans to home onto them. Later, when this possibility had been realised by the system's designers, a two-minutes-on, two-minutes-off automatic switch was fitted. The German homer, *Freya-Halbe*, which was being developed to track the *Mandrel* aircraft, was then relegated to the scrapheap. However, the Germans spread the *Freya* frequencies and also had switching gear incorporated to allow the *Freya* crew to select any of a number of frequencies. Originally two aircraft per squadron were enough to cover the band, but by July 1943 it would not have sufficed even if all Bomber Command aircraft had carried *Mandrel*. However, ground-controlled *Mandrel*, operating from stations along the South Coast, still enjoyed some success. In the summer of 1944 it was to be an important element in the 100 Group countermeasures campaign which so bemused the enemy that losses, particularly from fighters, were largely a matter of bad luck. Ground *Mandrel* had another incalculable advantage: it was not grounded by bad weather and could operate on any night to suggest to the Germans that an attack was imminent.

*Tinsel* was also an immediate success. The German controllers in the "T" huts communicated with the fighter pilots by radio-telephone, using the 3–6MHz band to vector them onto the bomber which had invaded their box. If these communications could be jammed even for a short period of time the chances of interception were reduced enormously. Since the actual frequencies used by the enemy varied each night, the British divided the band into 20 sections and assigned a wireless operator to each to sweep the whole section, listening for transmissions. As most wireless operators had no knowledge of German, anything not English was jammed to make certain. The jamming was produced by modulating the aircraft's transmitter with noise from a

39. See Glossary.

microphone fitted either in the engine nacelle or, later, inside the fuselage. The wireless operator's role had decreased in importance with the introduction of *Gee* and he had become more "a man for emergencies". But *Tinsel*, and to a lesser extent *Mandrel*, gave him a morale-booster: he was saving the lives of airmen and, even more important to him, those of his own crew. *Tinsel* was so successful that the Germans were driven to use VHF, which brought with it an entirely new range of problems.

1943 was not a lucky year for Kammhuber. His problems began early in January when *Tinsel* and *Mandrel* were first used operationally, and overnight two of the legs of his four-poster bed had got woodworm. His early-warning system was jammed and co-operation between controllers and pilots was being interfered with by the very aircraft they were trying to intercept. Frantic work on the *Freya*s to widen the band came first and then they had to be remodified to make it possible to switch quickly from one frequency to another. The medium-frequency problem was more difficult to overcome: there were often so many bombers jamming that at times the German pilots and controllers spent more time trying to find a free frequency than they did on intercepting. The obvious answer was to switch to VHF, but even Kammhuber could not obtain sets for 15 *Gruppen* and hundreds of ground stations overnight. However, before the Battle of the Ruhr was a month old, he had given the "Y" Service something to talk about. Perhaps it was this quick change-over that persuaded Harris that his salvation lay in *Window*. The balance between attackers and defenders was delicately poised, and it was to swing first one way and then the other before finally coming to rest in favour of Bomber Command.

The enormous growth in the number of zones and boxes, combined with the inherent complexities of the operation, led to the creation of five Air Division[40] command and control staffs, each housed in a bomb-proof concrete headquarters. At first glance these structures looked like opera houses, and so striking was the similarity that they were referred to as "Battle Opera Houses" or "Kammhuber Kinemas". There were slight differences between the five, but in principle they were run on the same lines. Where in a normal theatre the safety curtain would be, there hung a 50ft-wide frosted-glass screen inscribed with a map of Germany divided into grids, a gigantic *Seeburg* in fact. On the side walls were weather maps and boards indicating crew availability by station and *Staffel* (squadron). In front were rows of seats and tables, each with a telephone. Behind and above was a row of projectors, each manned by a *Helferin*[41] wearing headphones. Behind the screen another group of women, each connected by phone to a control station, awaited news of the British bombers. The seats were for the C-in-C and his staff: ops officers, fighter controllers, the met man, liaison officers from all sections concerned with defence – FLAK, searchlights and civil defence, including the Air Raid Warning Service – and technical officers capable of giving expert advice if necessary. The HQ also housed a massive telephone exchange providing direct links with everything in the division which might be needed for the air defence of the Reich, and a teleprinter to confirm verbal orders.

As the first warning of an attack came from the *Freya*s – in the form of a grid

40. No 1 at Deelen, No 2 at Stade, No 3 at Metz, No 4 at Döberitz (near Berlin), No 5 at Schleissheim (near Munich).
41. Equivalent to a Waaf in the RAF.

reference (a letter and a number), estimated track and number of aircraft – one of the *Helferinnen* would project the information onto the relevant map square. The officer responsible for that area would then alert the night fighter station in the *Gruppe* and the *Staffeln* would be put on standby. It was now up to the C-in-C, and as soon as he considered that his division was under threat he would scramble his fighters and they would proceed to their *Little Screws*. When the fighters arrived over their beacons the controllers in the "T" huts would inform HQ and the *Helferinnen* in the Upper Circle would then project a green "T" onto the map to show the fighter in position. Meanwhile, the other group of *Helferinnen* had been showing the progress of the bomber force. The circles of the zones had been overlaid on the big screen, and when the bombers came within the *Würzburg*'s range their height would be added to the information already detailed. All information would also be updated as it filtered through. The liaison officers would by now have given an early warning to their various units. Although everything might be going like clockwork, an air of excitement always pervaded the whole scene. As a *Würzburg* picked up a victim, a white "T" appeared on the huge map, followed by another and another until the width of the bomber stream was covered. Then the greens began to close in on the whites as the controllers at the "T" huts vectored the fighters. Fingers were pointed as a green overtook a white, and a muffled cheer would go up when suddenly a white light was switched off and a green returned to its first position. Often there were heated exchanges between the spectators, but as adrenalin levels sank an air of tranquillity again descended on the scene. The C-in-C would be getting his reports, which no doubt included a crop of excuses.

Then would come the speculation about the route the bombers would take after the target. The night fighters had by now landed and were being refuelled. The armourers were busy checking the guns and replenishing the shells and bullets, fitters were checking for damage, and other ground crews were swarming everywhere in an effort to get the aircraft ready in case they were needed again. At HQ reports on the progress of the bomber stream were coming in, while someone kept an eye on the aircraft serviceability board as the aircraft letters reappeared. If, as the time crawled by, it seemed more and more certain that the bombers were taking another route home, then it became just another night, with the staff waiting for the end of the shift.

July 24, 1943, was a beautiful summer day at Stade and, taking advantage of the unusual spell of fine weather, some of the evening staff had dozed off in the sun. As they came on duty that evening in Division 2's HQ there were some red faces and sore shoulders. It was still quite hot outside but the air-conditioning made this one of the most pleasant places to be. There were those who liked the excitement of the frenetic 25 minutes when fighter and bomber were in mortal combat; those who enjoyed it but hated the let-down; and those who liked it peaceful, as it had been for some time now. Most were wondering what the night held in store for them.

The rumours started flying, for reports of activity on the English bases had come through. Short nights usually meant the Ruhr, and certainly not Berlin; there they could sleep peacefully tonight. As the evening wore on news came in from Deelen – a large force travelling in an easterly direction – and it looked as if Division 1 was going to have another quiet night. From Cuxhaven – with its massive *Freya* placed high on a tower to give it a range of 120 miles – came the report that the bombers were holding the same track. The force of Halifaxes, Lancasters, Stirlings and Wellingtons had taken off from bases in the eastern counties of England, from the North Riding of Yorkshire to Suffolk, and joined up over the North Sea at 54°45N 07°00E.[42] From there they had proceeded eastwards in a broad stream parallel to the European coastline, comfortably out of night fighter reach. Two big questions were on *Leutnant-General* Schwabedissen's[43] mind: what was the target, and was his airspace about to be invaded? Kiel and Lubeck were the obvious choices. Rostock was just a possibility, but that was the limit since otherwise the return flight would be in the first light of dawn, and that was too much to risk. Only time would answer these questions, and Schwabedissen knew he must get his fighters airborne so that a sudden turn south to Bremen would not catch him unawares.

He ordered his aircraft to scramble. Lüneburg, Kastrup, Stade, Vechta, Wunstorf and Wittmundhafen all came to life. Crews – all briefed earlier – rushed to their aircraft and the noise of engines starting was followed by a deafening roar as they were run up. Then came comparative quiet as the pilots taxied to the end of the runway. The runway lights were switched on, a green signal lamp gave a single blink, and then came the roar of engines again as the first Me110 took off, closely followed by the others. The messages came back from the bases: "All aircraft airborne."

In the HQ building the tension was mounting, with all eyes on the screen. The Green Ts were being projected onto it, first in penny numbers and then suddenly in scores. The next move was up to the enemy. The general hubbub had subsided and a stranger might have become aware of the constant drone of the air conditioning, a feature of all such buildings. All this time a narrow stream – the watchers had seen the same picture so many times that they knew it was the Pathfinders – was pushing on ahead of a broader flood. Then the incredible happened: the tail stopped moving and, as the minutes ticked by, there it remained, steady. Anxious calls to the "T" huts produced the same reply: "We have so many blips that it's impossible to select one, and they are all static." Anxiety mounted to panic and spread from Division to the "T" hut. In one ear: "*Herr Leutnant*, the *General* wants an explanation." Who didn't? In the other ear: "What's happening down there?" from the fighter pilot. "I'm getting dizzy chasing my tail." The operators checked the equipment to satisfy themselves that the trouble on the screens was not internal. The transformation from normal to impossible had been well nigh instantaneous: flashes of light danced up and down and from side to side on the screen, dark bars would sweep across, and then the flashes of light would begin again. The reports throughout the division had a disturbing similarity. On the premise that "your guess is as good as mine," someone suggested that atmospheric conditions might be to blame.

*Mandrel* sets were now playing their part, and for two minutes at a time the *Freya*s were blind, then clear, then blind. The night fighting system was complex enough without someone throwing a spanner in the works. Conditions in the "T" huts became more chaotic when the wireless operators began to use *Tinsel*: conversations between air and ground, which for the past 15 minutes had been strained to say the least, now became positively abusive. However, most of the pilots gleaned from the snatches of talk which were distinguishable through the constant whine that they must find the

---

42. This was the actual position; the Germans could only have made an approximate guess.
43. Commander of Division 2.

bombers for themselves. One was optimistically informed: "Everything will be explained when you land." The pilots were in fact probably the first Germans to learn the truth. There was no lack of targets on their *Lichtensteins*, and as they closed in for the kill they found themselves flying through clouds of paper reminiscent of a New York ticker-tape celebration.

Now it is time to leave the Stade bunker and the pandemonium; the "T" huts in complete disarray, with their controllers exhausted from the aural battering they had received both from the ground and from the air; the *Würzburg* operators staring in bewilderment at cathode ray tubes still obliterated by hundreds of blips which refused to go away; the Messerschmitt and Junkers pilots searching for a grain of wheat amidst all the chaff. There was no immediate solution to all their problems.

Mere human beings had become important again now that science had outwitted science. The corps of observers watching and listening throughout the Reich could not be jammed, and it was they who reported the route markers dropping over Dithmarschen, near Meldorf. That signified a turning point, but in which direction? Telephone bells were ringing frantically at all the observer posts for miles around. Their reports showed that the bombers had turned to the south-east, parallel to the Elbe. Hamburg, it had to be Hamburg. The warnings were sent out to Hamburg, and searchlights and gun crews, already on the alert, were brought to action stations. They too were in for a surprise.

*Oberst-Leutnant* Zimmermann was not too popular with his commandr, *Oberst* Nissen: he was away playing football too much for Nissen's liking. The *Oberst* put his duty before everything and thought that everyone else should do the same. Zimmermann was in charge of the FLAK battery at Harbighoorst, which was one of the first to be called into action. At 2317 hours the *Würzburg* was switched on. The *Oberst-Leutnant* was given a height of 10,000 feet and he ordered his battery to fire. Then suddenly the interference started: instead of one or several pulses the screen was a mass of zigzag curves, making it impossible to distinguish anything. Zimmermann tried most of the amateur routines, even to turning it off and on several times, before reporting the trouble to an unsympathetic Nissen: "You may be good at football but you're obviously no good with radar. Report to me tomorrow." Zimmermann looked at the telephone, shrugged his shoulders and replaced it carefully. He tried the *Würzburg* once again but nothing had changed, and so he switched off the set and went to help the fire defence unit.

Nissen was already annoyed by Zimmermann, so when three minutes later the Glendau battery made a similar report, followed by Falnden and Billstedt, he was ready to put his whole command on a charge. There were 54 heavy and 26 light FLAK batteries and 22 searchlight batteries defending Hamburg, and all of them reported the same tale of woe: the *Würzburgs* were jammed. Hundreds of zigzags were flashing up and down on the screens, extending beyond the calibrated range. When Zimmermann eventually heard the news he breathed a sigh of relief: amidst all the confusion and among so many similar reports, his would not stand out.

At Z−3[44] the flares from the Illuminators burst over the city and then the reds of the

44. Z = zero hour, the scheduled time for the attack to open; Z−3 means 3 minutes before zero hour; Z+3 = 3 minutes after zero hour. Sometimes H (hour) is substituted for Z.

Visual Ground Markers went cascading down. The "eyes" of the bomber force were there on time, whereas the eyes of the defence, both on the ground and in the air, were blind. The FLAK was ordered to put up a barrage and look for searchlight cones; it would at least keep the bombers high and boost the morale of the civilians, who were already in the bunkers and had no idea of the problems facing the defences. Among the defenders the inexplicable events had produced a change from calm precision to complete disarray and a sense of impotence brought with it a feeling of foreboding. Something terrible was about to happen to Hamburg.

# Chapter III

# First Act of the Tragedy

THE FIRST chapter showed the meticulous care taken by everyone, from the Air Chief Marshal down to the lowliest AC2,[1] to ensure that the attack was a success. It left most of the bombers spread out over the North Sea looking for the yellow TIs which would mark their turning point.

The main purpose of this chapter is to follow the fortunes of the force to the target and back to their bases, where once again the ground organisation got into top gear, correlating all the information and supporting evidence which would reveal to the C-in-C the results of the night's work.

After the last aircraft had roared down the runway the whole station seemed to go into a state of suspension, though it was quiet only in contrast with the deafening noise of four engines at full boost. For most of the people involved their task was over for the day. It was too late to get a beer at the NAAFI – it closed at 2200 hours – but a cup of tea was possible at the Sally Ann,[2] which was open until 2300 hours.

For the senior staff on duty there was a pile of papers waiting for a quiet hour, but very often these were regarded with unseeing eyes. Through the ages women have coped with such situations far better than men: they manage to do nothing and everything quietly, efficiently and apparently unemotionally. Those with nothing to do could always find an eyebrow to pluck, a nail to file or "a hopeless sock which never gets done"[3] to knit. So the Waafs coped far better with the vacuum until the bombers returned.

Up to a certain point the intolerable waiting and anxiety were shared by everyone; the "early returns"[4] (crews who for various reasons had been unable to complete the sortie), 46 on this night, might have broken the monotony but they also heightened the tension. However, W/T (wireless telegraphy) silence, normally observed except in extreme circumstances, was now to be broken for the first time on a raid. Six selected crews from the Blind Markers were to broadcast to PFF HQ the wind, computed from their first H2S fix on the enemy coast and their last *Gee* fix. The duty navigator at Pathfinders, with Bennett, an expert navigator, breathing over his shoulder, had to average them and phone the result to Bomber Command HQ and thence to the other Group HQs. This (code-named *Zephyrs*) was then relayed to the crews at 0030, 0100 and 0120 hours. Theoretically all crews would then bomb on the same wind.

All Pathfinder crews were expected to be able to perform any of the Pathfinder duties – Route Markers, Blind Illuminators, Blind Markers, Visual Markers and Backers-up

1. Aircraftman 2nd Class, equivalent to Army Private.
2. Salvation Army.
3. Rose Macaulay, *Many Sisters to Many Brothers*.
4. Also called "boomerangs", initially by the RAAF.

– though senior crews with seasoned bomb-aimers were usually chosen to act in the Visual Marker role. For the *Newhaven* on the 24–25th all five duties were used. Four Lancasters from 7 Squadron and two Halifaxes from 405 Squadron were detailed to drop the initial yellow route markers: one LBTI each at 54°11N 08°50E. These six aircraft had a triple role as Route Markers, Blind Illuminators and Blind Markers. After completing their first duty they proceeded to the target and dropped 4 × 4 bundles of white flares and 2 × LBTI yellows.[5] There they were joined by four Lancasters of 83 Squadron, three Lancasters of 156 Squadron and seven Halifaxes of 35 Squadron acting in the dual target role. The timing of this group was not up to standard, and many of them were late. They should have dropped their flares and yellow TIs by Z−3, whereas only 11 out of 16 had dropped by Z+6.

By contrast their accuracy was very good, with several yellows falling very close to the aiming point. Unfortunately their tardiness affected the Visual Markers; instead of having 80 sticks of flares to help them identify the aiming point, the most they saw at any one time was 9, and of the 8 crews[6] detailed only 3 marked. The first group fell two miles to the south-east of the aiming point in the Baaken dock area, straddling a line of warehouses and close to the Grasbrook gasworks; another salvo fell between Wandsbeker Chaussee and Hasselbrook suburban railway station. The third fell in the Altona area two miles west; F/O R.A. Fletcher dropped a red in error, his bombsight being U/S (unserviceable). It also fell in Altona, and in fact his was the nearest to the aiming point. The Backers-up showed no favourites, as indeed they should not, so each red was supported by greens. As the first wave of bombers was also impartial, the attack opened with four distinct concentrations.

There can have been few people in Bomber Command who had a more eventful ten days in their operational tours than W/O R.J. Walters. In fact it was not until his sortie to Mont Lucon on September 15, 1943, that he had a trouble-free trip as captain of his own crew. On the night of July 24 he was there as a spectator, though no doubt he did a stint dispensing *Window*. It was common practice in Bomber Command for new pilots to do a sortie with an experienced pilot to see conditions over the target before being responsible for the lives of a crew. Walters was understudy to P/O R.G. Hartwell, who had struggled all the way across the North Sea in trying to persuade his Stirling to climb above 10,000 feet. The port outer, which had been causing concern for some time, burst into flames when the Stirling had almost reached the turning point, with the yellows dead ahead. Hartwell jettisoned the bombs, shut down the engine and turned for home. The fire died out and the disappointed crew began the long, dreary journey back to base. Although they got within sight of the enemy coast it would not count as a sortie.

The night fighters, tied as they were each to a small zone, were thus spread over a wide area. Now that the bombers were entering the Reich in large numbers on a narrow front, this approach had become uneconomical, so the Germans had formed a new group of freelance single-engined fighters, later to be called *Wilde Sau* (Wild Boars), to intercept the enemy at the target and harass them en route. It was a return to the old *Cat's-Eyes* method but with certain advantages: the flak would be restricted to height when they were in the vicinity, methods of signifying the bomber's route were devised,

5. The flares and TIs were dropped blindly, using H2S to assess the aircraft's position.
6. Three from 97 Squadron and one each from 7, 35, 83, 156 and 405 Squadrons.

and signals between fighter and ground were arranged. This was their first big night, and already some bright boy had realised that it would be reasonable to expect to find bombers around the route markers. As has already been recorded, the "tied" fighters had also been told by the harassed ground controllers to go and find their own bombers. Crew reports indicated that three outbound aircraft had been shot down by fighters, one each at Itzehoe, Meldorf and Heligoland. In view of this Hartwell was lucky not to have been picked up as he approached the turning point, where his flaming engine would have pinpointed him; on the other hand, it might have been his saviour, persuading the enemy that he was already under attack.

Night fighters were certainly in the vicinity, as Sgt A. Fletcher of 51 Squadron discovered. He had just crossed the enemy coast at 54°00N 08°50E, slightly north of the yellows, when Sgt R.S. Smith saw an enemy aircraft 200 yards astern. *Monica* had been sending out its monotonous pips for some time – which was not unusual because it did not distinguish friend from foe – and as the pips had increased neither in volume nor tempo the natural conclusion was that the following aircraft was a friend. It was Smith's first trip and, even if he had been conned by *Monica*, his reflexes were not impaired. He swung his turret and both bomber and fighter opened up simultaneously. Smith was too busy to bother with aircraft recognition but realised that the fighter was twin-engined when the starboard motor burst into flames. The night fighter broke away by diving steeply to port and made a red glow as it disappeared into the cloud below. It was fortunate that Smith's aim had been true, because after that all his guns jammed. He claimed the fighter as destroyed, but rules are rules and as no one saw it hit the ground the word "probably" was added to the official report. His gunnery leader's comment must also have taken away some of his elation: "Should have seen sooner, but compensated by some excellent shooting."

Five minutes earlier, at 0110 hours, P/O W.H. Benton in "K" of 207 Squadron was intercepted by a twin-engined fighter. Benton turned to port but the fighter pilot followed the manoeuvre. When it was 500 yards away both Sgt J. Fernandez and Sgt F.E. Holbrook, the gunners, opened up with a discouraging burst of gunfire and the enemy aircraft broke away. The combat report goes on to say that there was no co-operation with searchlights. This was hardly surprising if the given position of the attack, 54°25N 08°05E, was correct, because the Lancaster was still 35 miles from the enemy coast.

By 0119 hours the last red had burnt out and the control now lay with the Backers-up and, more importantly, with 11 crews attacking as Recenterers. As soon as the primary markers were out the Backers-up had to assess the central point of all the TIs burning and then fly on for two seconds before releasing their greens.[7] The Recenterers were not bound by these rules: provided their H2S was working efficiently they tried to bring the attack back to the aiming point. As the red TIs to the east and south-east died out, the weight of the attack was concentrated in the districts to the west of the Alster.

All went well until the third wave arrived at 0118 hours, but after that the rot set in. The scourge of Bomber Command attacks, creepback, became pronounced and as the raid progressed a carpet of incendiaries stretched back for seven miles along the track to the aiming point, most of them falling in open fields. Not all the crews in the fourth and

7. In an attempt to prevent creepback.

fifth waves were guilty: many waited until their ETA[8] before bombing and their HEs[9] kept the firefighters in the shelters.

It is possible to understand how men's courage could drain away or why they turned back when the aircraft or their defensive equipment was faulty, but it is difficult to comprehend why a crew would risk all the dangers of a sortie and then drop the bombs short of the target. It would be unfair to make this censure without highlighting another major reason for creepback. The Mk XIV bombsight was superior to the old Course Setting Bombsight in practically every aspect. It did have limitations at heights above 20,000 feet, and the Mk XIVA, modified to eliminate these errors, had a ceiling of 25,000 feet.[10] One drawback was the fact that there was no provision in the terminal velocity setting for bombs having a velocity of less than 1,000 feet per second. Into this category came the 4lb incendiary, Bomber Command's main incendiary bomb. The resulting tendency to undershoot could have been eliminated quickly if cluster projectiles had received a higher priority, so Air Ministry inertia must take some of the blame for the wasted effort caused by creepback. They knew the disease and its cure, and were constantly reminded of the urgency by the C-in-C. That same cure would have helped in another sphere. As Harris put it in his "Despatch": The 4lb incendiary bomb's "lack of aimability when dropped from small bomb containers . . ." caused ". . . great risk to our own aircraft from showers of loose bombs." On this night a Lancaster and two Halifaxes were hit by British IBs, and there were similar incidents on every raid.

On the 24–25th the route planners must also take some of the blame. The Pathfinders correctly dropped route markers where the track crossed the enemy coast to gather the wayward into the bomber stream, where they could enjoy the obvious advantages of *Window*. The track then continued for 55 miles[11] before the turning point to Hamburg. As soon as the TIs started to fall only the conscientious would go to the turning point, the majority of captains heading directly for the TIs. Thus few navigators would have a correct ETA even though they did have the advantage of *Zephyrs*. The aircraft would also be approaching the target from the wrong angle. Many captains made a shallow dive as they approached the target to get through the danger zone as quickly as possible, and although the extra speed would tend to offset the effect of bombing below the scheduled height, it did result in an undershoot. Finally, when the loss rate was high, about 25% of the force was made up of inexperienced crews with less than five sorties to their credit, and the majority of them bombed the first fires they came to.

*Window* was exceeding all expectations in its effects on flak and searchlights: the FLAK were reduced to putting up a barrage – firing without aiming – to keep the bombers high and make the bomb-aimer's task more difficult, and the searchlights were weaving across the sky "clueless," as 83 Squadron summed it up. Occasionally two searchlights would meet, the others would quickly zero in and make a cone, and the FLAK would then pepper it even though there was no victim. F/O G. Turner in a

8. Estimated time of arrival.
9. High-explosive bombs.
10. As only Mosquitoes bombed above this height no serious efforts were made to overcome this limitation.
11. Although many navigators did not work in nautical miles, the obvious advantages when plotting on a Mercator chart seemed to outweigh the fact that some aircraft airspeed indicators were in mph and Ordnance maps used land miles. Similarly, good navigators took fixes at six-minute intervals (or multiples of six) because degrees of latitude and longitude were divided into 60ths on the charts. Nautical miles are used throughout this book.

Stirling of 75 Squadron was one of the few unfortunates to be caught. Just after he had dropped his bombs the whole cockpit lit up. He realised immediately what had happened and dived to port before the other searchlights could home in effectively. Suddenly the whole aircraft shuddered from a terrific impact. The aircraft became almost impossible to handle and it was some minutes before he could get it under control. The next ten minutes were spent in sorting out the extent of the damage and how it would affect performance. Four feet of the starboard mainplane had been torn off, the starboard aileron had been ripped off also, and the aileron controls were no longer working. However, the Stirling lived up to its reputation[12] and seemed as unwilling as the crew to spend the rest of the war in Germany. When everything had settled down the skipper asked, "What the hell was that?" The crew, who had waited in silent apprehension while the flight engineer, Sgt. J. Thomson, and bomb-aimer, P/O A. Howlett, helped the pilot to sort out the problems, all tried to tell the story in unrehearsed unison. A Ju88, trying to find a victim the hard way and probably blinded by the searchlights, had crashed head-on into the starboard wing. This unequal confrontation resulted in the Ju88 turning over on its back and diving headlong towards Hamburg.

Bomber Command made a practice of recording the number of aircraft damaged by flak, but these incidents never received the prominence given to a combat. Provided that one side fired, it was compulsory to make a report of an interception even if neither combatant sustained damage. The exposure to danger would seem to have been the same in both circumstances, yet a combat, particularly a successful one, seemed to excite ground crews. In their view they only "lent" the aircraft to aircrew, and to bring it back damaged by flak showed lack of care for someone else's property. However, to the crews involved a flak strike was as serious as a combat, and with no opportunity to fight back.

Even on the first of the *Gomorrah* raids the effect of *Window* on the efficiency of the flak and searchlight batteries was apparent. There were only ten incidents of flak damage over the target, of which five occurred during the first 10 minutes before *Window* saturation had been achieved. Thus the Pathfinders and the first wave of bombers suffered more flak damage than crews in later waves. One Main Force crew, captained by W/Cdr A.D. Frank, were over the target at 0115 hours when they were engaged by predicted heavy flak and their Halifax was hit. While the damage was only superficial, an oil leak in the starboard inner engine required constant watching. F/Lt A.J.F. Davidson of 35 Squadron was given no peace from 12 miles short of the target until he was well south of the city, and only by taking continuous evasive action was he able to prevent his Halifax from being severely damaged. On the run-up to the target P/O H. Gowan of 405 PFF Squadron was the victim of predicted flak. One shell burst near the mid-upper turret, seriously wounding Sgt C.C. McLellan in the thigh and abdomen; sadly, these injuries proved fatal and he died on August 2. Another piece of shrapnel struck the H2S and made it unserviceable, but most of the damage was to the rear of the cockpit and Gowan made a safe return to Gransden Lodge.

Five aircraft were shot down over the target, three of them definitely by flak after they had been coned. How the other two were destroyed is not certain but there were night

---

12. The type was noted for its ability to take a great deal of punishment and still remain airborne.

fighters aplenty over Hamburg that night. Two minutes after leaving the target F/Sgt R.D. Morrison, F/Sgt J. Webster's tail gunner, sighted a Ju88 1,000 yards astern and closing fast. Webster made a steep dive to port but the enemy aircraft followed the manoeuvre. Morrison opened fire and scored hits on the Junkers' starboard mainplane. The German came on relentlessly, but flying through the rear gunner's lead spoiled his aim and at 200 yards he was forced to break away. The Halifax was undamaged. In keeping with 77 Squadron's policy the mid-upper gunner was dispensing *Window*.

About the same time as Morrison was handing out his warning another Junkers pilot was probably receiving the shock of his life. Having dropped his bombs on the target and checked for hang-ups, P/O W.S. Neathway clambered into the front turret. He had barely settled into his seat when he noticed a twin-engined aircraft below him. "Twin-engine, Wellington? No." The Lancaster was approaching the enemy too quickly for Neathway to get in a shot, so he warned the gunners to search the starboard quarter down. The Junkers pilot must have been cruising around hunting for Wellingtons and Stirlings, for he seemed totally unaware of the Lancaster above. The rear gunner, Sgt T. Goodwin, first sighted him at 400 yards on the starboard quarter down. "Junkers 88, dive starboard Skipper, go." The German pilot reacted quickly when he saw the tracer flying past and he broke away to port in a dive. Nor did he apparently feel vindictive, for he just disappeared. Sgt R.D. Large, the captain, could afford to smile, since not very many crews bothered to man the nose turret.[13]

W/Cdr P.N. Jennings, CO of 207 Squadron, was one of the captains selected to bomb in the first wave. After dropping his bombs he continued on his southerly track to the first turning point on the return route. His navigator, Sgt G.W.E. Stanford, gave him a course of 306° and told him to look out for PFF route markers cascading down dead ahead within the next few minutes. Cutting across this conversation came the urgent voice of Sgt D.R. Dearman, the rear gunner: "Skipper, fighter on the port quarter above, corkscrew port, he's moving astern, Fw190" – and then for the sake of P/O R.C. Etheridge, the mid-upper gunner – "he's coming in." The Focke-Wulf opened fire at 200 yards and broke off at 100 yards. Fortunately he needed more practice in night combat[14], for the cannon shells went harmlessly by. Both gunners replied with short bursts and showed why they had been selected to fly with the Squadron CO: with only a few seconds to take aim and fire they both saw their tracer hit the fighter, which dived away. The searchlight crew, attracted by the sound of gunfire and seeing the tracers, started sweeping the sky in the area. Jennings was held momentarily but slipped clear without much trouble. At 0128 hours, with the enemy coast still some 50 miles away, Etheridge's voice came over the intercom: "Corkscrew port, Skipper, go," and, for Dearman's benefit, "port quarter up, 400 yards." The fighter opened fire, dived down to 300 yards and then broke away. Etheridge got in a short burst to show the gunners were on the alert. It was all over so quickly that the gunners were unable to identify the fighter beyond the fact that it was single-engined. It may well have been the same Fw190, since the aim was poor and the pilot did not risk a close exchange of shots.

---

13. Frontal attacks were very rare at night.
14. Most trained night fighter pilots found the corkscrew a difficult manoeuvre to follow, so converted day fighter pilots were completely confused until they had gained experience. A corkscrew to port consisted of: dive port – climb port – roll – dive starboard – climb starboard.

Ahead of Jennings the six crews who had marked the route outward dropped their last LBTI yellows at 53°43N 08°36E to mark the homeward route. The same Backers-up who had kept the initial turning point lit and had then dropped their greens to keep the pot boiling at Hamburg were responsible for keeping the homeward turning point marked.

Three of the 20 Wellingtons manned by Polish airmen who took off from Hemswell[15] received the special attention of the German defences. The courage and daring of Polish personnel in the RAF was a byword, but the Operations Record Book (PRO AIR 27/1657) seems, to put it mildly, somewhat terse. Recounting the three incidents, it reads: "W/O W. Koczwarski's Wellington was hit by flak over the target and the trailing aerial was shot away. At 54°00N 07°30E, 'S' of 300 Squadron sighted a single-engined enemy aircraft 200 yards ahead and 100 yards above. Our aircraft dived to port, losing height to 16,000 feet, and the fighter was not seen again. Sgt S. Grzeskowiak crash-landed two miles north of Trusthorpe due to petrol shortage caused by an attack thought to be by a Ju88. The crew were safe." There is no account of the combat even though Bomber Command required a report of all encounters with the enemy, no matter how trivial, compiled by the captain and the gunner(s). Not all station and squadron historians recorded the airmen's deeds with the greatest lucidity, but they usually managed to excel themselves when the lives of the crew had been in jeopardy. So it would seem that a language problem existed.

There were many reasons why the fighters seemed to make more interceptions on the homeward route, one of the main ones being the fact that bombers were silhouetted by the target fires and the fighters were able to assess the general direction of the bomber stream. Of equal importance was the tendency of the stream to spread laterally and so give the German ground controllers a better opportunity to select isolated aircraft. Many captains said "Let's get the hell out of here" and made a beeline for the coast, ignoring the laid-down route.

It would certainly appear that F/O J.S. Cole had done this, because he was intercepted near Cuxhaven. One of the plans to help the night fighters was for a searchlight to swing backwards and forwards to indicate the bomber's track, whereupon any *Wild Boar* in the vicinity would come roaring over. Cole was prepared to go into a corkscrew as soon as either P/O J. Sarginson or Sgt G. C. Thompson, his gunners, told him to "go," for a searchlight on the port beam had been signalling for some time and *Monica* was bleeping her warning. Then the unexpected happened: the searchlights formed a cone around a tiny dot in the sky, an Me109. The German pilot switched on a nose light and the searchlights were doused. As the yellow light dived towards the Lancaster, Sarginson opened fire but did not call for a combat manoeuvre because his intercom was unserviceable. Thompson, following the mid-upper's tracer, picked up the Messerschmitt while it was still some 700 yards away. He ordered "Dive port" and opened fire. The enemy continued diving but the combined firepower of the British gunners forced him to break off the attack without actually firing a shot.

Either the crews of 158 Squadron were poorly briefed or some of their crews did not pay enough attention. Although the last red went out at 0109 hours, one bomb-aimer bombed with a red TI in his bombsight – having seen it cascade at 0123 hours – and

15. Thirteen from 300 Squadron, seven from 305.

another reported seeing reds cascade at 0131 hours, though they had gone out before he could bomb them. One crew from 100 Squadron claimed to have bombed a red at 0145 hours. In fact, 25% of the force reported seeing reds long after the Visual Markers had left the Hamburg area, though many of them realised they were decoys.[16]

As reported elsewhere,[17] as early as May 1943 the Germans had been firing decoy TIs and had succeeded in deceiving the bombers on more than one occasion, so this night they got busy firing reds. Bennett, ever the perfectionist, was most critical of the crews who were deceived. This was only natural because his crews were always blamed when attacks went awry and the Main Force seemed to enjoy being able to report seeing TIs in the wrong place. Unlike the newspapers, which on occasion are known to make retractions, Bomber Command HQ never admitted it could be wrong. Bennett was correct in saying that there was really no excuse for bombing decoys, but few airmen had his professional approach. While they wanted to beat the Germans as fervently as he, they considered themselves amateurs in a highly professional occupation and were quite content to leave it that way. Nevertheless, bombing of decoys would not have happened if attention had been paid at briefing and navigators were confident of their ETAs.

* * * *

The Germans firing the decoy TI reds were by no means the only busy people at Hamburg. Already the fire services were swamped with calls for help. Believing themselves to be one of the best organised in the Reich, which indeed they were, they were horrified to find themselves completely out of their depth. They were so inundated with calls it was almost a relief when the telephone services failed. This happened after only 15 minutes in the western sector, and scouts had to be sent out on motor cycles to report on conditions in the area.

The districts of Altona, Hoheluft and Eimsbüttel were burning with growing intensity and the wind was gaining strength by the minute. The port area had not escaped and the fires in the waterfront area of St Pauli were still attracting some of those crews who liked bombing fires – and there were plenty of those in Bomber Command. The Reeperbahn was burning on both sides of the road and, from the old boundary between Hamburg and Altona as far as Altona Station, the narrow streets were becoming impassable as houses collapsed and flames leapt from one side of the road to the other.

The German public were kept in ignorance of the extensive damage done by Bomber Command, and although rumours about the devastation caused during the Battle of the Ruhr had percolated through, there were few eyewitness accounts. Even the fact that it was a year since they had experienced a major attack did not alert the citizens of Hamburg to the fact that they were high on Harris' list. After 134 previous raids Hamburg had comparatively few battle scars – a house here and there, mended factory roofs, some damage in the port area – and the people had become *blasé* rather than inured. The last five raids had all been nuisance attacks by Mosquitoes which caused the people to curse the nocturnal disturbances and wish that the night fighters would

16. According to German sources it was the first time they had been used in the Hamburg area.
17. *Pathfinder Force*, by the author of this book.

shoot down "the few *Tommis*" who disturbed their sleep. However, reluctantly maybe, grumbling certainly, many did go to the shelters when the alarm sounded.

Frau Thea Lahaine always went to the shelter. She had three children, of which the eldest had only recently been evacuated with his school and the youngest was still a baby. The baby always cried when the guns fired, and the muffled sound in the cellar was not so terrifying. Her husband was fighting on the Eastern front, so she felt wholly responsible for the children's safety and even the ribbing of her friends could not break her resolve. On average, people with children did behave more responsibly. Even so, when the sirens dragged the citizens from their beds with Sunday hardly 30 minutes old, few could have imagined what the night held in store for them.

The underground shelter in the Industrial Palace[18] in Caffamacherreihe, St Pauli, had filled up with families from the neighbourhood soon after the alarm sounded. The guns were firing and the searchlights weaving across the sky. The *Luftschutzwart* (air-raid warden), Herr Kumiercvyk, had witnessed this many times before, but it was a fascinating sight and he had total faith in the defences, so he waited by the door both to observe and to be on hand for any latecomers.

A load of incendiaries fell on the houses opposite and they were soon engulfed in flames. The warden was going to see if he could help when he heard the whistle of falling bombs and ducked inside the shelter just in time. The blast tore the steel door off its hinges, benches and people were thrown about, the electric lights fused, plunging everything into darkness; women shrieked and children cried in fear.

The shelter was equipped with reserve lamps for such an emergency, and after these were lit some semblance of calm was restored. Mercifully no one had been killed, and although the room was filled with dust the air was still breathable. The injured were taken care of and then the warden went to look at the other exits lest he have to evacuate the shelter. Escape was impossible, however: all the exits were blocked with rubble and the door frames were burning. He explored along the passage which led to Beckstrasse and there found a hole in the wall, but as the street was ablaze he decided not to investigate further until the fires had died down. He went back to the people, now huddled together in family groups, and told them that although the exits were blocked they were in no immediate danger and that they were infinitely safer inside the shelter than in the streets outside. Such was their faith in him after the confident way he had handled the initial panic that they accepted his judgement without demur.

The fire engines had all been manned and in position by 0110 hours, but 60 minutes later the total strength had been called out and there was not a single engine left to cover any further emergency. The Police Presidency was in urgent need of help and had to be evacuated when the fire quickly got out of hand. The control room of the *Luftschutzleiter* (air protection leader) was engulfed in flames and evacuation was extremely hazardous. The large office blocks in the area had proved ideal kindling for the thousands of incendiaries dropped in the early part of the raid. The HE bombs too played their part, keeping the firefighters in the shelters and so allowing the IBs to take maximum effect. They also burst the water mains so that the fire services had to rely on the static water

---

18. Industrial shelters were built underground to house the workers and staff of commercial firms or factories. They were designed to withstand all but the largest bombs, contained several connecting rooms and were equipped with electric lights and air conditioning.

tanks and canals. The streets became so blocked with rubble that even the reconnaissance officers on motor cycles found it almost impossible to get through and succeeded only after making long detours.

* * * *

The first crews to arrive back were those of 8 Group, and soon afterwards flying controls in East Anglia and Yorkshire were hard at work as crew after crew asked for permission to land. Trouble came early at Wyton when G/Capt J.H. Searby arrived over the airfield to find the visibility down to a quarter of a mile. He called up for permission to land and was given a height of 1,000 feet[19] as the runway was in use. From this height on the crosswind leg he could barely make out the flarepath. Realising that the conditions called for the utmost vigilance, he forced the tiredness from his mind and muscles. Suddenly, coming towards him out of the gloom, a black shape appeared immediately ahead. He thrust the control column forward and there was a horrible crunch as the black shape sliced off the mid-upper turret; fortunately P/O J.H. Coley had made a timely exit only seconds before. The Lancaster yawed madly and it was obvious the controls had been damaged. By using the engines and keeping heavy pressure on the rudder bar Searby managed to keep the aircraft on a straight course, though it was still see-sawing about. He ordered the crew to don parachutes and be ready to leave immediately. The engines were not affected, however, and he found that he could maintain height. Flying Control gave him a priority landing but it needed a master's skill to manoeuvre the Lancaster – minus starboard rudder and fin – into a good position for the approach. In the "funnel" he had great difficulty in controlling the aircraft as power was reduced, and then, just as he was all set for landing, a 139 Squadron Mosquito nipped in and landed ahead of him. To go round again was out of the question, so he landed on the grass parallel to the runway. Captain and crew survived the ordeal without a scratch, but the Mosquito pilot's ears must have been burning.

Meanwhile, at Warboys S/Ldr S. Hall of 156 Squadron was calling for a priority landing. He too landed safely, with the starboard outer on fire and dangling from the mainplane of his Lancaster. A split-second decision had saved the lives of 14 airmen, while a stupid act had put seven of them in jeopardy again. Fortunately there were only a few irresponsible pilots in a trade where one was too many.

F/O Turner of 75 Squadron arrived over Mepal at 0410 hours and was immediately given a priority landing. Dog-tired after three hours of struggling to keep his Stirling on course, like Searby before him, he realised that full concentration was vital for a few minutes more. Howlett had been standing by continuously against the time he might be required to help his captain; he too knew that the slightest error could mean disaster. On the approach the sight of the flare path seemed to go to the Stirling's head, and as the power was reduced it took all Turner's and Howlett's strength to hold the nose up. It could not be classed as one of Turner's best landings but, on the premise that "all landings are good ones if you can walk away from them," no one was complaining.

---

19. Warboys and Wyton both operated left-hand circuits, "though it seems incredible now," as Searby says. Where the circuits of two stations were contiguous or overlapped, to avoid crashes one of them usually orbited right-handed. When stations were close sometimes one "stacked" at 500, 1,500 and 2,500 feet, the other in between at the even 1,000s.

As the crews landed Flying Control logged the time and the information was passed to Group, where the landing times were entered against the captain's name on the crew board. The weather forecast for bases had been: "Clear for take-off with clear skies and moderate visibility. Towards dawn visibility would deteriorate but at 0400 hours 75% of the bases would still have visibility of one mile and this would still be true of 50% at 0500 hours. 6 Group however might have a few problems." Curiously, 6 Group did not have the expected early morning mist and, with one exception, all stations landed their crews without difficulty. Holm was the exception, but Riccall came to the rescue and six aircraft of 76 Squadron were diverted there. It was south of the Humber, in 3 Group, where visibility was falling off rapidly as dawn approached, and 21 Stirlings had to be diverted, two of them outside the Group.

Eventually the time was reached when all hope that any outstanding bombers could still be airborne had faded. A total of 12 crews had not returned, but it was a gratifyingly small loss from a force of 791. *Window* had exceeded all expectations. Harris breathed a sigh of relief as the last Stirling landed and he dashed off to get a few hours of sleep before starting another busy day, less than 4½ hours away.

A great deal of time and trouble went into crew debriefing after an operation, but there was a feeling that much of it was a waste of time. There were good reasons for this: the crews were tired and hungry, and in many cases nothing out of the ordinary had happened. Suggestions and complaints rarely seemed to have any effect, many reports would be similar and there were too many people nagging for answers. Again, as in every branch of the service, the quality of the Intelligence Officers varied and many of the questions seemed pointless. Having myself been through the ordeal many times and having studied the results thirty years later, it is obvious that much of the work, by ORS for example, was totally irrelevant to what should have been the main concern: how to win the war in the shortest possible time with the lowest loss of life.

The argument about whether 5 Group's low-level marking was better than 8 Group's *Oboe* attacks was out of date by the time a report was issued and its findings were no longer true when averaged over a longer period. It also referred to a series of raids which were history by then. What is perhaps more to the point, neither Bennett nor Cochrane[20] was influenced by the report, nor had they had the slightest intention of changing their methods.

The analysis, which showed that H2S operators who took more fixes per hour were on the average more accurate than those who took fewer, ignored the fact that while most navigators worked flat-out for the duration of the sortie, some worked more quickly than others. Nor were tests made to see whether the quicker ones would have been less accurate had they taken fewer fixes. Were they better operators in addition to being quicker?

Air gunners complained from the beginning of the war that they were outgunned by the fighters, yet after five years the position was the same, if not worse, since by then the enemy was firing rockets. Incidents in which friendly aircraft were hit by 4lb incendiaries were recorded by ORS but that did not speed up the introduction of "cluster" projectiles.[21] However, some of the information did bear fruit: when navigation

20. Air Marshal the Hon Sir Ralph Cochrane, OC of 5 Group.
21. See Glossary.

improved as a result of better navigational aids, route markers eventually helped the night fighters more than the Main Force, and they were consequently used sparingly.

The main purpose of debriefing was to assess the success of the raid, and no one objected to that. Nor were the crews averse to discussing the merits of *Window* and *Zephyrs*, the two novelties. In fact they reported anything new. At least three crews reported seeing a new type of flak which looked like a Catherine wheel. This information had reached Army Intelligence early enough for an AA major to go as a spectator on July 29–30.

There was also one crew who reported seeing a "scarecrow". This was the name given by aircrews to describe a shellburst which gave the impression of an aircraft exploding and disintegrating, and it is one of the unsolved mysteries of the war. The official view was that it was in reality an aircraft which had been hit by flak and actually exploded. More weight was given to this theory when, after the war, the Germans said that they had no such shell. Yet on an operation to Wanne Eickel on November 9, 1944, my skipper and I were flying at 28,000 feet on a marking run when we saw what looked like an aircraft disintegrating. It was a daylight attack and the only aircraft in the vicinity was being flown by friends of mine, F/Lt D. Tidy and F/Lt G.H. Barr, acting as Reserve. Flak was being thrown up at our height but a little behind on the port side. I had seen their Mosquito in that position only seconds earlier. We were naturally very upset and were later describing the incident to the Intelligence Officer at debriefing when a voice behind me said: "It certainly wasn't us." With immense relief we turned and saw our friends standing there. It seemed that they had realised we were going to "cope"[22] and so had turned away. Neither 105 nor 109 Squadrons lost any Mosquitoes that day, and there would not have been any other British aircraft at that height. What we saw definitely looked like an aeroplane exploding, and similar reports persisted all through the war.

Instances of freelance fighters operating over the target and of night fighters dropping flares and operating with navigation lights burning or with a headlight in the nose were quickly fed through the cumbersome bureaucratic machinery to become common knowledge on the stations within days.

The extent and type of damage to the target were first assessed from crew reports and then confirmed by PRU photographs. The conclusions were fed back to the stations and displayed in the Intelligence room. Good attacks were great morale-boosters.[23] Irrespective of whether crews liked debriefing or not, it was compulsory. So, having dispensed with the formalities at dispersal, the crew gathered all their kit together and waited for some transport back to the flight locker rooms, where flying kit was stowed away. There was the inevitable chit-chat with other crews, and always the skipper pleading "Come on, chaps, let's get to debriefing before there's a long queue." The debriefing room was usually at Station HQ. Seated behind trestle tables were various officers, including the Intelligence Officers, waiting to fill in the innumerable forms which, even in wartime, appeared to take priority over deeds. Just inside the doorway, on yet another trestle table, stood a large urn of tea with milk and sugar already added,

22. Code name for a successful *Oboe* sortie.
23. The lack of confirmation of damage to Berlin during the winter of 1943–44, combined with an increasing loss rate, sapped crews' enthusiasm and tended to increase the number of "fringe merchants".

undoubtedly to Air Ministry specifications. Most of the table was taken up by rows of cups neatly aligned as if dressed by an army CSM, although, as if in recognition of the informality of the proceedings, not all the handles were pointing at 4 o'clock. A Waaf on duty for that purpose filled and refilled the cups. Each crewman was allowed a tot of rum after every sortie. Some drank it neat while others used it to lace their tea. There were also a few who brought their tobacco pouches and used their ration to anoint the contents; it certainly enhanced the bouquet and may well have improved the flavour. Smoking was permitted but, as if in resigned recognition that the floor was a big ashtray, there was always a shortage of the more conventional receptacles. In the winter, when the windows were locked tight shut to keep in the heat and the operation had been "dicey," the atmosphere rivalled the old-time London fog for thickness and the floor was littered with cigarette ends.

After debriefing the Intelligence Officer would have to correlate all the stories, summarise them and get his report off to Group as soon as possible. Some of the data had already been entered: names of crew, type of aircraft, type and weight of bombs, duty of crew, previous number of sorties flown by the captain. The rest of the information had to be gleaned from the crews. The pilot usually started the proceedings by giving his version of the sortie, with promptings and confirmations from his crew. If the account did not contain all the information required for his report the Intelligence Officer would then ask questions.

Group and Command needed to know whether the method of marking was successful; the crew's assessment of the attack; whether there were any explosions and at what time; whether there were fires and smoke; and, if the aircraft was damaged, how, when and where it was sustained, and its extent. The navigator would answer most of the questions because he had noted all important details in his log. When the gunners were involved they were usually allowed to elaborate; it would have been impossible to stop them in any case. Next he asked if the crew had noticed any changes in the enemy's defensive tactics; their reply had to cover not only flak and fighters but decoy fires and TIs. Next came the technical questions about *Gee* and H2S, *Tinsel*, *Mandrel* and *Monica*; as *Zephyrs* and *Window* were being used for the first time, a special report was required for them.

One question was usually put rhetorically to the captain: "This is your fifth/sixteenth/twentieth operation?" It almost seemed as if credibility was proportional to experience. Then, when he felt he had bled them dry, he would ask, "Anything else?" followed by "Thank you" or, sometimes, "Thank you, gentlemen". His hands, which up to that moment had shown only knuckles, turned palm-upwards and the crew handed over their escape aids, target maps, destructible papers and, finally, the navigator's log and chart. As soon as the last crew left, Intelligence had to make a summary which was forwarded to Group. Group in their turn were expected, within four hours, to have their summaries at HQ Bomber Command, where they were again summarised for Harris.

The Photographic section had by now developed all the film and processed all the printable negatives. This was always a mad rush, since the Photographic section, like all specialist sections, was invariably undermanned. In addition, 8 Group sections had to develop and print 35mm film taken by marker crews. S/Ldr Lees had worked out a novel scheme whereby the H2S screen could be photographed at the exact time of TI release. Although this print did not show the position at which the TIs landed, it could be worked out accurately. Because H2S gave a picture of the ground irrespective of cloud and smoke, the position of the TIs could readily be assessed. With such pressures it was small wonder that at Wyton some colour film was accidently placed in the black-and-white developer tank. The finished prints had to be rushed to Group, in order to have them on the CO's desk by early morning. Copies were also sent to HQ Bomber Command and passed on to ORS.

All the other information was eventually passed to ORS, which in its own good time issued a Night Raid Report (July 24–25 was No 383). It gave a summary of all Bomber Command's activities for the night, the main target being treated in great detail. The proposed attack was described first and then came an assessment of how successfully the plans were carried out. The narrative of the attack was gleaned from the debriefing reports and confirmed or refuted by PRU photographs. Other topics included: how special equipment functioned on the night; H2S and *Gee*, with *Window* receiving special attention; the German defences, divided into flak and searchlights, and fighters. As a secondary proof of the effectiveness of *Window* on the AA guns the following was quoted: "Of the 10 incidents of aircraft sustaining flak damage over the target five of them occurred within the first 10 minutes before *Window* had achieved maximum saturation." Another interesting point, showing that the *Wilde Sau* were not yet co-operating with the ground defences: "Of the 5 aircraft seen to have been shot down in combat all of them were at least 20 miles from the target." The list of casualties followed the section on defences: number of aircraft missing (12); number of aircraft damaged (31), subdivided into flak (20), fighter (2), non-enemy action (9). The kills were divided equally between the two defences: 5 (or 6) flak, 5 (or 6) fighters. The majority of the aircraft seen to have been shot down were first coned by searchlights. However, by the

**NIGHT OPERATIONS July 24–25 & 25–26**

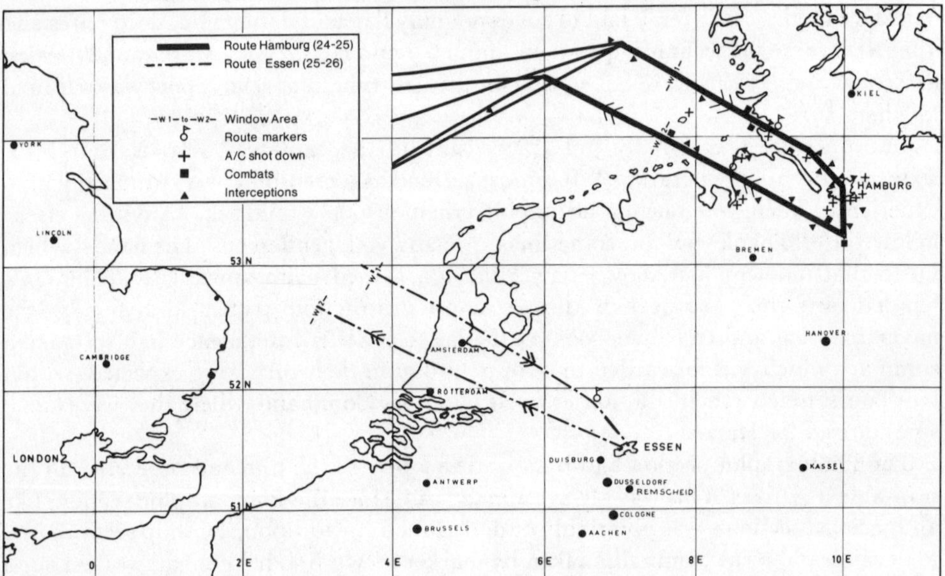

**The 8 Group operations board at 0925 hours, April 5, 1945, after a busy night. Over 240 successful sorties were flown, a sad "no news" being recorded after the names of three crews.** ***(Howard Lees)***

**A Mk IX Mosquito (MK 331) of 109 Squadron. This aircraft took part in the Essen raid of July 26-27, 1943.** *(Author)*

**Lancaster "C Charlie" of 153 Squadron. Judging by the bombs painted on the side she was one of the select group of aircraft (about 30) which completed more than 100 operations. The specially posed photograph shows in the foreground her massive bomb load: 1 × 4,000lb and 16 × 500lb bombs. The seven aircrew, standing behind the 4,000lb "Cookie", are wearing Mae Wests; the five armourers are grouped behind the 500s; three of the Lancaster's own ground crew are on the right of the picture. The petrol bowser was manned by two airmen and the group of four in the centre were part of the team of electricians, radio and instrument mechanics, and other sections who worked on the bomber to get her ready for an operation.** *(Author)*

**A hole in the cloud gave F/O F. Thompson and his crew an opportunity to land rather than bale out.** *(Author)*

**Final preparation for an op.** *(Author)*

**(Left) An operator cutting aluminium foil in the course of *Window* production.** ***(IWM)***

**A Ju88 (above) and an Me110 with British markings (below). Both these German aircraft were captured and later tested at Farnborough. The aerials for their AI equipment show them to be night fighters.** ***(PRO, IWM)***

**Lancaster Mk III of No 619 Squadron.** *(IWM)*

**Lancaster Mk III taking off for a raid on Hamburg. Waaf at the side of the runway wave farewell.** *(IWM)*

**Halifax Mk II on its way to Essen.** *(IWM)*

**Halifax Mk II of 10 Squadron in the light of a flarepath before take-off on a night raid.** *(IWM)*

**Wellington of No 466 Squadron.** *(Author)*

**Stirling of No 214 Squadron.** *(IWM)*

B-17s of the 532nd (code letters VE) and 533rd (VP) Squadrons (above) and 534th (GD) Squadron (below) of the 381st Bomb Group (code letter L), 1st Bomb Wing (▲), above the overcast and flying through dense cloud. This group took part in the daylight attacks of July 25 and 26. *(USAAF)*

**Bombs falling on the Hamburg docks from a B-17 on July 25, 1943.** *(USAAF)*

**Hits in the target area. The large white circle indicates a huge explosion.** *(USAAF)*

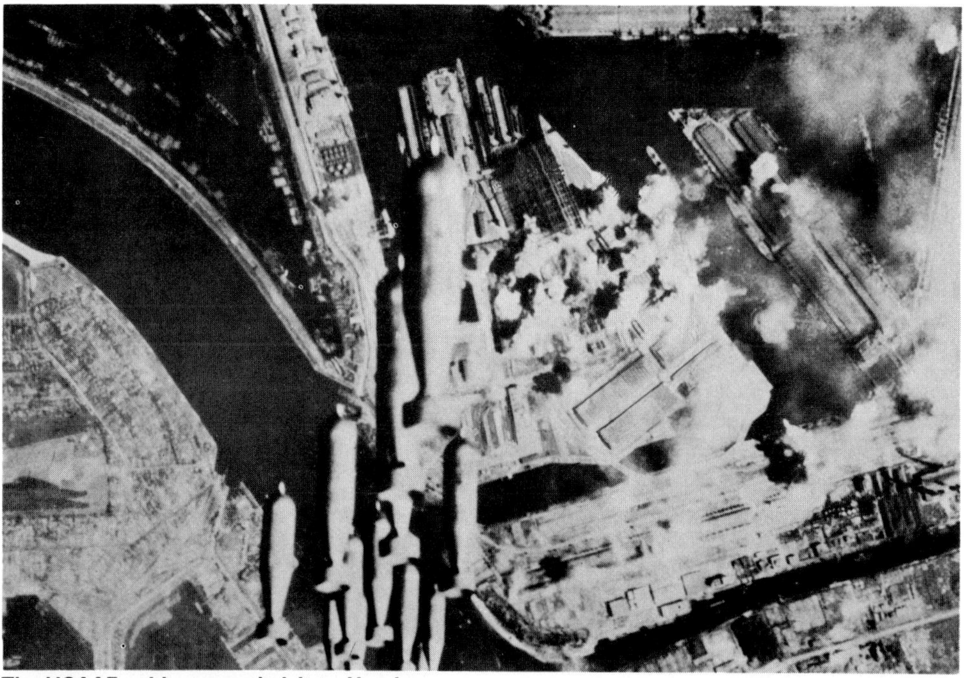

The USAAF paid a second visit to Hamburg on July 26. This photograph shows bombs winging their way down to the Howaldtswerke complex in the dock area. Several salvoes have already burst within the complex. *(USAAF)*

Another pattern of bombs falls slightly to the south of the initial bombing, scoring more hits in the shipbuilding yards and also seriously damaging the Neuhof power station (bottom right-hand corner). *(USAAF)*

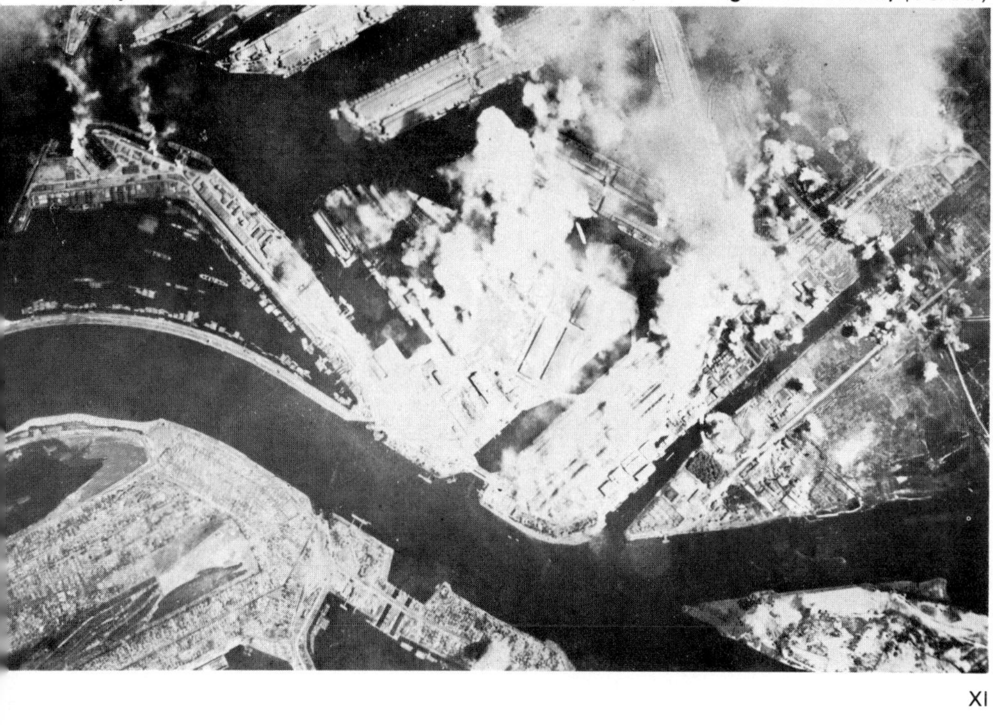

**Boeing B-17s over Hamburg dock area. Black dots are flak bursts. The two aircraft circled at lower right are Me109s about to attack.** *(USAAF)*

**Fires rage uncontrollably behind the demolished building in the foreground.** *(Staatsarchiv Hamburg)*

**This photograph of riverside buildings illustrates vividly the inexorable progress of the wind-driven fires. The building on the left has already collapsed into the river, while although the upper floors are ablaze in the building on the right, the fires have not yet reached ground level.** *(IWM)*

**St Pauli was heavily damaged on the night of July 24-25. The Reeperbahn, world famous for its nightclubs, and the red-light area around Seilerstrasse were demolished.** *(IWM)*

**Further west in Altona, damage was equally severe. This is a typical example of the devastation in the area.** *(Hans Brunswig)*

**Burnt-out wreck of a fire engine which had been taking on water from the Eilbek Kanal. This incident took place on the perimeter of the firestorm; trees less than 100 yards away were untouched.** *(Hans Brunswig)*

**Mangled remains of a fire engine hit by a high-explosive bomb.** *(Hans Brunswig)*

**Although the streets have been cleared, damaged trams still block Route 33.** *(Staatsarchiv Hamburg)*

**Queuing for fresh water near Harvestehuder station.** *(IWM)*

time the report was published the poor performance of the German defences on this night was history. The pendulum was already swinging the other way and continued to do so for the following nine months.

*   *   *   *

In Hamburg the "All clear" sounded just after 3 o'clock and people in the north and east left their shelters, stared unbelievingly at the mass of fire in the south and west, and went to bed to get a few hours of sleep or at least to rest. However, there was no respite that day for Hamburg's fire service, nor for those responsible for civil defence. The Harbour and East groups had managed to keep in touch throughout the bombardment, and neither envied the other its problems, but when the scouts returned with their reports from the western zone it was realised for the first time that by far the greatest damage was in that area. Besides the Police Presidency and the *Luftschutz* (Air Defence) control already mentioned, numerous other air-raid precautions centres were either destroyed or damaged. Four firemen had had a narrow escape when their fire engine received a direct hit which reduced it to a mangled wreck. Burst water mains rendered many fire engines useless, and others were trapped by fallen masonry. Static tanks proved their worth but were soon emptied, and to replenish them was well-nigh impossible because the streets were blocked with rubble.

One group of people who had been forced out of their burning shelter had literally jumped out of the frying pan into the fire. Flying sparks had forced them into nearby buildings, where reflected heat from the walls and the thick smoke made them distressed and brought them almost to a state of collapse. The buildings too were beginning to crumble when Werner Schlung, an officer of the fire service and the ARP on reconnaissance, stumbled across the group. First he led them out from their immediate danger and then pointed out their best way to safety.

In the area around the Bismarckstrasse a firestorm was raging; this was near the Police Presidency, where 1,000 people were trapped in a bunker. In spite of the heat and smoke, which was causing much distress inside the bunker, conditions outside were infinitely worse. Once it was realised that their plight was known and help would come as soon as possible the panic subsided and the people settled down to wait. As the reports filtered through it was obvious that the urgent need was to rescue people trapped in the cellars and bunkers; the big problem was reaching them.

The first reds in the Altona area had received a great deal of attention and as the fires started in earnest many bomber crews were drawn to this area, spreading the destruction east into St Pauli and north into Eimsbüttel.

Herr Kalix was a member of the Air Protection Police in Eimsbüttel. After his station had been bombed and put out of action, and since he would not be getting any orders from outside as his telephone had been dead for some time, he decided to go ahead and find trouble for himself. He did not have far to go, since most of the houses in the area were ablaze and many of them had their own cellar bunkers. He realised that this raid on Hamburg was unlike the previous ones, with an intensity never experienced before. First, together with two of his comrades, he scouted the area for an escape route, and then forced his way into the cellars, bullying the inhabitants into leaving these potential death traps. Once on the street he grabbed hold of a couple of children, dashed through the flames, and rushed to Emilienstrasse U-Bahn (underground railway station), exhorting the others to follow him. All Hamburg stations had air raid shelters and this one proved to be a sanctuary for hundreds as Kalix encouraged the people to brave the flames rather than stay and suffocate.

On one of his return trips he was intercepted by a watchman who said there were 150 people trapped in a public shelter on Fruchtallee. The shelter was under a house with a thatched roof (hardly an ideal place for an air-raid shelter) which, not surprisingly, was on fire. Herren Pourlewaki and Noewald, who were helping Kalix in his rescue work, went along with him to assess the danger. In the cellar were 90 foreign workers, some of them French. They seemed very agitated, particularly the Frenchmen. By contrast the Germans – old men, women and children – were displaying remarkable calm. Kalix explained that they were in no immediate danger and told them that there were many others in a far worse plight. His duty was to rescue the others first but he would keep his eye on conditions and come back to help if need arose. His promise seemed to reassure everyone and he went back into the street to help those in more urgent need.

However, the fire got worse and when it spread to the cinema next door it became obvious that the people would have to be evacuated promptly. The house was now burning at ground level and the shelter ceiling was hot; smoke had seeped in through the ventilator shaft and the air was almost unbreathable. The emergency exit was on fire so they had to make their way out through the flames. Kalix told the women to put towels over their thin clothing. The foreign workers were ordered to take care of the children and also to help the women. This was a good move because the responsibility made them behave rationally, and everyone first made their way to the centre of the street and then to the U-Bahn. The "All-clear" had gone some time ago, so the only danger was from falling masonry. The rescue was timely as the shelter had become very hot. Sweat was pouring off Kalix, soaking his clothing, and the smoke was blinding him. He made one last dash through the rooms, calling out to anyone who might remain, but got no reply. Finally he made his own escape, but only with great difficulty. The cinema was by now blazing so he had to find a new way out across a collapsed wall and through a store now burnt to a shell. The bunker survived the fire but one Frenchman and one German who must have crawled away from the group were later found dead of suffocation.

Hagenbeck Tierpark[24] lay on the bombers' route to the city and became a victim of creepback. In addition to its world famous zoo, the Hagenbeck Circus was encamped within its grounds, providing ideal kindling for the incendiaries: tents, wooden seating, travelling cages and caravans (at least 80 vehicles), all stored neatly together in one area. Also in a compact group were the zoo's restaurants, public house and office buildings, with the workshops close by; all of them were single-storey buildings and highly inflammable. The fires did a thorough job and the whole area was gutted. However, some of the animals survived and the younger elephants herded round the two leaders, who led them to safety without panic. Nor did the birds of prey take

24. Some sources say the bombing occurred on the 27th. A circus performing in Altona was also destroyed, and this may account for the confusion. The creepback on the 24th would have covered the area of Hagenbeck, whereas on the 27th it would have been stray bombs.

advantage of their freedom: they fed on the dead animals and then returned to their cages.

Curiously, it was not the lions and tigers roaming free in the park that struck fear into the hearts of people, but the bears. This may have been because their enclosure was on a knoll close to the entrance, so that they were always in plain view. That some of the animals had survived and were roaming around free and hungry was sufficient excuse for the army patrols to give the area a wide berth. Gossip takes the mind off one's own problems for a while; and the tales of the Wehrmacht's caution were passed along and embellished gleefully. Somebody else had seen mysterious flashlight signals from the Tierpark. As a great port Hamburg was a natural avenue for spies entering or leaving the Continent, and much information was passed on by sailors. After this attack the sin emporia of the Reeperbahn were in ruins, so the purveyors of secret information had to find a new rendezvous at which to transact their business. The rumour that the Tierpark was their meeting place for the next week or so still survives today, so there could be a grain of truth in it.

Meanwhile, Herr Kumiercvyk in St Pauli had paid several visits to the hole in the wall of the Industrial Palace. After the "All-clear" had sounded the fires had gradually died down. The sun had been over the horizon for some time when at last he found that the bricks surrounding the hole were cool enough to be pulled out. The passage to the shelter was 100 metres long and many people had to be carried because they were unconscious, but everyone got out safely. Kumierzyk inspired confidence and the people's behaviour was exemplary, with everybody helping one another. Their eight-hour ordeal had brought them close together, and in their troubles they had shared their comforts, particularly the drinking water, and helped those in distress. Under normal conditions the devastation outside would have made them weep, but the feeling at that moment was simple gratitude at just being alive.

At about the same time as the last person left the bunker in Hamburg, Harris was entering the one at High Wycombe to set the wheels in motion for another attack on the Reich.

# Chapter IV

# The Americans

ON JUNE 10, 1943, Air Vice-Marshal N.H. Bottomley, Assistant Chief of Air Staff, sent Harris his sixth directive of 1943. It later became known as *Pointblank* and remained in force until the war was almost won. It had to play second fiddle to any of the purely strategic directives such as *Overlord*, but at all times Harris was permitted to use his force as laid down in this directive when it was not required for special assignments.

Although the Nazi star was declining at the beginning of 1943, Bomber Command remained the only means of striking at the heart of Germany. Harris believed he could bomb the enemy into submission, but the Chiefs of Staff thought it would be imprudent to rely on this happening, even though the US 8th Army Air Force was about to reinforce the RAF in attacks on Germany. The Casablanca Conference was called in January 1943 to explore all the possibilities of Anglo-American co-operation. The Americans, who had prepared themselves mentally if not physically to open a second front in the spring or summer of 1943, had been made to realise that the task was impossible. The British, being closer to the problem, had realised that it would take until the spring of 1944 for the Allies to assemble a force strong enough to launch an invasion. It was also hoped that by then the Germans would be too weak to repulse it. Much emphasis was placed on the sapping of Germany's strength and, although the word "invasion" automatically reduced the bomber offensive to secondary importance, it was readily agreed that the bombers' contribution would be very significant before, during and after the invasion.

The British expressed the belief that the American bomber force would be wise to join Bomber Command in night assaults on the Reich, but US Army Air Force Commander Major-General H.H. Arnold, having discussed the question with Lieutenant-General I.C. Eaker, Commander-in-the-Field,[1] decided that the USAAF could serve the Allied cause more effectively if it stuck to the method for which it had been trained: daylight precision bombing.

The Conference agreed that a combined bomber offensive should be the aim, but how to achieve it, which was a thorny problem, was dumped unceremoniously into Sir Charles Portal's lap. This might at first seem irresponsible, but without an initial agreement to disagree[2] no directive could have been issued and much of the effort of both forces would have been wasted. As it was, to maintain accord practically every conceivable type of target was included in the Casablanca directive[3] and the list of priority targets would have been identical had there been no conference.

1. Harris' equivalent in the USAAF.
2. The Chiefs of Staff of both countries had divergent views, not on what had to be done but on priorities.
3. Sent to Harris on February 4, 1943.

The problem was one of fundamentals. The British were committed to area bombing, attacking the towns rather than specific factories, whereas the Americans believed in the selective bombing principle: that it is better to cause a high degree of destruction in a few really essential industries than to cause a small degree of destruction in many. The principle was in essence the one with which the RAF had entered the war and had been forced to abandon. Although the early-war Blenheim and Hampden could in no way be compared with the Fortress, the Americans certainly had a point to prove.

There were many interested spectators, not the least of them being Churchill, who believed that the Americans were in for a shock. Over France in the autumn of 1942 the Americans had proved that, provided they kept a tight formation, they could more than hold their own against the enemy fighters. However, the boast that the Norden bombsight was so good that they could drop bombs into a pickle barrel[4] from 30,000 feet ignored the fact that important German targets were defended by heavy flak. A close formation of bombers flying at heights within range was an AA gunner's idea of bliss, as the 8th had discovered when flying over "Flak City",[5] which was defended by 50 AA guns. After the ground defences had scythed holes in the formation the fighters' task became easier, though never a sinecure. The name Fortress was not a frivolous one, and stragglers always gave a good account of themselves, sometimes embarrassing the enemy by fighting their way clear.

Perhaps Portal was conditioned by Harris' insistence on "weather permitting" being added to any and every commitment he agreed to undertake, but Sir Charles was concerned that too little thought had been given to the effect of the weather, in particular the changing conditions that the USAAF would invariably encounter when making deep penetrations; not the least important of these was cloud over the target. There were numerous occasions when the bombers, although suffering heavy losses, fought their way resolutely to the target only to find it cloud-covered. Had the Americans been working to a timetable they would have failed miserably. Above cloud and flying into the sun, the day bomber was as blind as the night bomber.

The Eaker Plan (April 12, 1943), drawn up principally as a guide for the American forces, called for a combined offensive against six key segments of German industry.[6] Almost as if unaware that there was a difference of opinion, the plan assumed that the British would co-operate in strategy as well as policy. Curiously, Harris voiced no criticism and told Eaker that he was "in complete agreement with the policy recommended", but he added that if it proved inelastic in the event it would be necessary to modify it to meet the circumstances.

If Harris' real opinion of the Eaker Plan remained a secret because he was eager to see the 8th built up into an effective force actively striking at the German economy, his views on selective target bombing were well known and frequently expressed: to attack a specific target was to pander to the "panaceamongers". He believed that there were no key points in the German war economy which, if threatened, could not be dispersed

4. On April 14, 1945, 24 Liberators of the 467th Bombardment Group dropped all their bombs within 1,000 feet of MPI, and 50% within 500 feet. The target was a coastal battery near Bordeaux. Good visibility and a lightly defended target at last gave the crews an opportunity to prove the 8th's boast of 1942.

5. The USAAF's name for St Nazaire.

6. They were: submarine construction yards and bases, the aircraft industry, the ball-bearing industry, oil production, synthetic rubber and military transport vehicles.

and reactivated elsewhere, underground if necessary. Only total devastation in all the towns could bring about the disruption necessary to break down organised industrial activity. Nor were events in 1943 going to change his opinion. By June the main towns of the Ruhr lay in ruins and, without boasting, he could justifiably claim that the destruction was staggering. At the same time, the 8th Air Force had run into many of the problems which had been forecast. Harris has been branded as the arch-proponent of area bombing, but in fact neither the Germans nor the Americans were averse to using this tactic. The Germans had regularly employed the method against Poland, Holland and France in the early part of the war to terrorise the population prior to invasion. In fact they had sent the *Luftwaffe* to Spain during the Civil War to gain experience with these tactics. The German *Baedeker* raids on England in April–May 1942 were aimed at targets as poorly defended as Dresden and completely devoid of strategic value or industry. Exeter, Bath, Norwich and York all fell into this category. Earlier, at Coventry on November 14, 1940, the Germans, using a pathfinder force to drop incendiaries on the centre of the town to guide the other bombers, tore out the centre of the city even though there were dozens of truly strategic targets, few of which were heavily damaged. The V1 and V2 rockets were prime examples of area bombing, since neither could be aimed with any degree of accuracy. The Americans also carried out area attacks. For example, on October 10, 1943, when the 3rd Division attacked Münster, the city centre was the aiming point. It was a clear day and the town offered many selective targets, but the purpose of the attack was to disrupt the working population. Roger Freeman says:[7] "That they [the American crews] were deliberately being sent to kill and make homeless civilians apparently did not produce any moral qualms amongst the airmen. It is recorded that some cheered this news at briefing, their own sufferings having bred bitterness." Much later, in 1945, the Americans carried out area raids on Japan; on March 9 of that year General Curtis Lemay led a force of USAAF bombers to Tokyo for the first of the firebomb raids. The attack was carried out at heights between 5,000 to 7,000 feet and only incendiary bombs were dropped. The town was particularly vulnerable to this type of attack, being built chiefly of wood. A 25 mph wind fanned the flames, which swept across the city, leaving a trail of death and destruction. The bravery of the men who undertook this hazardous mission is beyond question, but no one can deny that it was area bombing. The supreme examples of area attack must surely have been the dropping of atomic bombs on Nagasaki and Hiroshima. Area bombing was therefore indulged in without any qualms by the three main protagonists, when and where the strategy called for it or the capabilities of the air forces necessitated it.

Harris considered that new directives, particularly if they came with monotonous regularity like unpaid bills, showed a lack of purpose in planning, and were designed to divert part of his Command away from its primary task. The *Pointblank* directive, as adopted May 18, 1942, met with his approval, however. It confirmed that the primary object of the bomber forces remained as set out in the Casablanca directive: "the progressive destruction and dislocation of the German military, industrial and economic system, and the undermining of the morale of the German people to a point where their capacity for armed resistance is fatally weakened." This was exactly what

7. *The Mighty Eighth.*

Harris claimed he was doing, and earlier in March he had written to the Air Staff stating this fact, but in the process rephrasing the words to make them agree more precisely with his own thinking. It would be naive to believe that the alterations went unnoticed, but they certainly drew no comment.

*Pointblank* also included modifications to the Eaker Plan and promoted to first priority attacks on the German fighter forces and the industry upon which they depended. The 8th Air Force priorities were listed, and then came the watered-down version of the Eaker Plan. The selective bombing paragraph was omitted and the directive went on to state: ". . . While the forces of the British Bomber Command will be employed in accordance with their main aim in the general disorganisation of German industry their action will be designed as far as practicable to be complementary to the operations of the 8th Air Force." Then it pointed out that in most instances the selected industrial areas were identical with those of Bomber Command.

The original directive and the Eaker Plan sent out after the Casablanca Conference unfortunately showed a complete lack of understanding of the vastly different operational requirements of day and night forces, and assumed that the weather would remain constant over the target and bases for almost 24 hours. Nor did they consider that the type of weather most suitable for each force was not necessarily the same; the state of the moon, for example, affected Bomber Command but not the USAAF. Also ignored was the fact that there are only two equinoxes a year and that short days or nights would place limits on combined deep penetrations.

The first five months of 1943 had been very chastening ones for the 8th, and only because of the supreme courage shown by the men was the daylight offensive maintained. Shortages of crews, aircraft and spare parts were contributory factors which should never have arisen. Inclement weather was something the natives had learned to live with, but to the Americans it was an intolerable frustration. Finally, the German defences, both on the ground and in the air, had proved far more resilient and inventive than the Americans had foreseen. So by the third week in July 1943 there had as yet been no effort on either side to begin a combined offensive.

The last week in July, known in American Air Force history as "Blitz Week," was the first time that the two air forces attacked the same target within a short enough space of time for the raids to be classed as a combined operation. This week of concentrated effort exemplified the problems facing the daylight bombers. On the 24th the effective strength of the 15 Fortress groups was approximately 330 aircraft and crews; by noon on Friday the 30th, when Lt W. Harry brought his badly damaged B-17 to rest across the runway at Boxted, it was less than 200, with the equivalent of 90 crews classified as missing, killed or wounded. In addition, more than 100 of the remaining B-17s had been damaged in varying degrees by the enemy. The Fortress groups were non-operational for two weeks as they worked to get crews and aircraft back to strength.

The differences between the two bomber forces were not confined to policy. The main one was the fact that the Americans flew in daylight and, more distinctlvely, in formation. Later, in 1944 and 1945 when the *Luftwaffe* was a spent force, the British did return to daylight bombing but flew in a "gaggle". The Americans were able to defend themselves against the *Luftwaffe* by flying in formation, but British survival by day depended to a large degree on how much petrol and ammunition the enemy had left when the bombers were intercepted. Perversely, the Americans were more exposed to barrage and predicted flak because they had to hold formation, whereas the British gaggle was not so vulnerable because each aircraft could take individual evasive action.

If the Americans had not spoken a language which sounded somewhat like English the differences would have been more obvious. The disimilarity in terminology began at the top. The RAF had a Bomber Command, the Americans a Bombardment Command. The Americans flew missions, not sorties; a mission was an attack by any number of aircraft on a single target, and the number of aircraft was called the attacking force. The 8th Bombardment Command was divided into Wings,[8] Groups[9] and Squadrons. The Squadrons, like the British Flights, were the smallest units and so suffered a high degree of anonymity, while Groups, in the same manner as the RAF Squadrons, tended to claim the glory. The formations, referred to as forces, were each composed of boxes which could contain as few as three bombers or as many as 21. All aircraft in a box bombed as a unit, releasing their bombs at the same time as the leader.

By comparison, until the introduction of Master Bombers, the captain of each aircraft in Bomber Command was the sole arbiter of where, when and whether a crew attacked. The criteria of success were vastly different too: the yardstick in Bomber Command was to bomb within three miles of the aiming point, though if PFF TIs were awry the Main Force claimed that as an alibi. The requirement in the American camp was seemingly more stringent, within 1,000 feet of the aiming point, but as the bombers dropped in formation the bombs fell in a pattern (**Figs 4A, 4B**) and the mission was declared a failure only if no box had more than 5% of its bomb load within the prescribed area. An increase in altitude, the size of the force or the size of the box tended to decrease the accuracy, though in the last two cases it improved the chances of the mission being classified as successful. The requirements were as different as the language, the dangers as diverse as the strategy.

One of the earliest concessions in language was made by the British boffins, who used the American word "radar" instead of the British equivalent "radio". An Englishman might be forgiven for being a little bewildered when hearing an American Top Sergeant (Warrant Officer) describing the procedure for mounting a mission (preparing for an operation). "As soon as the alert [stand by] was received at a bomber base [station], engineering sections would ready [prepare] the aircraft, checking and testing most of the night. The ordnance and chemical men [armourers][10] who handled the high-explosive and incendiary bombs would begin loading while it was still dark; ammunition was put aboard and turrets given a final go-over [check]. . . . . . . cameras for strike [target] photos loaded and set. . . . . . . navigators would have to study routes and schedules, bombardiers [bomb-aimers] their targets. . . . . . . every man on the base played his part in preparing for a mission [sortie], each knowing that at any time from the Field Order [A or B notice] coming in on the tele-type machine [teleprinter], to the Group's formation approaching the enemy coast, the mission could be cancelled. . . . To the crews under pre-combat [pre-ops] tension this was no relief. . . ."[11] In British

8. Wing was the equivalent of the British group.
9. Each Group controlled four Squadrons. A Squadron's nearest equivalent in British terms was a flight.
10. The Americans used the word "armourer" but only for men working specifically on mounting, checking and maintenance of guns.
11. The excerpt is from *The Mighty Eighth*; the RAF equivalents are in brackets.

terms a "combat" was a confrontation between a fighter and a bomber. The Americans' "targets of opportunity" were comparable to British "last resorts".

The differences may have been manifold but in the final analysis it all came down to the airmen, and in this sphere there was mutual respect. Both forces were aiming for the same end and each man put his life on the line unselfishly in the hope that, if the supreme price had to be paid, the world would be a better place as a result of his sacrifice.

The Germans had been quick to realise that the lead aircraft in a formation was highly important because, while all bomber aircraft carried navigators, the one in the lead aircraft was responsible for the course and timing of the whole formation and chiefly responsible for getting it to the target. They had discovered also that the B-17's weakest spot was in the nose area. A frontal attack therefore reduced the chances of being shot down and enhanced the possibility of hitting the bomber in the vital cockpit area; engines and mainplane were also probably easier to hit with head-on attacks. There were snags, however: with a closing rate of 600 mph the risk of collision was high and the aiming time practically nil. Yet if it was hair-raising for the *Luftwaffe* pilots who knew what they were going to do, it was surely far worse for the bomber pilot, who had to sit there, fingers crossed, with nothing between himself and the enemy except perhaps a heart-felt plea to "Jeeesus". He knew he could take no evasive action for fear of breaking up the formation, and was only too well aware that the German pilots had on occasion made errors which proved fatal for all concerned by colliding with the bomber. *Oberstleutnant* Egon Mayer used the tactic of attacking head-on as early as November 1942, but it did not become a regular hazard until 1944, partly due to the fact that many of the German pilots were confronting the Americans for the first time, having been pulled back from the Eastern Front. Yet many of the attacks did come from the front quarters, if not from dead ahead, with the lead aircraft the main quarry.

For reasons of safety the three groups comprising a combat wing flew at different heights. Originally the low group had led the attacking force, but after the frontal attacks started it became doubly vulnerable. So the middle group took over the lead and the high group brought up the rear, protecting the group in "Purple Heart Corner"[12] from direct assault by the fighters. This formation was first used at Bremen on April 17, 1943, and thereafter became standard. The leading group bore the brunt of the initial fighter attacks and the low group was accorded the special attentions of the ground defences. No one liked flying in the low group, so a system of rotation was instituted.

The Germans, British and Americans all developed automatic bomb releases. That of the Germans – a mechanical clock which was fitted in their pathfinder aircraft of 1940 – was the crudest. The British one was perhaps the most sophisticated, being triggered by ground stations in England to release bombs over targets in Germany.[13] The American system was used in conjunction with the Norden bombsight, which itself was probably the best in the world.[14] Almost all the essential information could be pre-set before take-off and the more important, like ground speed and drift, could be

---

12. Nickname for low group. See Glossary.
13. In truth it was not actually used operationally to release the bombs, although this was possible. In practice a signal was sent and the navigator released the bombs manually.
14. Some of the specialised sights were probably technically as good.

# PATTERN BOMBING

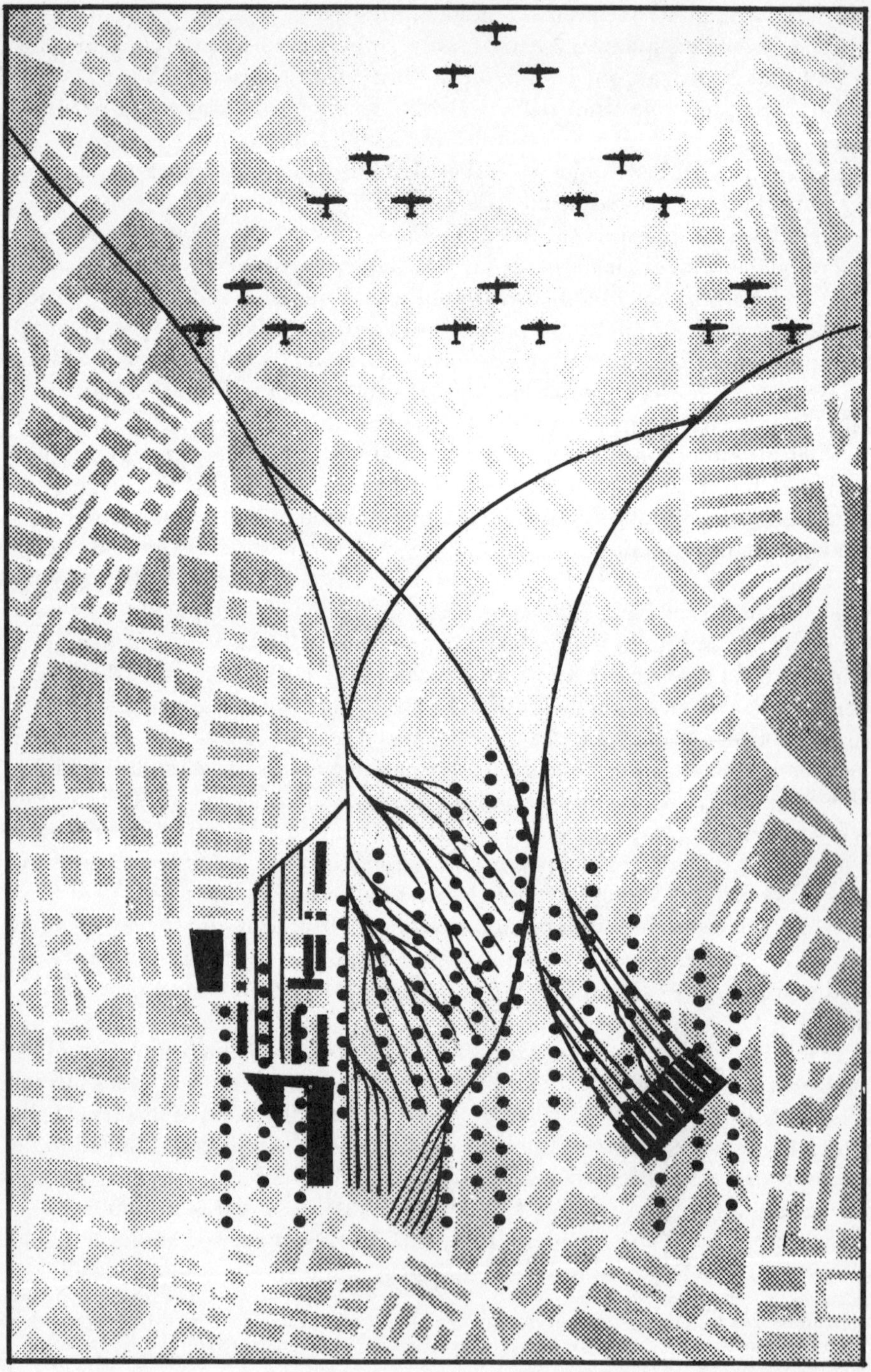

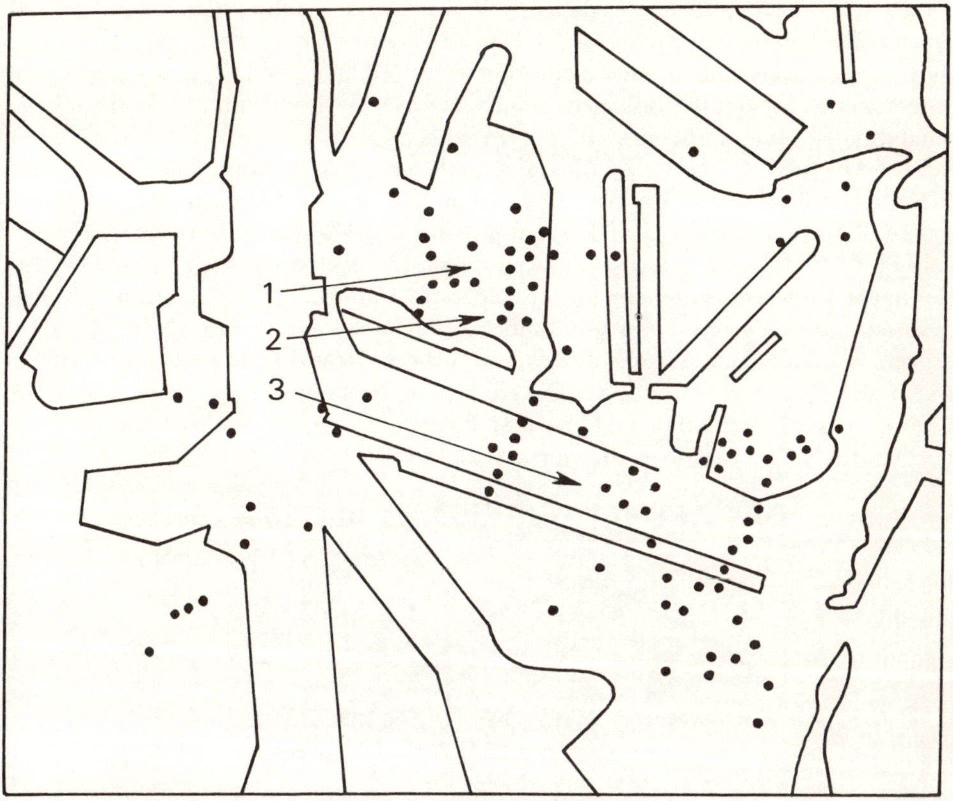


When aircraft fly in formation and the bombs are released simultaneously they fall in a pattern on the ground. Although some bombs are wasted, in general the majority fall on the target. In **Fig 4A** (*left*) the lead aircraft was to starboard of track yet most of the bombs hit their mark. Another formation behind would fill the gaps. **Fig 4B** (*above*) is a bomb plot of the USAAF's attack on Hamburg on July 26, 1943. Only positions from well defined prints were used. 1 = Howaldtswerke AG. 2 = MAN. 3 = Neuhof power station.

altered in flight. It had shortcomings but in the American heavy bombers, for which it was designed, they were not apparent. For example, the gyro toppled if the aircraft banked at more than 18°, but violent evasive action was not part of the American scene. When the gyro was uncaged it had to be levelled, a slow and arduous process if done by hand; in the B-17 levelling was automatic. The requirement for a long run-up to the target was a disadvantage, but this was balanced by the fact that the bombardier could alter the timing in flight and corrections could be made up to the last second, in fact until the crosshairs which ran along the sight reached the aiming point, when the automatic release began to function. Used in conjunction with the automatic flight control equipment (AFCE), it made precision bombing a mere formality. AFCE[15] allowed the bombardier to steer the aircraft during the bombing run. This complex system was linked with "George", the automatic pilot. When the bombardier started his bombing run the captain switched over to automatic pilot and handed over control.

15. First used successfully on March 18, 1943.

Naturally, if the aircraft was in danger the pilot could switch to manual and regain control. The bombardier could make precise alterations, whereas it was very difficult to convey by verbal orders the amount of adjustment necessary, and the time lag between order and execution was eliminated. Lead bombers were fitted with AFCE, though its reliability left much to be desired.

Saturday July 24 saw the opening of the 8th Air Force's "Blitz Week", when 324 B-17s took off to attack Heroya, Trondheim and Bergen. Only one bomber went missing[16], so the campaign got off to a propitious start. The Americans were pledged to help in the *Gomorrah* attacks, so following the night attack of the 24–25th by Bomber Command the 8th could be seen assembling over Cromer in the early afternoon. To be more accurate, only glimpses of the bombers could be seen because the cloud, although broken, was once again making life difficult for the crews as they struggled to find their group and force formation. The new method of assembling over different *Splasher* beacons proved successful, and the first three forces proceeded on schedule in a north-easterly direction over the North Sea.

**DAY OPERATIONS USAAF July 25 & 26**

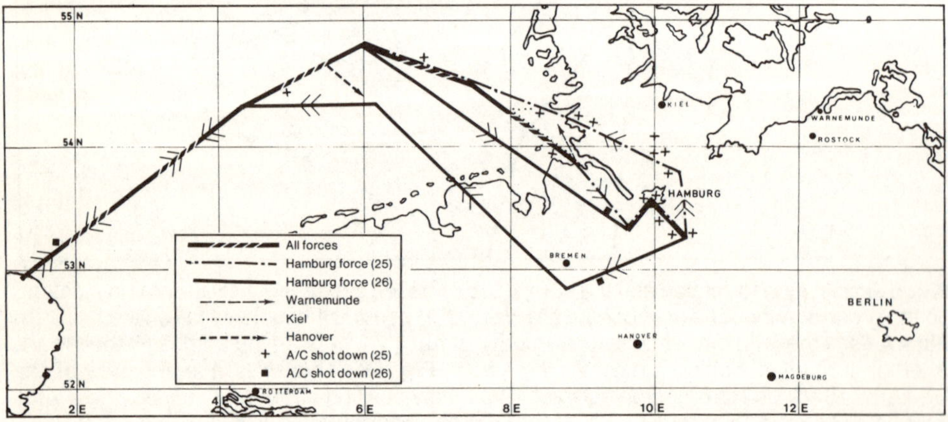


Five bomber forces were engaged – three from the 1st Wing and two from the 4th – and three targets were to be attacked: Hamburg, Kiel and the Heinkel aircraft factory at Warnemünde, on the coast 14 miles north of Rostock. The factory was assembling Fw190s, so the Americans really did need to destroy it, but cloud came to the aid of the Germans on the 25th. The plan of attack was somewhat elaborate for the time and demonstrated the high regard the Americans had for the *Luftwaffe*. Similarly, the size of the enemy force put up to oppose them showed how seriously the Germans were treating the new precision bombing threat. The *Luftwaffe* fighters in North-west Germany and the Low Countries had been increased from 270 in April 1943 to 600 in August specifically for this purpose.

The five forces, each consisting of three groups, took the same route as far as 53°50N 08°55E, the Kiel force and the two for Warnemünde preceding the two Hamburg forces to that point by 40 minutes. This feint at Hamburg was intended to get the fighters

16. It actually crash-landed successfully in neutral Sweden.

airborne long before the Hamburg force arrived in the area and to draw them away from the target. From this point the 4th Wing groups turned north and flew parallel to the coast, later to turn to the east and proceed to Warnemünde. The Kiel force turned back on their track and, it was hoped, after 20 minutes would meet the real Hamburg force; they were then to proceed to Kiel. The Germans rose to the bait and the Hamburg warning was sent out at 1440. They may have been confused by all the to-ing and fro-ing, but a B-17 going in any direction was a target in their eyes. Ironically, however, the decoys met with little opposition; diversionary raids by Marauders, Mitchells and Bostons to the Low Countries did attract some fighter attention but did nothing to alleviate the pressure on the Fortresses.

Fighters from Heligoland/Jever and Nordholz were the first to make contact, encountering the two Hamburg forces at 1614 hours as they approached the enemy coast near the Elbe estuary. The first wave, the 103rd Combat Bombardment Wing, was engaged by the *Staffeln* from Heligoland, the attack coming mainly from the starboard, level or below, the tactics varying from line-abreast to "in train" (line-astern); there were also attacks by single aircraft. This battle lasted four minutes.

The second wave, the 101st Combat Wing, was attacked 12 minutes later, this time from above, probably because the force was nearing Cuxhaven and the fighters did not want to be caught in the imminent flak barrage. The sun had by now passed its zenith so the Nordholz fighters climbed to the south-west of the bombers' track and, coming out of the sun, dived down from 29,000 feet. The Hamburg formations were described as good and this was probably why the fighters made little impression. That is not to say that life was not very hectic, as cannon shells came pouring towards the B-17s. However, it was no picnic either for the *Luftwaffe* pilots to dive through a fierce hail of lead aimed at them by determined gunners. The second wave was also sighted by a *Staffel* from Oldenburg which did not attack because this force was already under heavy fire from the ground. From the moment the bombers crossed the enemy coast and for the whole of the 55 minutes they were over enemy territory they were harassed by flak or fighters, and afterwards the fighters even pursued them out to sea for 30 miles. The welcoming committee at Cuxhaven greeted them with great enthusiasm, as if to warn them they could expect a peppering from below whenever they came within range of the ground defences. The Americans had long since learned the hard way that if they allowed the flak to break the formation the fighters would have a field day; they just had to sit and take it.

That Sunday in North-west Germany was a brilliant summer day for everyone except the inhabitants of Hamburg. There was no sunshine in the port, with sky darkened by the mushroom of smoke and dust which hung over the city. There was no gas, electricity or water, and people could be seen wandering around with buckets looking for an undamaged hydrant. Individuals were trying to salvage what they could from their damaged homes, the fire services were still fighting a losing battle, and the rest of the defence services were labouring to clear the streets and main thoroughfares of fallen masonry, overhead wires and telephone lines. The sirens had sounded at 1440 but it proved to be a false alarm. Suddenly, however, the drone of bomber engines could be heard to the south of the river. There had been no air-raid warning and the defences had not received the usual 30-minute and 15-minute alert signals, nor indeed any advance warning that enemy aircraft were approaching. The alarm eventually sounded at 1620 hours, but only the deaf did not know by then that a raid was imminent. At the first sound of aircraft the people of Hamburg dashed for safety, while the defence services thought that the attack was designed to hinder their work.

The whistle of bombs in the distance, followed by the distinctive crunch as the bombs struck home and exploded, intermingled with the boom of the AA guns. This was Hamburg's first experience of pattern bombing. The impact of dozens of high-explosive bombs hitting the ground almost simultaneously seemed to make the ground rise and fall as in an earthquake, and few would have been surprised had the buildings around them collapsed. The occasional rat-tat-tat of cannon fire proclaimed that the *Luftwaffe* was at hand. German aircraft flying low over the harbour to lay a smoke screen caused perhaps as much apprehension as the approaching bombers. Then came the gradual diminuendo as bombers and defences continued their argument while the Americans fought their way from the port to the coast.

Col M.A. Preston,[17] CO of the 379th Group, was the captain of the lead aircraft of the 103rd Combat Wing, and Capt A.K. Dutch, his navigator, had brought the wing to the German coast dead on track. After crossing the coast the Hamburg formations set course for Hollenstadt, south-west of Hamburg, their turning point[18] to the target. Capt J.A. Brown, the bombardier, was using special pinpoints to keep the force on track. Just after leaving the IP Preston switched to "George" and Brown took over control using AFCE. Dutch seemed to have found a good wind, for Brown had to make no alterations for ground speed and drift, two of the main ingredients of a satisfactory bombing run. Smoke from the previous night's attack and the smoke screen laid by the German aircraft made target identification very difficult, but 30 seconds from ETA, as if by magic, the Blohm & Voss works came into Brown's bombsight. The jubilant bombardier yelled "All bombs away, she's all yours." The leaders in the other boxes bombed as they saw the lead aircraft's bombs wing their way down. Dutch entered 1637 hours in his log; this was eight minutes late but the bombers were not scheduled to meet a fighter escort, so no one was worried. This wave made an accurate run and held very steady in spite of intense predicted flak from the heavy batteries surrounding the port and, more particularly, from the battery at Wilhelmsburg, practically on their track to the aiming point.

The four squadrons[19] comprising the leading group, the 379th, had survived the initial fighter attack without loss and, although they did lose two aircraft, it was not until after they had left the target. The high group, the 303rd,[20] lost one aircraft, again on the homeward run. So these two groups, each comprising 20 Fortresses armed with 10 × 500lb medium-capacity, dropped their full complement of bombs.[21] In stark contrast, the low group, the 384th, suffered the highest losses: seven Fortresses shot down and three others aborted; the other 11 dropped 16 × 250lb of incendiaries each.

Because of the cloud and smoke spreading over the port area only the 351st Group of the second wave, the 101st Combat Wing, were able to see their target, and 17 Fortresses from this formation each dropped 40 × 100lb incendiaries. The 351st were

17. One of the longest-serving group COs in the 8th Bombardment Command.
18. The Americans called this the Initial Point (IP).
19. The 524th, 525th, 526th and 527th.
20. *Knock-Out Dropper*, the first B-17 to fly 50 missions, flew on this raid with the 303rd Bombardment Group.
21. The 379th put up 21 B-17s and one of them was allowed to drop 10 × 500lb on a convoy *en passant*.

the low group but surprisingly (when compared with the 384th) they suffered very little damage, losing only one aircraft, and that was after the bombers had left Hamburg. The 91st Group, who should have led the second wave, had trouble with assembly and, although they later caught up with the wing, Major D.G. Alford decided to take up a position in the rear of the formation. They attacked on a heading of 034° True. This heading was intended to take the Fortresses over the Klockner aero factory but because of cloud and smoke haze the leader dropped on ETA. The 351st Group, led by Major C.F. Ball, commander of the 511th Bomb Squadron,[22] also dropped on ETA, but the 381st retained their bombs. Over the target a B-17 of the 351st Group was hit by flak which set the starboard inner engine on fire, and as it fell out of formation it was pounced on by fighters and shot down.

Both combat wings turned starboard after making their bombing runs in order not to be exposed any longer than necessary to the murderous onslaught from the flak batteries of the well-defended port. Although a *Staffel* of Fw190s was harassing them from the rear, the manoeuvre appeared to surprise the enemy. Again, when the force reached Lüneburg and turned north, skirting Hamburg to the east, the fighter controllers were caught unprepared.

Two aircraft crashed in this area, though not necessarily due to fighter action; the fighters in general stayed out of range, waiting for stragglers. The raiders were intercepted again just south of Neumünster, where three bombers were seen to go down, but again the credit could not be definitely attributed to the *Luftwaffe*. Two further B-17s crashed as the bombers made for the coast.

The 103rd Combat Wing crossed the coast in the vicinity of Meldorf, where the AA gunners certainly needed the practice. True, they were unaccustomed to seeing their prey, but they certainly would not have been flattered had they known the Americans' summary of their shooting: "Meagre to moderate, and inaccurate."

It is arguable that formation flying did help morale, but when their ranks were being decimated by the enemy on every mission the American crews needed a lot of guts to hold on to a bomb load for 40 minutes longer than expected, while being constantly harassed by fighters and peppered from below by flak at every opportunity. However, they were determined to succeed, whatever the cost, and they were not found wanting. The patient crews from the 381st Group who had not dropped their bombs over the target were able to use them to good purpose when they chose Heide as their target of opportunity. The bombs fell in a good pattern and did some useful damage in the railway sidings and the town. Two B-17s exploded in this area, but some of the airmen were seen to bail out.

If half their troubles were over, the American crews had no time to appreciate it, for the German fighters from Husen, some on their third sortie, and others from Jever on their second chased them out to sea well beyond Heligoland. After two hours of constant harassment even the Americans were too exhausted to talk, whereas in fact there was much to discuss: not only the cannon shells that whistled past, so close one could feel the breeze, or the flak, so thick one could walk on it, but also the strange appearance of B-17s on either side of them, shooting from the waist positions. Perhaps

22. Many of the 511th Bombardment Squadron's B-17s used *Ball* as part of their insignia, e.g. *Fireball*, *Screwball*. The Major's aircraft was *Linda Ball*, named after his baby daughter.

even more perplexing were the smaller aircraft, painted white and also flying alongside, which made no hostile move and, as the coast came up, turned and followed two twin-engined night fighters back into the Reich.

Fighters from Schiphol intercepted the bombers during the latter stages of the mission, and this caused some moans at debriefing. It was suggested that the confrontations could have been avoided if the return route had been planned further north. In truth this was not the fault of the planners, the navigator in the leading aircraft having cut his corners and put the bombers 40 miles south of their allotted track. Fortunately the Germans did not catch the gunners off guard, as they had done six weeks earlier. Some gunners of the 94th Group, believing they had left the fighters far behind, had begun to dismantle and clean their guns. This was a post-operational chore and the quicker it was done the sooner they could dash off to Bury St Edmunds to study the local form.[23] When only 30 miles off the Norfolk coast 12 black-painted Ju88 night fighters appeared out of the evening mist in a neatly planned and efficiently executed foray and shot down nine bombers before the Americans had time to react. On the 25th, however, the tally was one for one.

Of the 102 aircraft put up by the 1st Wing to attack Hamburg and Kiel only 68 bombed their primary, all at Hamburg; a further 31 bombed the target of opportunity (Heide). The Kiel force did not bomb. Some 15 Fortresses from the wing were lost and a further 67 damaged, one of these seriously. Flak caused the major damage and four aircraft were definitely known to have been shot down by the ground defences.

Much effort was expended by the *Luftwaffe* for meagre rewards. A conservative estimate was that the fighters flew at least 300 sorties. For the Americans it was like an aircraft recognition test: Fw190s, Me109s, 110s and 210s, Ju88s and Do217s, all tried their hand. The Americans claimed to have shot down 38, probably destroyed a further six and damaged 27. In exactly the same way as the British fighter claims during the Battle of Britain were found to have been grossly exaggerated when the German figures were captured at the end of the war, so most of the American claims had to be modified. For the moment, however, they were an enormous morale-booster. The 384th Group, for example, had 70 personnel missing from one station alone,[24] and to have hacked 10 fighters out of the sky was some consolation for the losses they had suffered. They felt that the constant loss of 30 or more fighters on each mission must be making holes in the German front-line strength. Irrespective of the truth, there was certainly plenty of lead flying around. The 1st Wing used more than a quarter of a million 0.5in shells – 284,830 to be precise – on this mission.

At 0300 hours on Monday the 26th, as the British bombers were making their way back from Essen, crews of the 8th Air Force were being awakened to attend a briefing at 0345 hours. The two main targets were Hamburg and Hanover, and the plan of attack was again devised to confuse the enemy as to the target and the strength of the forces employed.

From 0700 hours the *Freya* crews along the Continental seaboard from Cuxhaven to the English Channel were on the alert as Fortresses began to take off from airfields in East Anglia. A message to the German defence headquarters warned that the signs indicated that a daylight force was gathering over the Norfolk coast. As yet no accurate

23. The 94th had taken off from Earls Colne and were to land at their new station, Bury St Edmunds.
24. Each B-17 was manned by a crew of ten.

assessment of the number, nor the direction in which they would be heading, could be obtained.

Although the Americans were using *Gee* and *Splasher* beacons to assist in assembling the formations, cloud in the area made life difficult. The 4th Wing and one force from the 1st were the early birds, bound for Hanover. These forces set course an hour ahead of the two bound for Hamburg. The plan was for them to precede the Hamburg force and, from 54°40N 05°30E, make a feint at Bremen. Their track took them over Baltrum, and from there they would bypass Bremen on their way to Hanover. The Hamburg forces assembling an hour later found the cloud just as troublesome, but the 101st Combat Wing, made up of 24 B-17s of the 351st Group, 18 from the 381st and 20 from the 91st, set course on time. The 103rd Combat Wing made a valiant effort to sort out their formation en route, but only the 303rd Group succeeded, and they tagged onto the 101st Combat Wing when the 379th and 384th groups were recalled. They took the same route as the earlier forces but maintained their track to 06°00E, where they turned south-east to the German coast, making for Hollenstadt, the same initial point as on the 25th. Their track took them to the west of Heligoland and Cuxhaven.

Fighters from Heligoland were vectored south-west but missed the bombers on their first sweep and were later sent to Wangerooge, where part of the formation came near enough to the island for the ground defences to go into action. Stade was determined to prove it was a good place to avoid. The four groups had been on the previous day's raid, and although the flak was intense and the fighters seemed to be coming from everywhere, everything somehow seemed to go more smoothly. It was the Hanover forces that felt the venom of the defenders.

Capt J.T. Stewart, with Major E. Lidoux as co-pilot, led the 351st Group (the leading group of the 101st Combat Wing). Stewart's navigator was Lt L.P. Stover; like Dutch on the previous raid, he performed well and the force made landfall on track. The bombardier, Lt Stevens, had flown with Ball on the 25th, and as the IP was Hollenstadt again he had little difficulty with the pinpoints. Flares were dropped over Hollenstadt to help the rest of the formation. The run to the target was almost a replica of Brown's. In the early stages it was possible to check ground speed and drift, but as the aiming point got nearer smoke and a smoke screen, haze and cloud prevented Stevens from seeing the ground. However, he considered the run accurate enough to release on ETA. The 381st, 91st and 303rd Groups had the same problems and they too followed Stevens' lead, three groups dropping HE and the fourth IBs. Although the flak on the bombing run and at the target was just as heavy as on Sunday and was bursting all around the bombers, no one was shot down. This was principally due to the fact that it had to be a barrage because of the smoke cloud. In one B-17 a 500-pounder stuck in the rack and Tech Sgt N. Michel climbed out of his turret and kicked it free. At 29,000 feet dashing around without oxygen is courting disaster, and Michel quickly lapsed into unconsciousness. The formation was in the process of turning away from the target and before anyone could reach him he was thrown about in the aircraft and sustained concussion and back injuries. Again the bombers turned south-east to Lüneburg but from there they went to 53°00N 08°45E, making a dogleg to ensure that no one gave the German AA gunners at Bremen any practice. Then they retreated along the return route of the Hanover forces out over the North Sea to 54°20N 06°10E. From this point they flew for 90 miles before heading for Cromer.

The American gunners had little respite. The force was pursued the whole of the time they were over enemy territory, apart from the run-up to the target, for barrage flak was dangerous to bomber and fighter alike. The attacks were however sporadic and not pressed home. In general it seemed as if the enemy were waiting for stragglers, but in fairness it must be said that the fighters were never in sufficient numbers to risk a serious confrontation.

The Sunday and Monday of Blitz Week were frustrating days for the 91st Group, who were naturally keen to maintain their reputation as one of the most effective groups.[25] On the Sunday they were scheduled to lead the 101st Combat Wing, but trouble with assembly had forced them to bring up the rear. On Monday their problems were entirely different. Some 20 B-17s took off from Bassingbourn and experienced little difficulty in assembly over the field, but when Capt J.C. Bishop in the lead bomber set course for Cromer, five of his group had already landed because of mechanical or technical failures. Two more turned back just after leaving the English coast, and another while the formation was still over the North Sea, making a total of eight who returned early. Of the 12 aircraft that reached the target only nine released their cargoes. The group considered themselves fortunate that the opposition was only on a small scale; had it been the strength of the previous day their losses would have been much higher. Because their formation looked invitingly small and they were bringing up the rear, the majority of the enemy attacks were concentrated against the 91st and two B-17s were shot down. Only over the target was the flak a real menace, and although the 91st were the high Group they sustained more damage than the other groups. No bombers were shot down by the ground defences but two had to make forced landings in England, one at Sculthorpe and the other at Polebrook; the crews were uninjured.

When the Americans first came to England they thought water was something that came out of a faucet (tap), but they soon realised that, except when attacking France, to invade enemy airspace they had to spend hours over water. Ditching[26] was something they had not thought about seriously and many crews were drowned unnecessarily. Lt Hargis and his crew had practised the drill assiduously and on the 25th their industry paid off. Hargis had been losing engines and height at a rate which meant that, unless he remustered to the Navy within the next 30 minutes, he would be out of his element before reaching the English coast. About 30 miles north-east of Cromer he had no engines and only a few hundred feet of height left. He made a perfect dead-stick landing on the sea across the swell, and within minutes the crew were safely in their dinghies. About two hours later, at 1940 hours, they were aboard rescue boats and on their way back to England. Later in the evening they left Bassingbourn for a rest camp; there must have been easier ways of getting seven days' leave.

The 1st Wing's performance must have evoked some enquiries from HQ; of 127 bombers which took off for Hamburg only 53, less than 50%, attacked the port. Two Fortresses were missing and 17 damaged, 2 of them irreparably. Six enemy aircraft were destroyed and the wing used 195,406 shells.

---

25. They already had a unit citation for their attack on Hamm on March 4, 1943, the 8th's first visit to the Ruhr.
26. Landing on the sea.

The fact that the Americans flew in formation and that each box bombed as a unit resulted in the bombs falling in a pattern. The advantages and disadvantages of this will be discussed later; for the moment the 8th Air Force could feel satisfaction at a good job well done, as the strike photographs proclaimed. On the 25th the Blohm & Voss submarine yards were well and truly hit and dock installations in the area were also damaged. The tool store and smithy and the construction shops were blanketed with bombs and their own power station damaged. The liner *Der Vaterland* was under construction when the war began but work ceased on her when the Government turned the yards over entirely to munitions. The partly built ship was moved to the Steinwarder wharf and used as a timber yard, chiefly for storing poles and posts for building the stocks and slipways. A direct hit by a 500-pounder raised the bow out of the water and ignited the timber, which for some reason was allowed to burn itself out. Another ship, the *General Artigas,* berthed close by in Kuhwerderhafen, was being used as a training school by the Navy. The Americans claimed only a near miss, though the Germans say she sank. Two floating docks were hit: one of them sank and the other keeled over. Howaldtswerke, another government-owned factory, was, like its big brother to the north, employed in submarine construction. Here a few bombs did scattered damage, but its turn was to come on the morrow, when the whole factory was blanketed with bombs, causing severe destruction, including fire damage. Maschinen Fabrik Augsburg und Nürnburg (MAN), manufacturing diesel engines, received direct hits, and two floating docks were extensively damaged. Altogether it was a bad day for submarines: scheduled production for August and September was 58 boats, of which only 43 were completed, and that was achieved only after an enormous rescue operation by companies outside Hamburg. As later boxes released their cargoes further south, bombs straddled the Neuhöfer Canal and fires were started in an oil storage depot. A large explosion, which told of one tank which would not hold oil again, brought an instant feeling of satisfaction to the American crews.

On the 26th the damage was in the same area but the main concentration was at Howaldtswerke, where IBs caused extensive fire damage. MAN, which also suffered heavily, received a direct hit on the aircraft assembly hangar and three on the boiler-house, and the power station was severely damaged. One floating dock was sunk and another received a direct hit. A third floating dock was sunk in the Stülcken yards. Blohm & Voss escaped almost completely. The merchant vessel *Leuna* was set on fire and four acres of warehouses in Hansa Hafen were burnt out, including Hansa Mühle, whose stocks of soya oil, soya beans and sunflower seeds burned so fiercely that adjoining warehouses were set on fire within a short space of time. Kleine Grasbrook was a congested industrial area to the east of Blohm & Voss, and there it was more difficult to miss a factory of importance than to hit one. The whole area was a patchwork of railway sidings, which suffered extensive damage. Two gasholders in the municipal gasworks were hit.

Perhaps the most important damage caused by these two raids affected the Neuhof power station, which took weeks to repair, although some of the effect was offset by the grid system. In general the damage to the services caused more loss in industry than any direct damage to a factory. The British attack on the 24–25th did cause destruction south of the river, but no one could question the fact that the daylight attacks were responsible for the mayhem in these districts. On the 25th one of the selected targets was the Klockner aircraft factory, but cloud prevented the Americans from attacking the complex. In the event the bombs would have been wasted because the plant had been evacuated the previous week. North of the river, in Altona and St Pauli, the Americans claimed some "overs" (overshoots) which caused damage in the Altona *Hauptbahnhof* and in the goods yards at Adolfstrasse, though obviously most of the damage in these areas was caused by the night attacks, chiefly on the 24–25th. Other damage here affected H. Stag's aluminium works, and a grain silo went up in flames. In St Pauli many slaughterhouses and wholesale meat storage depots were destroyed. Holstenstrasse Station was gutted, the Police HQ and the local barracks were destroyed, and an acre of warehouses was burnt out. In addition to the Police Presidency and the control room of the Air Protection Leader, many other police HQs and public offices were either severely damaged or destroyed, including the police station at Eimsbüttel and the fire station at Hohenfelde. The headquarters and offices of the main commercial firms were in the city and many of them were completely gutted by fire.

Many factories on both sides of the North Sea, which in peacetime employed skilled workers to make precision instruments, had since been turned over to war work. Messaps were makers of clocks, and their expertise was directed into the making of clockwork time fuses for shells of 75 and 150mm calibre. To cope with the demand a subsidiary was opened in Schanzenstrasse, where it occupied the top three storeys of a six-storey building. On the night of July 24–25 the whole building was burned out and the machinery fell through to the ground, 80% of it being completely destroyed. Due to damage and absenteeism after the raids Messaps lost two months' production.

Damage to residential property was widespread and on a scale far exceeding that which the people of Hamburg thought possible. Firefighting was impeded by the extensive damage to the water mains, and fires could not be prevented from flaring up again and again. Many individuals already had their winter store of coal and coke, and this was the main cause of the fires breaking out afresh. By July 27 the fires were under control and the main thoroughfares cleared – chiefly by the *Wehrmacht* – but the state of emergency was still operating. To the west of the Alster there was no gas, water or electricity and production was virtually at a standstill. South of the Elbe conditions were little better, and even where production was possible absenteeism reduced it to a minimum.

# Chapter V

# The Night of the Firestorm

HAMBURG had been selected by Harris as the main target for the night of July 25–26, with Essen as the alternative. However, a 1409 Flight Mosquito reported that Hamburg was shrouded in smoke from the previous night's raid, so the force was sent to Essen. The raids to Hamburg and Essen had been maximum efforts, so, in keeping with the C-in-C's usual policy, the third night was a stand-down for the heavy squadrons. Provided the weather held, Tuesday the 27th would be a maximum effort and, weather permitting, Hamburg would be the main target. So it turned out to be.

The instructions from Bomber Command HQ for the 27th were in most respects identical to those of the 24–25th. The zero hour and the aiming point were the same, and even weather conditions at 1 Group bases for the return were problematical, as on the Sunday morning. The track was similar but went some 40 miles further before the turn to Hamburg. If this ruse was designed to make the Germans think that the force was going to Kiel or Lubeck, it was a complete waste of petrol: after the two American daylight raids and the Mosquito night attacks, everyone in Hamburg was convinced that the RAF would be back in strength as soon as conditions were favourable. The main differences were that *Zephyrs* were not being used on this occasion, and a second lot of route markers were to be dropped 15 miles south of Lake Plönen as a checkpoint on the route to the target.

The Pathfinder method was to be *Newhaven*,[1] as on the 24–25th, and the TI colour pattern was identical. The reconnaissance Mosquito returned from Hamburg with the report that "dust and smoke haze covered the town". After hasty consultation between Bennett and Saundby it was decided that TIs would be visible but the Visual Markers would not be able to pinpoint within the target area, so the method was changed to *Parramatta*. There would be no reds dropped in the target area, and the Main Force would bomb the centre of all the yellow and green TIs. The changed orders were phoned to the Groups and they informed the stations. The order to PFF squadrons was: "Visual Markers will act as Blind Markers, except 97 Squadron, who will operate as Main Force." That entailed a last-minute switch of bomb loads. "Blind Markers will retain their flares, all other crews as ordered." A total of 787 aircraft were despatched, the largest number of the four nights, and they dropped the heaviest load, 4,417 tons, a new record for Bomber Commmand. Take-off time was again around 2200 hours.

F/Lt A.H. Crowe of 106 Squadron must have had one of the earliest returns on record in Bomber Command. Just after take-off, a mere 100 feet in the air, the starboard inner engine of his Lancaster caught fire. The engine was cut and the extinguisher fired,

1. Webster and Frankland, in *The Strategic Air Offensive Against Germany*, say the raid was planned as a *Parramatta* because the Blind Markers had done so well on the first raid. This is not true, and it was in fact planned as a *Newhaven*.

and just when it looked as though he would be forced to land with the engine still alight, the flames began to die down, and so he did a second circuit. That was not his only problem, however: the safety weight for landing a Lancaster was 53,000lb and Crowe's aircraft, with a full bomb load and full tanks, was 9,000lb above this weight. To jettison the bomb load was very dangerous because cookies had a nasty habit of exploding even when dropped "safe". The blast might make the other bombs explode in sympathy and, with the Lancaster still only 100 feet up, to open the bomb doors, which would induce extra drag, could make the difference between remaining airborne and crashing. To risk landing with the extra weight was stretching his faith in Messrs A.V. Roe's undercarriage beyond even their own limits. The safety of the crew had also to be considered; at 100 feet there was no hope of baling out safely. In the event Crowe took his chances on the landing gear and lived to tell the story, which speaks volumes for the design and manufacture of the undercarriage.

There was cloud on the route at 05°00E but it was mainly in layers and so posed few problems except in the vicinity of the cumulo-nimbus, where static was encountered. Beyond 08°00E it began to thin out and the German coast was clear. The toil (by now considered a labour of love by the bomber crews) of dropping *Window* began at 54°27N 07°32E and would continue until the aircraft reached 54°15N 07°15E on the homeward route. Nine out of 25 Blind Markers were detailed to drop yellow route markers at 54°18N 08°40E and these were to be backed up by 4/11 Recenterers and 14/49 Backers-up. Of the remaining Blind Marker crews, 6 dropped check route markers at 53°52N 10°25E, and they were similarly backed up by 2 Recenterers and 6 Backers-up.

The German fighters were up in strength and both single- and twin-engined aircraft were operating. The Me109s and the Fw190s were working in co-operation with the searchlights, whereas the Ju88s and the Me110s were being advised by their ground controllers but were being sent on freelance interceptions. There was almost no vectoring but advice was given on course and height to help them infiltrate into the bomber stream. These untypical instructions reaffirmed the conclusions of the previous nights that *Window* was indeed making it impossible for the ground controllers to vector the fighters in the usual manner.

One of the controlled fighters claimed a success at 0115 hours but, contrary to the usual practice (returning to his *Little Screw*), he was ordered to remain in the area and search for other bombers. Later he reported interference on his AI, so *Window* was having some effect on the airborne equipment too. The *Wild Boars* were also informed of the track and height of the bombers and when one was caught in the searchlights the call went out to the fighters.

Several aircraft had multiple clashes on both the outward and homeward routes. In addition to the target area the fighters congregated around the route-marker TIs, and the majority of the interceptions were in these areas. When S/Ldr J.R. Watson heard a microphone click he sat up a little straighter, ready to go into action immediately. The yellow route markers on the coast were dead ahead, so a change of course was not imminent. It could only be trouble, a fighter most likely. Their combat drill was that, when under attack, the captain would perform a corkscrew, and he was all set to carry out the manoeuvre. Sgt S. Eastwood, the mid-upper gunner, had spotted a Ju88 on the starboard beam, at their height, 19,000 feet. It looked as if the Germans were unaware of the Lancaster's presence, and Eastwood decided to fire while surprise was on his side. "Corkscrew starboard, Skipper," and then for the sake of the rear gunner, Sgt R. Clifford, "Ju88, starboard beam". Eastwood opened fire as the Lancaster made its initial starboard manoeuvre. The fighter turned to port and opened up with a short burst of cannon fire which passed well astern, but when Clifford got a bead on the Junkers it maintained its course, diving away to port. Watson continued to corkscrew until the gunners were certain the enemy was not coming in to attack again. Sgt R. Crawshaw, Watson's navigator, had made a mental note of the time, 0017 hours. Members of the crew not involved usually remained inactive during a combat, partly from tension but also because they were aware that any distraction, however slight, might endanger everyone's life. The entry in Crawshaw's log had to wait.

It was easy to relax with relief after surviving a combat but they were an experienced crew and when, at 0035, Eastwood again broke the silence to announce an Me109 on the starboard quarter up, Watson instantly dived to starboard, losing 600 feet. Eastwood and Clifford both opened fire, scoring hits on the Messerschmitt, which dived away to port without attempting an attack. Wide-awake gunners were often a sufficient deterrent for fighter crews who were not already committed to making an attack. The thinking was quite rational: "Why raise the odds when there is easier prey aplenty?"

Watson resumed his course for the last turning point but did not waste time climbing again. Seven minutes later Eastwood sighted a Ju88 on the starboard quarter and slightly above the Lancaster at 600 yards range. He ordered a corkscrew to starboard and, as the combat manoeuvre began, fired a two-second burst. The Junkers dived away to port and was not seen again. It would appear that all three combats were chance encounters, although the Ju88 may have had AI equipment. No searchlights, track lights or flares were used by the enemy to indicate the bomber's position, and the fighters were not displaying any recognition lights. Watson resumed course for the target and was left in peace to drop his bombs and return to base.

About the same time as Eastwood was giving his third set of orders to Watson, Sgt O. Roberts was saying the same words to his captain, Sgt R. Petty. The outcome was identical, too. Petty was 10 miles nearer to the target than Watson and he too reported no activity on the ground. However, Lancaster "C-Charlie" was carrying *Monica* and she was pipping her warning with monotonous regularity. But *Monica* could not distinguish friend from foe, and, although she did get more excited as an aeroplane approached, increasing her rate of pips, the Ju88 and Me110 were not so much faster than the Lancaster that they could be distinguished with certainty. However, the difference between a bomber and the Me109 or Fw190 was readily discernible. Although *Monica* was still bleating, Petty resumed course and the gunners continued to search the sky for anything that moved. It was Roberts, the rear gunner, who first saw the Ju88, this time on the port quarter, and ordered, "Dive port, go". The Junkers was now only 400 yards away and Roberts, sighting between the red and green navigation lights, waited for it to draw closer. Sgt E. Smith, the mid-upper, joined in the action and, to the immense relief of the captive audience, the Junkers dived down on fire and exploded. *Monica* must take some of the credit for this action, for it was her constant nagging which had kept the crew on its toes. Once again, alert gunners had taken the initiative and kept the enemy too busy to return their fire.

At 0050, shortly after crossing the enemy coast, Sgt T.B. Rowan, Sgt D. Brown's rear gunner, sighted an Me110 200 yards astern and slightly below their Halifax. The enemy opened fire with cannon and machine guns, scoring hits on the starboard tailplane and fuselage, but he broke away to port when Rowan opened up and Brown went into the combat manoeuvre. When the fighter pilot flew on a parallel course to the bomber on the port beam his aircraft was silhouetted against the northern light; this made Rowan suspect a trap, so he searched the dark part of the sky in case the Messerschmitt had assumed the role of decoy. The German pilot must have been watching the rear turret because as soon as the rear gunner swung his turret he made his attack from the port beam. Brown made a diving turn to port which caused the night fighter to pass overhead, and it was not seen again. *Monica*, although switched on, gave no warning and Sgt H.T. Smith, the mid-upper gunner, was at the flare chute throwing out *Window*. The night fighter pilot probably saw the Halifax in the glow of the yellow TI route markers which had just cascaded down behind the bomber.

The first TIs went down at 0055 hours and by 0100 (zero hour) 15 salvoes had been dropped. With the exception of one or two strays, they were all in the Billwerder district, 1½ to 3 miles east-south-east of the aiming point. The Main Force was early, probably because crews had taken a short cut to the second group of route markers, and 87 of them had bombed by Z+2, which was the scheduled time for the first wave to begin bombing. There could be very few complaints about the standard of bombing: fires started around the yellows and the attack had got off to a good beginning – a prerequisite for any outstanding raid. There were a few crews who bombed to the north and south, but they were completely put to shame by the remaining 100 bombers in the first wave.

* * * *

The German system of air-raid precautions was as good as the British in every way. The basis of the system was self-protection (*Selbschutz*). The individual was taught in the first instance to take care of himself and his own property, and secondly to join with his warden in mutual help, such as taking care of the injured and helping to rescue neighbours. There were almost as many ranks in the ARP as in the Army, with responsibility passing from the house wardens (*Hauswarte*), through the ranks of the precincts to the districts, and then to the groups, of which there were three in Hamburg: East, West and Harbour. Over them all was the ARP leader (*Luftschutzleiter*), who was himself directly responsible to the Police President. In general the system worked very well and the authorities in Hamburg considered that they were highly proficient, which indeed they were under normal conditions. The factories too had their own Protection Service men enlisted from their workers, and recruiting became easier when shelters were built for them. The *Wehrmacht* (armed forces) provided two patrols – one to cover the dock area, the other the town centre – to look after premises that did not have their own ARP service.

The Germans claimed that they laid more stress on saving lives than protecting property, and if the number of different types of shelters is any criterion then there may be some substance to the claim. The eight different types to be found in Hamburg were designed to house a total of 378,000 people, though it has been estimated that 500,000 actually crowded into them. Although the Germans did not have small shelters like the British Anderson or Morrison, they were provided with more deep shelters per head of population. Where cellars and underground facilities did not exist huge surface shelters were built – they were mainly of two types, round and rectangular – and the largest were designed to accommodate more than 1,000 people. They were made of solid reinforced concrete and were considered to be bomb-proof and blast-proof, but were in fact vulnerable to the larger bombs. They had a number of floors and most amenities; some of those built in Hamburg are today used as office blocks. In addition there were tunnel shelters, underground splinter-proof shelters and 246 surface emergency shelters,[2] rather like huge army posts, which were places of temporary refuge only.

Hamburg had particular problems because of its numerous canals and waterways. The older part of the town was well endowed with cellars, but many of them were below water level and therefore vulnerable to flooding. Those that were considered safe were reinforced and an extra exit was made, usually into an adjoining cellar, so that each cellar could be evacuated without having to go out into the street. These exits usually took the form of a steel connecting door, but during the *Katastrophe* they proved to be more a liability than a help in most cases. The steel door expanded with the heat and jammed, or was too hot to touch. The house cellars, similarly modified, had additional hazards because, apart from the usual clutter normally found in cellars, many people had stocked up with coal and coke for the winter, and once this caught fire the inhabitants had to evacuate or die of carbon monoxide poisoning.

There was someone in charge of each cellar or bunker, and if he could not save his charges it was his duty to go out and get help. However, no one envisaged that the demands for assistance would be on such an enormous scale locally or covering such a large area generally. The public shelters were adequate for – in addition to those already mentioned, totalling around 2,000 – the railway stations also provided shelters. Though primarily erected to accommodate passengers and staff, these shelters did not close their doors to anyone seeking refuge. The appalling carnage in the streets during the Firestorm was not caused by shortage of room but because the heat made the shelters untenable.

The Germans had two air-raid warnings. The early warning (*Kleinalarm*) was given when the enemy was still some 15 minutes away and consisted of three 15-second wails of the siren with a five-second interval. The people were not compelled to heed the warning, and in general most of them took little notice of it. *Der Alarm*, the second warning, took the form of 15 wails per minute and was given when a raid was imminent.[3] In Hamburg many people usually switched on the wireless and tuned in to the local station to hear a progress report from the State Secretary, Georg Ahrens. Since the early raids in 1941 he had come on the air whenever the city was about to be raided, voicing reassurance and advising the citizens of when it would be prudent to go to their shelters. These soothing messages earned him the nickname *Onkel Baldrian* (Uncle Sedative). His audience rating on July 27–28 was definitely low.

After the heavy attack on July 24–25, when more than 1,200 people were killed and storm fires had swept through the districts west of the Alster, few of the citizens needed persuading to go to the shelters when the warning alarm was given, for by comparison

---

2. Sandbag constructions against walls for protection against shrapnel if caught in the open.
3. Part of the alarm system had been put out of action on the night of the 24th, so the AA guns within the city boundaries fired a warning salvo to warn everyone that an attack was imminent.

with previous raids it had been a devastating attack. As the Hamburg Police President put it: "The continuation of the first raid by daylight and nuisance raids during the period from the morning of July 25 until the morning of July 27 disclosed the enemy's intentions." So, like the English during the blitz on London in 1940, the people of Hamburg decided it was wiser to take their families and sleep in the shelters at night. The adults sat around chatting or playing cards to while away the evening.

**NIGHT OPERATIONS July 27–28**

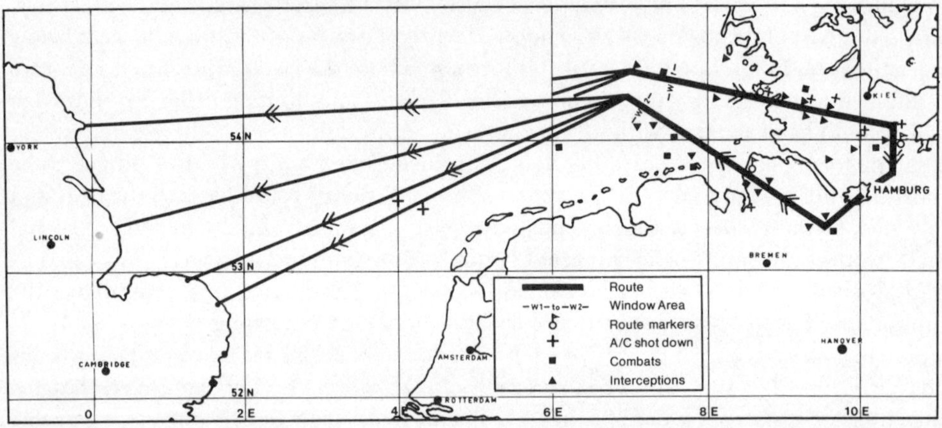


July 27 had been a sweltering hot day; the shelters seemed airless and sleep was far away. The Mosquito attacks on the nights of the 25th and 26th had disturbed most of Hamburg's population just when they had managed to drop off to sleep in spite of the heat. So on this occasion most of them resolved to wait up, especially since the raid on the 24–25th had not started until one o'clock in the morning. As one o'clock approached they went outside for a last cigarette and a breath of cool air coming from the river or canals. Some of the older folk were forecasting a thunderstorm. Then the alarm sounded. To the west the searchlights could be seen weaving across the sky, and when the sound of Ack-Ack gunfire could be heard like distant thunder in the still night they realised that this was no Mosquito attack. They were filing calmly into the shelters when suddenly the flak was bursting overhead and the bombers could be heard, followed quickly by the whistle of falling bombs. The boom of the guns was reassuring and the rattle of machine-gun fire from the sky meant that the enemy was not having it all his own way. Some of the heaviest bombing in the early stages was in the region of Berliner Tor, where Sergeant-Major[4] Schmidt was in charge of a bunker in Spaldingstrasse. His military air had already inspired the local inhabitants with confidence and his bunker was filled almost to capacity with 400 people. Such was their trust in Schmidt that the people remained quiet and orderly in spite of the crunch of bombs plunging into the ground nearby and exploding; one, extra close, shook the foundations and put out the lights. The storm lanterns were lit and Schmidt strolled among the people to reassure them.

4. Equivalent German rank *Feldwebel*.

Less than a quarter of a mile away, in Frankenstrasse, Herr Bey was in charge of the shelter at No 38. He too was very popular and had acquired a large band of "regulars". When the alarm sounded he advised everyone to get inside while he took a walk round the block to hurry along those who might be strolling in the neighbourhood. The falling bombs made him realise, like Schmidt, that the danger was more imminent than he had originally thought, so he rushed back and exhorted the people to take cover quickly. Seeing the unmistakable light-blue glow of incendiaries burning in the nearby streets, he posted his guards outside with instructions not to let anybody out and to check for phosphorus contamination before letting people in. Then he went inside and closed the iron door. The Hamburg shelters had one common denominator: the lights went out as soon as bombs began to fall. Psychologically it had its advantages because it enabled the warden, by producing secondary lighting such as candles or storm lanterns, to reassure everyone that everything was under control.

Most of the early bombing was to the south-east of the aiming point, and fires had taken hold in Hamm, Hammerbrook and Rothenburgsort by Z+9, when the second wave of bombers arrived over the target. Some of the first wave bombed further to the north – in Barmbek and around the Stadtpark – but their loads chiefly comprised HE and proved to be only a foretaste of what was to happen there on the 29–30th. The Lancasters and Halifaxes of the second wave poured their loads into the fires. They of course knew nothing of the complicated meteorological phenomena that had been set in motion, but they did notice the speed with which the small fires united to form a large conflagration which, by 0112 hours, was raging in the Billwerder district. Meanwhile, a carpet of incendiaries had been laid north-east into Hamm and westward beyond the Alster. St Georg and Ullenhorst were also well ablaze. The Mackensen and Hindenburg barracks were set on fire during this stage of the attack.

* * * *

At about this time F/O J.G. Claridge was less than four minutes away from the target, flying straight and level. From 20,000 feet the target was an impressive sight: huge fires dotted with spots of green and, every now and then, small eruptions of flame leaping skywards as another salvo of HE burst on the ground. Larger bursts were immediately identified as cookies. Then came a bizarre impression that a group of people had gone berserk on the ground and were running around switching on electric lights at a furious speed. This effect was created by a load of incendiaries bursting on the ground and looking, in the initial stage, like powerful bulbs giving off a strong bluish-white light.

The searchlights were weaving around but were causing Claridge no concern for the moment; nor indeed was the flak, which was bursting well below his Lancaster. The wireless operator, Sgt H.C. Jones, had taken over from the bomb-aimer the task of pushing *Window* down the flare chute.[5] The bomb-aimer, Sgt J.C. Bell, pleased to be

---

5. The crew member who performed this task varied between the Groups and even between crews. No one wanted the unpopularity that would result from stating which crew member should perform the task, so Command passed the buck to the Groups; they passed their own policy to the Squadrons, which tacitly suggested it to the captain, who had to take the abuse.

relieved of the task, was settling himself down in the nose in preparation for dropping the bombs. The Lancaster was yawing slightly, but that was comforting for it meant that the gunners were wide awake, rotating their turrets as they searched for the enemy. The serenity was broken when Sgt S. Graves, the rear gunner, called to Sgt T. Ross, the mid-upper, to keep his eyes peeled on the starboard side. "I have an Me109 in my sights on the port beam 500 yards away. The bastard's got a bloody great spotlight in the nose. I think he may be a decoy." Graves' calm assurance helped to keep the tension to a minimum, but even so Jones stopped pushing out the *Window* without realising it and F/Sgt L. Bending, the engineer, turned round—a purely reflex action. "Dive port, Skipper, he's coming in." The enemy aircraft seemed to skid across the sky and quickly closed to 300 yards, but Graves, who was ready for such a move, opened up with a very accurate burst. The apprehensive spectators felt a glow of admiration as they observed the tracer wing its way towards the tiny object which could be so lethal if given a chance. The Messerschmitt burst into flames and fell away to the starboard quarter. Graves watched it all the way down and actually saw it hit the ground.

Claridge decided that some evasive action would not come amiss, so he started to do a standard corkscrew. It was a difficult choice: many captains favoured a shallow dive and made a beeline through the target, others thought that the extra time taken for weaving was well spent, since few fighters or AA gunners found a corkscrew easy to follow. Jones suddenly realised that he was standing doing nothing and resumed dispensing *Window* at a rate far exceeding the specified one; it was a normal reaction, as if to make up for the time he had stopped. Bell had just settled down again when both gunners switched on their microphones almost simultaneously. A Ju88 with navigation lights burning was closing from the starboard quarter, but when the German saw tracer come pouring towards him from two sources he hastily switched off his navigation lights and broke away without firing a shot. Graves had been so quick on the draw earlier that the Me109 pilot had not had time to open fire either.

Sgt P.J. Drane was intercepted three times, twice in the target area and finally out over the North Sea long after he had left the enemy coast. Shortly after leaving the check route markers Sgt R.E.C. Buck, the rear gunner, sighted a single-engined aircraft at about 600 yards on the starboard bow and flying at 90° to the Lancaster's track. Buck informed his skipper and told him to be ready to dive to port if the fighter had spotted them. Sgt J. Henderson, the mid-upper gunner, swung his turret into position in readiness. Everything went quiet in the Lancaster and then Buck's voice broke the silence: "Go, go, go." In that time the fighter had cut down the distance to 400 yards and cannon shells were winging their way towards the bomber. The pre-combat preparation saved the bomber, and as Drane dived to port the tracer shells hurried on past him. The gunners claimed to have damaged the fighter, which dived away and disappeared from sight. The actual combat was over in less than 10 seconds; the racing pulses would take much longer to get back to normal.

W/O Walter's experience as second pilot on the 24–25th[6] was a picnic compared with Sgt D.A. Board's introduction to operations. Board was acting as second pilot in F/O R. Waugh's Lancaster. Just before the target the aircraft began to vibrate violently, and immediately afterwards the starboard inner caught fire and the captain

---

6. See Chapter III.

ordered the crew to don their parachutes.[7] The engine was stopped but the fire did not go out and the propeller would not feather. When the revs began to drop on the port inner and the port outer too became temperamental and started misfiring, Waugh ordered "Abandon aircraft". The navigator, wireless operator, bomb-aimer and the two gunners baled out, but Board and Sgt F.J. Watson, the flight engineer, elected to stay. The immediate problem was the fire. Waugh jettisoned the bombs and dived to 6,000 feet without affecting the flames, but he decided to try another dive and when he levelled out at 2,500 feet the fire was out. Fortunately the dive seemed to have a rejuvenating effect on the port engines and he was able to gain height and once over the North Sea he set course for England. The port inner started playing up again and Waugh was forced to shut it down. The aircraft could not maintain height on two engines and the simple sum of (height of aircraft) minus (loss of height per mile × miles to England) left them in the red or, in this case, the North Sea. Board and Watson set about throwing overboard everything that could be detached. The Lancaster was down to 3,000 feet when the English coast came in sight, but by then it was equal to the task of maintaining height. It eventually touched down at Mildenhall at 0345 hours. The captain received an immediate award of the DFC and the two sergeants DFMs. The citation spoke of "great courage, coolness and determination". Perhaps the remainder of the crew would not have been so charitable. There is a tail gunner roaming round London still hoping to catch up with the pilot who ordered him to bale out yet managed to bring the aircraft back to England safely. The gunner spent 2½ years in an NCOs' prisoner of war camp where the food ration was so meagre the airmen concentrated on conserving energy in order to survive.

As the raid developed the bombing drifted eastwards until the centre was now 3½ miles due east of the aiming point. There was however no evidence of creepback, the inferno below being too strong a magnet. The 11 Recenterers and the remaining 25 Backers-up were completely powerless, their TIs merely adding a touch of colour to a sea of fire. Equally ineffective were the decoy reds of the Germans, fired initially some 10 miles to the west of the town. Although they moved closer to Hamburg in the later stages of the attack, they did not seem to realise that they were wasting their time, even had they been firing the correct colour. Saundby wrote: "The penchant for bomber crews, both English and German, to bomb fires was exploited on both sides of the Channel. Dummy fires were started outside the main target area and it is unbelievable the amount of attention they received."[8] The Hamburg decoy fires were lit, but from above they must have looked like someone stoking a camp fire compared with the huge conflagration stretching for miles over the eastern and south-eastern districts of the port.

Many squadrons could look back on the *Gomorrah* raids and the first ten days of *Window* with immense relief; six excellent attacks and no losses, and in some cases no combats either. Yet for 76 Squadron it was a period which many of the crews wanted only to forget, none more so than F/Sgt W.E. Elder's. From the reports it would appear

7. Only the pilot and rear gunner wore their parachutes, which were packed on seat-type containers, throughout a sortie. The rest of the crew stowed their 'chutes in some handy place where they could grab them at a moment's notice. Their parachutes were clipped chest-high on a harness. There was scarcely room for two people to pass in a bomber, and wearing parachutes would have made it impossible.
8. *Air Bombardment*, Air Marshal Sir Robert Saundby.

that in some instances the mid-upper gunner was dispensing *Window*, so some of the trouble was of their own making. Elder had been compelled to shut down the port inner engine before reaching the target but had pressed on and dropped his bombs. Almost immediately afterwards his Halifax was attacked by two enemy fighters. F/Sgt J. Heggarty, the rear gunner, was partially blinded by searchlights and glare from the raging fires below and did not see the dark speck diving towards him until tracer was hammering into his turret. Immediately he ordered a corkscrew to port and engaged the enemy. The mid-upper, Sgt A. Smith, was not in his turret, and so a second fighter coming in from the starboard was not observed and, being unopposed, came in close, pouring cannon shells into the bomber. Smith, standing by the flare chute, was killed during the attack and Sgt W. Berry, the flight engineer, was wounded in the leg. Berry had however managed to haul himself into the mid-upper turret before the fighters made their second attack.[9] The sequence of events during the next hectic 20 minutes, as disaster followed disaster, was impossible to unravel. Elder remembers the struggle to carry out the evasive action as three engines tried to do the work of four. He also remembers that the intercom must have become unserviceable early in the fray. He recalls the sudden silence and then seeing the call lights[10] wink on as Heggarty indicated which way he wanted his skipper to turn. The crew were thankful when *Monica* went U/S; they were only too aware that they were being attacked and the incessant bleep, on top of the tension, was nerve-wracking. The rear gunner remembers being wounded twice: he was hit once in the leg and then he felt a searing pain as a bullet grazed his face. He realised that the intercom was shot up because Elder did not respond to his instructions, and he immediately pressed the indicator button. The turret suddenly stopped rotating and he knew the hydraulics were severed. Fortunately he had no problem with his guns and every time a combat manoeuvre brought one of the fighters into his sights he blazed away, teaching the enemy a little respect. The mid-upper turret would not rotate either, so Berry, whose only knowledge of deflection aiming was what he had gleaned from "line shooting",[11] started firing long before the fighter came into his sights and kept the triggers pressed until it had passed out the other side. Eventually the fighters broke off the engagement and, as the bomb bay was burning furiously, it was assumed that they considered the bomber doomed. Although other bombers did escape in similar circumstances, it was out of character, for the Germans usually followed a doomed aircraft down until it crashed.[12] Other equally valid reasons for breaking off the combat were the possibilities that the fighters were running out of petrol or had expended all their ammunition.

Although Berry had been aware of the fire in the bomb bay – he was sitting directly above it – he was much too involved to worry about it. However, as soon as it was certain the combat was over he leapt down, grabbed a fire extinguisher and crawled to

9. It is interesting to note the extent to which individual trades had become specialised by 1943. Navigators no longer dropped the bombs, and wireless operators, who at one stage of the war were trained additionally as gunners and took over their duties when the gunners were wounded, now had so much equipment to look after that their training took longer than the earlier combined courses.

10. Indicator buttons were fitted in gun turrets against the possibility of intercom failure. The gunner pressed either the port or starboard one to indicate in which direction he wanted the pilot to turn. When the button was pressed a light winked on in front of the pilot, who turned in the indicated direction.

11. Exaggerated boasting of one's exploits.

12. The Germans, like the British, were not given credit for a kill unless they actually saw the aircraft crash or explode.

the bomb bay. By now the outer fabric had burned away and the wind was fanning the flames, which blew into his face. The extinguisher was equal to its job, but Elder was now faced with the unenviable task of nursing an extensively damaged Halifax across 360 miles of sea on three engines. The prospects, although bleak, were not hopeless: the bulk of the damage was behind the cockpit, and neither the engines nor the petrol tanks had been hit.

Elder asked for a direct course to England and the wireless operator kept in constant communication with base. Eventually the Halifax limped across the coast near Great Yarmouth. East Anglia teemed with aerodromes yet Elder apparently did not attempt to land at the first one he saw, but he continued west, passing over Norwich, until he reached Shipdham, a USAAF station. Under happier circumstances one would have smiled approvingly at his choice, which guaranteed breakfast with lashings of bacon, tomatoes, sausages and more than one egg, toast, butter and marmalade aplenty, jugs of steaming hot coffee, bowls full of sugar and a basket overflowing with packets of the most popular brands of American cigarettes. Elder had no such frivolous thoughts. With the undercarriage U/S, he was forced to make a crash landing because of the wounded engineer and rear gunner and the dead Smith. First he ordered the other members of the crew to bale out, which they did successfully without injury, although Sgt G.A. House, the bomb-aimer, was somewhat bemused by the nightmare trip and, according to the medical officer who examined him, was suffering from "mental confusion". Elder made a successful crash landing and the Americans sprayed the Halifax with foam to extinguish the fire while medical orderlies carried out the wounded and the unfortunate Smith. The feeling of solid earth under his feet was a tonic for the gallant Elder.

Sgt S.J. Troake, also from 76 Squadron, had just left the Hamburg fires behind him when Sgt R.S. Orr, the tail gunner, sighted an Me109 on the starboard quarter, flying level 800 yards away. Orr reported the fighter's position and gave the preliminary order "Prepare to corkscrew". The fighter made a curve-of-pursuit attack, and when it was 600 yards away Orr shouted "Go, go, go" and opened fire. The combat manoeuvre was so violent that Orr was unable to direct his fire accurately, but the fighter pilot had seen enough. He made a shallow dive below the Halifax and then a climbing turn on the reciprocal and headed back to Hamburg. At the time of the attack the mid-upper gunner was dispensing *Window*.

The advent of *Window* threw the whole of the German night defence system into complete confusion, with the result that ground and air defences were ready to co-operate in any way, at least until some organised defence was worked out. A system was hurriedly devised, but the numerous different ways the fighters adopted to identify themselves to each other and to the ground were crude and, untypically, lacked organisation. Burning navigation lights was one simple method which required no modification, though one bomber crew noted an occasion when the red light was on the starboard and the green on the port, the opposite of the normal practice. The Me110 which attacked F/Sgt K.L. Wright had an orange light on each wingtip. Lights in the nose and underneath the fuselage were also used for identification purposes. Sometimes the lights appeared to be used also as a ploy: the "torch-bearer" maintained a respectful distance out of reach of the rear gunner's four machine guns, thereby attracting his attention, while a colleague then attacked from another quarter.

The Germans did shoot down aircraft, so perhaps some of the methods were reasonably successful. On the other hand, moving lights attract attention and also provide gunners with a useful point to aim at. However, the reluctance of the German night fighter pilots to mix it proved the importance they attached to getting in the first blow. While it is easy to talk glibly about the night fighters' idiosyncrasies in peacetime 35 years later, at 18,000 in 1943 feet over Hamburg the click of a microphone switch did the stomach no good at all. Similarly, the crews of 83 Squadron happily commented that "the searchlights were clueless," and so they appeared to be – until someone was caught in one. Then the speed with which the other searchlights zoned in and made a cone had to be experienced to be believed. Nor did it take much imagination to see the determined look on the ground gunners' faces as they feverishly poured shells into the searchlight cone, even when there was no aircraft trapped. Opportunities to aim were so rare as July drew to a close that they seldom went begging. Sgt C.G. Hopton was coned over the target and immediately heavy flak came shooting up to 19,000 feet. Evasive action did make life more difficult for the Ack-Ack boys, but the searchlight crews were very tenacious. "Sideslip and lose height" sounded easy but in fact it was not a simple manoeuvre, and before Hopton managed to get clear the Lancaster was hit and the port inner engine was set on fire. It went out quickly enough when the feathering and extinguisher buttons were pressed, but not before an Me109 pilot, who had been enjoying the fun as a spectator, had decided it was time to get a piece of the action. British gunners were repeatedly warned not to look at the fires because it would impair their night vision; searchlights also tended to blind them. The mid-upper gunners suffered least of all the crew in this respect because the fuselage protected them. So it was Sgt R. Dunn's excited voice which called "Dive port, Skipper, dive port," followed by "Me109 port quarter up" for the benefit of Sgt P.C. Lambert, the rear gunner. Both gunners opened fire and their combined effort forced the fighter pilot to break off the attack and dive away to safety. He had sighted his cannon on the burning engine, raking the port wing and, as the bomber turned to port, tearing holes in the fuselage and tail. Fortunately no one was hurt and the fighter did not risk a second attack.

The general opinion of crews was that the ground defences had been increased since the previous attack, and certainly the railway mobile batteries (*Eisenbahnflak*) which had been sent to the Ruhr were rushed back to Hamburg after the raid of the 24–25th. Two Pathfinders were among the 29 crews who suffered flak damage on the 27–28th. F/Lt R.E. Fawcett's Lancaster was hit by flak and the starboard windscreen was shattered. None of the crew was injured, but the flight engineer had to endure a cold and draughty return flight. S/Ldr J.H. White, also of 156 Squadron, was able to confirm crew reports of the 24–25th that the Germans were using a new type of flak: his Lancaster was hit by rocket-type flak. The same night F/O J. Reynolds's Halifax was holed in the mid-upper turret area but the crew suffered no injuries. F/Sgt F.R. Joy's Lancaster was hit by flak and the port inner was damaged. The resulting fire went out when the engine was stopped. Joy made a safe return to England on three engines and landed at Wickenby without mishap. F/Sgt R. Stewart also had an engine hit by flak and set on fire, but this too subsided when the engine was shut down. In addition the hydraulics were hit, so Stewart had to land without brakes.

Flak damage was insidious: many of the crashes, well away from the target area, were due to flak damage affecting the aircraft long after the apparent danger was past. When F/Sgt R. Heazlewood landed at Scampton at 0356 hours on the 28th his Lancaster crashed because the undercarriage collapsed as a result of a burst tyre. Although this was not specifically attributed to flak, the tyre had probably been punctured by a piece of shrapnel unbeknown to Heazlewood. Sgt R. Marks of 166 Squadron was coned and hit, an engine nacelle being damaged. Like Heazlewood, he discovered that he had a burst tyre when he landed at Kirmington.

The FLAK was more efficient when the aircraft was coned, and this was the main reason why the searchlight batteries were taken from Kammhuber in 1942. Sgt Hopton, whose combat with an Me109 has been recorded, was first coned and then hit by flak, which set the port inner on fire. The night fighter seemed to use the fire as an aiming point, adding to the damage already sustained on the port side. Many crews found it difficult to escape from the searchlights once they had been coned, and Sgt G. Welch, who was held for nine minutes, lost so much height taking evasive action that he deemed it wiser to drop his cargo on Kiel. F/O A.J. Belsay was coned for 25 minutes but, like White, he took such violent evasive action that both flak and fighters were unable to engage his Lancaster.

As the raid progressed the effect of *Window* became more pronounced: when the *Würzburg* screens of the ground defences were swamped with spurious echoes the searchlights groped blindly and the gunners were reduced to throwing up the flak in barrage form. Bomber crews repeatedly reported that the flak decreased in intensity later in the attack, though there seems no logical reason for this unless the gunners became discouraged. F/Lt F.J. Garvey of 83 Squadron, who was usually at the forefront of the attack, was among the last group of PFF marker crews on the 27–28th, and he was astounded at the weakness of the defences. Other 8 Group crews, operating with the Main Force, were carrying canisters of anti-personnel bombs. They had fun locating the AA batteries and then dropping this new weapon[13] on to the gun crews. The immediate effect was very gratifying: the batteries stopped firing.

When the fourth wave arrived over the target area at 0124 hours the incendiary carpet had spread as far east as Wandsbek, where a near-miss by a bomb had caused the road bridge over the railway to collapse. The troop depot in the vicinity was in urgent need of assistance in putting out the fires, which were rapidly getting out of hand. This was one night when "fringe merchants"[14] did some good, but only because the storm-force winds on the ground encouraged the small fires to join and eventually make one huge conflagration. However, some of the bombers had the patience to wait until they were over the centre of the fires before releasing their loads. By 0128 hours the Grasbrook gasworks were surrounded by flames and seven minutes later crews reported a violent explosion when a gas-holder in the Tiefstack plant blew up. F/O J.W. Leitch of 7 Squadron reported a line of warehouses one mile long ablaze. It was almost embarrassing for the fifth and sixth waves, for by now the fires had spread to the west of the Alster and even south of the river into Wilhelmsburg and Harburg. There were isolated fires as far west as Altona, already devastated by the previous night attack

13. New to the European theatre of war. AP bombs had been used very successfully in North Africa.
14. Those who bombed on the edge of the fires.

and the overspill from the American missions. "Is your journey really necessary?" was a wartime slogan; some of the later crews must have asked themselves that question.

Towards the end of the attack the smoke was boiling up to 23,000 feet, spreading out at the top like a huge cumulo-nimbus cloud. The mid-upper turret of Sgt G. Ogilvie's Lancaster was covered with black smuts. One crew of 83 Squadron said they could feel the heat from the fires in the aircraft and other crews reported being able to see the glow from 200 miles. The havoc created by the bombing was nothing compared with that caused by the firestorm, which raged for hours after the bombers had left the target.

It was at this point that the troubles of many crews really began. Giving the enemy a headache was only a part of the operation; getting back to base in one piece was vital too, particularly to the crews themselves. More losses occurred on the homeward journey than at any other time during a sortie. This was for a variety of reasons: the bomber stream tended to be less concentrated; crews were tired or relaxed after the excitement of witnessing a good attack or depressed if it was a poor one; the fighters had infiltrated the bomber stream and were waiting to pounce on the unwary.

In a letter to Saundby dated July 2, 1943, Air Marshal Cochrane (OC No 5 Group) said that if gunners would show a greater willingness to open fire then they might "convert the German nightfighter trade from one of the safest in the German Air Force to one of peril". Cochrane realised the inherent dangers of such a policy and callously dismissed them as inconsequential: "In the process, we shall, no doubt, put a number of .303 bullets into our own aircraft, but I doubt whether that would matter very much." His views were no doubt well known in 5 Group, and seemingly the crews were willing to put their comrades' lives at risk to preserve their own. It could be argued that night fighters were smaller than bombers, particularly the single-engined types, but at that time Bomber Command was still operating the Wellington, which was twin-engined and had a useful turn of speed. More important, new tail-warning devices like *Monica* were coming into service, and although they were very useful, they all had two drawbacks: they did not distinguish friend from foe and they heightened tension. Claridge (2), Drane (3), McClelland (1), Parker (2), Petty (2), Reid and Wright (1 each) were all captains of 5 Group crews, and between them they accounted for 12 of the interceptions. The gunners, without exception, gave a good account of themselves. No doubt with Cochrane's edict in mind, they did display a "willingness to open fire".

Sgt A.M. Reid was homeward-bound from Hamburg. There had been some conversation on the intercom, first to tell his navigator that the route markers were dead ahead, and then to warn the gunners to keep a sharp look-out as a searchlight was sweeping back and forth parallel to the Lancaster's track. Sgt C.M. Pearse, the tail gunner, called: "I see him, Skipper, Ju88 crossing to starboard, about 300 yards." Pearse opened fire immediately but the night fighter continued on his course, disappearing from sight. It was all over so quickly that Sgt J. Kirkham, the mid-upper, did not have time to swing his turret into position. Reid had begun a starboard corkscrew as soon as Pearse warned him of the enemy's presence. The Junkers reappeared a few seconds later on the starboard quarter, about 300 yards away but not closing, and next performed a movement similar to that of the Me109's pilot, described above, by skidding to get into position astern. Pearse and Kirkham both opened fire and claimed that they had damaged the Ju88. Certainly the enemy did not like the odds, for he dived away without opening fire.

F/Sgt N.M. McClelland was nearing the first turning point after leaving the target. His ETA was 0141 hours and as it was now 0140 he was expecting his new course from the navigator at any moment. But the voice that came over the intercom was that of Sgt K.L. Worden, the rear gunner: "Dive to port, Skipper, Focke-Wulf 190." The fighter was on the port quarter level with the Lancaster, almost 600 yards away, and Worden opened up instantly. The enemy closed to 500 yards but the 0.303s were coming too close for comfort and he dived away without replying.

A chronological sequence does have its virtues, but when 787 bombers are attacking over a time span of 50 minutes it can also be very confusing, with individual aircraft as much as 200 miles apart and some crews being intercepted on more than one occasion.

From the position of his first combat, 54°10N 08°25E, it would appear that Sgt F.E.S. Parker had not continued south through the target to the turning point at Wenzendorf but had turned right after bombing and taken a cruise down the Elbe. Once the aircraft had taken off the captain had sole responsibility for where it went, and many pilots performed what seemed to be irresponsible acts but which to them were calculated risks. A Ju88 followed Parker out over the North Sea and Sgt C. Wharton, the rear gunner, spotted the Junkers when it came out of the smoke cloud a mere 200 yards away on the starboard quarter down. The enemy must have been tracking the Lancaster on AI because he was not set to attack. Wharton's reaction was lightning-fast, and his bullets were tearing into the night fighter before the enemy had recovered from his surprise at finding the Lancaster so close. The Junkers turned on its belly and dived away; it was claimed as destroyed. Parker thought that it was time to join the bomber stream but while still north of track (52°59N 08°10E) the Lancaster was intercepted by another Ju88. Wharton, this time joined by Sgt J.K. Read, the mid-upper gunner, fired a scare burst at the night fighter while it was some distance away. The enemy took the hint and veered away without firing.

The Ju88s and the Me110s appeared to be having more success than the *Cat's-Eyes* fighters, the Fw190s and the Me109s.[15] Of the 17 British aircraft missing, 5 were seen to have been shot down over the target area, 3 by flak and 2 by fighters. It was in this area that the *Wild Boars* were expected to excel, but the switch from day fighting to night fighting was not easy and the techniques were not learned overnight. A total of 49 RAF aircraft were damaged, the bulk of them (38) by flak. Two bombers were hit by incendiaries, which fortunately did not ignite. ORS credited the night fighters with 7 successes and 4 damaged; the RAF gunners claimed to have shot down 8 enemy aircraft and damaged another 4.

Just beyond the target Sgt Drane's Lancaster was intercepted for the second time. An unidentified twin-engined enemy aircraft was sighted on the port quarter at 400 yards. The fighter closed to 350 yards before opening fire, but by then Drane was already diving to port. Buck and Henderson replied with what they termed "defensive action". The night fighter broke off the engagement and was not seen again. Drane was left unmolested for the next 30 minutes, during which time he made steady progress to the German coast and out to sea. Drane was 90 miles north-east of Bremerhaven and just

15. The purists use the prefix Bf instead of Me, as this was the German prefix. In wartime they were known as Me110s by the RAF, the USAAF and the public alike. Similarly, flak was the forces' name for German AA gunfire, whereas in Germany it was a body of men.

short of the turning point at 54°20N 07°00E when, as Henderson swung his turret to port, he saw a Ju88 on the port quarter up and 400 yards away. "Dive port, Skipper." He opened up promptly but the enemy closed the gap until he was only 150 yards away. Henderson saw tracer enter the nose of the Junkers and as it broke away he fired another burst into the tail; at that distance it was almost impossible to miss.

Sergeants Buck and Henderson were no doubt ordered to spend some of their spare time in the aircraft recognition room, because they identified only one of the three fighters which intercepted them.[16] That would seem to have been a poor reward for damaging two of their three adversaries. The gunners had a dangerous and difficult task: they were out-gunned (the night fighters were equipped with cannon) and the bombers were slower, less manoeuvrable and much larger targets. Once in contact the fighters had all the advantages. Who cared which type of fighter it was? Certainly not aircrew.

It is almost certain that Sgt Drane's third combat was the Germans' final attempt to increase their tally for the night, but there remains one more combat to recount. F/Sgt E. Roberts was homeward-bound when he was attacked by two or three Ju88s. His Stirling was alleged to have been at 53°32N 07°20E, which would have put him due east of Wilhelmshaven, 55 miles off track, but the report says he was approximately five miles to port of track. 08°20E would have put him too close to Bremerhaven for comfort, particularly as he was only at 10,000 feet and there was no searchlight action or flak reported. At 09°20E he would have been to starboard of track. He was certainly on the correct course, 300° Magnetic, and still over enemy territory, but exactly where would seem to be anyone's guess. The problem of whether there were two or three Junkers is understandable: the attacks followed each other so quickly that it would appear to have been impossible for the first aircraft to have positioned itself in time to make a second attack, particularly as fighter pilots found a corkscrew a most difficult manoeuvre to follow.[17]

The first attack developed from the port beam. P/O J. Hayden, the mid-upper gunner, sighted Junkers "A" about 600 yards away and slightly higher than the bomber. Hayden ordered a corkscrew to port and when Roberts began the combat manoeuvre the enemy realised he had been spotted and began his attack. All three gunners opened fire – the front turret was manned[18] – and the night fighter moved around to the port quarter, closing all the time. The German replied with a short burst of cannon fire which slipped harmlessly by before he dived away to starboard. The gunners were certain that they hit Junkers "A", preventing it from making a direct

16. Such nonsense reminds me of a scheme designed to improve navigation. Navigators' logs were marked after the operation and the best navigators, it was alleged, were those with the highest average marks. Marks were given for wind-finding, taking astro shots, and getting loop bearings and pinpoints, with bonus marks if they were used. After a few weeks the Group Navigation Officer came down to the station to interview those at the foot of the table. I was one of the four on the carpet. We were receiving a very painful "stripping" when suddenly one of the boys started laughing: "Look at the top eight, sir." Seven of them were missing and the eighth had been completely lost the previous night; his captain had been calling "Mayday, Mayday" when they were over the centre of London. The Navigation Officer ripped down the sheet and stormed out of the operations room. Incidentally, three of the four at the bottom survived the war.

17. The *Luftwaffe* admitted this after the war.

18. By the bomb-aimer, P/O J. Giles.

attack. As it dived away, Junkers "B" came in from the port beam down, but before it could get a bead on the corkscrewing bomber Hayden fired a short, accurate burst, forcing the enemy to dive away to starboard. Immediately afterwards, Junkers "C" (or "A") came in from the starboard, almost astern and below. Sgt D. Haub, the rear gunner, fired a long, accurate burst but the Ju88 came relentlessly on, ignoring the bullets and even following the corkscrew. He refused to be deterred even when Hayden added his fire. From less than 100 yards away he raked the Stirling from stem to stern with cannon and machine-gun fire. The front and mid-upper turrets were put out of action, the starboard bomb doors shot away, the fuselage and wings severely holed and a petrol pipe severed. Miraculously, no one was wounded. Haub and Hayden had poured more bullets into the night fighter before it disappeared underneath the bomber, and it was probably too damaged to continue the combat.

By now the bomber stream stretched for over 200 miles across the North Sea as more than 700 aircraft hurried home, gradually losing height to gain a little speed. At about 3 o'clock the Observer Corps reported the first bombers approaching, and stations in East Anglia came to life. Flying Control at Wyton were already searching the sky because a Mosquito of 139 Squadron was long overdue from Duisburg, but soon they would be too busy to worry as 83 Squadron Lancasters arrived back from Hamburg. Oakington was the only PFF station to have any trouble. P/O G.R. Woodward had had a trouble-free sortie and was patiently waiting to land when suddenly two engines cut. The Stirling crashed into a tree beyond the runway and was a complete write-off. The crew escaped with minor cuts but as they were all suffering from shock they were detained in station sick quarters for 12 hours.

On Monday morning Sgt G.L. Coxon had arrived back over Langar with only two serviceable engines and landed successfully. Back he was again asking for a priority landing on the morning of the 28th, this time with one engine unserviceable.[19] "Once you've landed on two, three's a piece of cake."

At Mildenhall Flying Control had already dealt with one emergency when F/O Waugh arrived back, but by now 13 of the 18 aircraft 15 Squadron had sent to Hamburg were safely down and life was not so hectic. Then Sgt D. Jackson called up and asked for a priority landing because he was short of fuel. His aircraft, Z-Zebra, crashed on the runway, burst into flames and was burnt out; the crew escaped unhurt. Three of the remaining four were diverted to Newmarket, where they landed safely; the fourth was missing.

In Flying Control at Scampton all eyes were on F/Sgt Heazlewood's Lancaster. The Flight Sergeant had made a good approach and S-Sugar sank beautifully to earth, raising puffs of smoke as rubber met concrete. Then the Lancaster slewed round as the undercarriage collapsed, and came to rest in the middle of the runway, the victim of a burst tyre. The crew were flung around in the aircraft but no one was hurt. Four crews of 57 Squadron were therefore diverted to Dunholme and F/O N.B. Morrison was advised to go to Wittering, where the runway was longer, because his Lancaster's flaps were unserviceable.

When the debriefing reports reached Harris he was delighted. *Gomorrah* was going better than anticipated and reconnaissance photographs confirmed the glowing reports

19. The ground crew were not to blame: it was a different aircraft.

of the crews. Many citizens of Hamburg still blame Harris for what happened, but the Firestorm was the real culprit. Harris, quoting from the Bible, once said: ". . . they [the Germans] have sown the wind, and they shall reap the whirlwind." Hamburg certainly reaped the whirlwind on the night of the 27–28th.

* * * *

During the blitz on London it was noted that when great numbers of incendiaries fell in a short space of time (roughly 20 minutes) it became impossible for firewatchers to report all the incidents; similarly, the firefighters were unable to prevent some fires from taking hold. The work of the fire services during the raids became very hazardous if incendiary bombs were alternated with HE. In addition, if the HE burst the water mains the firemen were almost powerless. Bomber Command made full use of this information and, while the tactics were not novel to *Gomorrah*, the German defences had not found a solution, as the extensive damage of July 24–25 had shown. In the small hours of the 25th the fire defence in Hamburg had been overwhelmed by the weight of the attack combined with the extent and ferocity of the fires, hampered by the alternation of incendiaries and HE bombs, frustrated by the lack of water and isolated by the breakdown in communications. On the night of July 27–28 conditions were immeasurably worse.

Hans Brunswig says: "When . . . the sirens sounded no citizen of Hamburg could have had a presentiment of such a catastrophe as the city underwent in the following hours. . . . today, after 30 years, it is still not possible . . . to give a comprehensive picture of the Firestorm."[20]

By chance the weather conditions over the city[21] were primed to exaggerate the effects of the bombing beyond all belief. A small rise in temperature (5° or 6°F) on the ground would be sufficient to break the uneasy peace established between a small pocket of warm air trapped over the city and the far colder air above and around it. When that happened the pocket would act like a chimney and the rising air would be sucked upwards, the cold air above offering little resistance. If the initial heating was caused by an incendiary fire then, provided the updraught was maintained, the replacement air would be sucked in as if by a flue, and the fire would thrive and become a firestorm.

The position on the ground was never clear and, although a log of events was kept at the HQ of the Fire Watch in Berliner Tor, the incidents noted were isolated in both space and time. Some were confirmed by the Fire Service patrols but conditions were changing so rapidly that seemingly contradictory statements may have been true. The reports of the bomber crews were consistent: viewed from the air the whole area east and south-east of the Alster appeared to be a mass of flames and smoke was rising 20,000 feet. So it seems incredible that a patrol travelling from Berliner Tor to Wandsbeker Chaussee between 0200 and 0230 hours should state that in their opinion the fires were extensive rather than intensive.

---

20. *Feuersturm über Hamburg*.
21. See Chapter VI.

The last aircraft had left the target before 0150 hours, by which time the machinery creating the firestorm had already been set in motion. Can it be that when the incendiaries (not the fires) burned themselves out in some areas there was a lull before the full effects of the firestorm were felt? This would account for the number of people caught in the open. When the crashing of the bombs ceased and the thunder of the Ack-Ack stopped they had leisure to assess their own situation. Many concluded that they would be safer away from their shelters. The report from HQ Berliner Tor stated that the post was thrown into turmoil from 0130 hours onwards as fugitives from neighbouring areas sought refuge there. Many had come from Hammerbrook, where the bombing had been particularly heavy, and they were still in a state of shock and wholly bewildered. Most of them were suffering from burns, bruises or abrasions, all had suffered harrowing experiences, and many had had miraculous escapes. They were in various states of *déshabillé*, and some were even naked, having stripped off their burning clothing. A great number were dripping wet after jumping into the Fleet (a canal) to escape the heat. Herr Brunswig, who was on duty at Berliner Tor, reported that one woman, completely naked and in an advanced stage of pregnancy, came staggering through the yard gate and shortly afterwards gave birth. In sharp contrast, the patrol mentioned above stated that the Wandsbek area was completely deserted.

It is impossible to give a clear picture of what happened on the ground because the firestorm brought chaos and all sense of time was lost. The entries in the log of the Fire Service are so few that a stranger reading it for the first time receives no suggestion of disaster, no hint of the total destruction and carnage. The log, as befits that of a fire HQ, records many incidents of fire and such news as the arrival of outside help – fire engines, for example – some from as far away as Dresden. It also records several instances of people trapped and requiring urgent assistance, but the word "firestorm" appears only once. Yet the HQ itself was near the centre of the storm and the house on the other side of the street portrayed a typical firestorm sequence (see pages XVIII and XIX). The heat from it was so intense that the paint on the HQ window frames was burned; the wind was so powerful in the courtyard that strong men, six feet tall, had to crawl on hands and knees, and to stand erect was absolutely impossible without holding on tightly to the railings. In the open it was only possible to run before the wind, always in danger of being hit by flying beams. The storm wind picked up timbers and beams as if they were matchsticks, dumped them into fires, picked them up again and hurled them blazing into houses bereft of roofs, which had been blasted off by high-explosive, burned by incendiaries or ripped out by the clawing wind.

There are many reports of flying, burning timbers, but Heinrich Johannsen's account seems to be the only one which records someone being knocked over by one. Half an hour after the alarm had sounded Johannsen saw green TIs cascading down to the north over Eilbek. The bombers, coming in from the north-east, seemed to be making directly for Hamm, so he beat a hasty retreat into the shelter. His calculations proved more precise than he would have wished because very soon afterwards a shower of incendiaries fell on the roofs and in the street. These were followed within seconds by HE bombs, one of which exploded so near that the blast blew out the splinter-proof glass in the cellar, giving Johannsen a clear view of the street, which was lit up by burning IBs, and the fires that were beginning everywhere. Someone upstairs who had not come down to the bunker shouted: "The house is burning on the third floor."

Johannsen went up with others from the bunker to see how serious the situation was. From the stairwell they could see the restaurant on the other side of the street ablaze. They tried, unsuccessfully, to put out the fire, which was quickly reaching the ground floor. When more HE began to drop they retreated to the bunker, realising that they were risking their lives and achieving nothing. It was fortunate that they did so because seconds later a salvo of bombs fell in the street and all the doors in the house were blown off. The lights went out and several men, perhaps because they panicked but certainly without orders, made a hole in the wall, presumably in an effort to escape from the cellar. They quickly realised their stupidity when the hot wind from the street rushed in, bringing with it showers of sparks. Even if the first action could be excused by the need to find an alternative escape route, their next one was unbelievable. They stuffed into the hole a number of straw bales which were in the cellar. With smoke now pouring into the bunker, survival and evacuation were synonymous. There was only one exit remaining: up the stairs, into the hall, through the doorway and into the street.

Johannsen was one of the last to leave the cellar and was at first surprised to find everyone gathered in the hall, but when he looked into the street he understood the reason: the raging inferno outside was composed of sparks as big as hailstones, the wind was roaring at everything in its path as it made its headlong dash to the vortex, and oxygen-hungry flames leapt across the street. All around them could be heard the drone of bombers, the whistle of more bombs, the unmistakable sound of cannon and machine-gun fire as fighter and bomber duelled above, and the previously comforting boom of the Ack-Ack guns. The yawning cellar behind meant death from smoke poisoning, while to remain in the hallway was only postponing the inevitable; to Johannsen they were not alternatives worth considering. He wanted to live, and although the odds against survival outside were daunting in the extreme, he had to challenge them. He grabbed his wife's arm and pulled her to the doorway. She in her turn dragged along her parents, and then others followed their example and ran out into the street. Johannsen considered that the better chance lay in running against the wind, reasoning that the flames would pass them quickly and they might buy themselves a few seconds in which to find some refuge, but he had miscalculated the strength of the wind they could make no progress. "One step forward and two steps back" best expresses the Johannsens' battle against the hurricane. Turning back at first seemed even worse, as they were almost lifted off their feet by the storm-force winds. They could only control their pace by hugging the wall, where the eddying wind only buffeted them along.

They had passed four houses before they found one not yet on fire, and the four of them pushed their way in. Even in that short space of time they were breathless, particularly the parents. The hallway was crowded with other refugees, most of them having second thoughts about braving the storm. Johannsen knew that the house was doomed and that it could only be a temporary sanctuary. He searched the apartments on both sides of the hall for water, their most urgent need, and was lucky to find a full bath. He soaked his uniform and advised the others to soak their clothes, dip their towels and blankets in the bath and then wrap the blankets around their bodies and make turbans with the towels. They all did as he advised calmly and methodically. He found out from the local inhabitants that the nearest open space was a construction site some 200 yards away, fortunately in the direction of Landwehr, towards which the wind was blowing. The crowd stood huddled together, hoping that by some miracle they would be saved without having to venture out again into that raging inferno. However, the fires on either side refused to be denied and soon smoke was pouring into the hallway. The brief interlude was over.

They rushed out into the open in the hope that speed would lend them courage and conquer fear. It was a close call. The immediate obstacle was a hot pile of rubble over two feet high, debris from houses which had collapsed. Fearful of being left alone, people threw away their possessions in order to keep up, and the wind seized these avariciously. Waves of fire pursued the fugitives down the street, adding terror to their flight and splitting up the group. Flying sparks stung like a swarm of angry bees, and burning timbers struck Johannsen several times in the back, one of them knocking him flat on his face. He struggled to his feet and was thankful to see the building site directly ahead.

In the open space everything appeared relatively quiet. About 150 people had come there in the hope of finding sanctuary, and most of them were lying down with their faces hidden in their arms. Johannsen's wife was shouting "Heinrich, Heinrich," almost hysterical because she had become separated from him and had also lost contact with her parents. To pacify her he went to look for them, although he knew it was an impossible task in such appalling conditions. After a fruitless foray he lay down to assess their own situation, at the same time spotting a heap of white bricks stacked along the side of the site. They were in the process of piling these over themselves as protection when they heard a small boy sobbing: "I don't want to burn, I don't want to burn." Johannsen took him in his arms under the wet blanket and asked him how he came to be wandering around alone. His story came flooding out: his mother had caught fire and died with his little brother, Manfred, in her arms; his father was on the Russian front. Johannsen promised to take care of him and shielded him with his body.

The temptation was to go to sleep after their exertions. The feeling of comparative safety, the reaction to fear-inspired adrenalin flow, the excessive heat: all combined to create an overwhelming drowsiness. The Johannsens agreed it was important to stay awake and so they kept talking to one another to make sure that they did, for peril was never far away. The storm was still raging and every now and then a wave of flame would sweep across the site, disgorging a shower of sparks. The fantastic heat had by now evaporated the last vestige of moisture and everything inflammable was ready to burn at the slightest encouragement. A spark on clothing, if not immediately brushed off, meant certain death. They had seen people wake up screaming, leap up and, within seconds, fall down again, dead. The term "flash-over"[22] and its scientific explanation were unknown to them, as indeed it was to most people in 1943, but they witnessed its deadly effect. A woman nearby caught fire and, terrified that the flames would leap over to them and aware that Heinrich could not leave the boy, Frau Johannsen leapt up to try to pull her further away. By the time she reached her the woman was dead. To keep as far as possible from the flames she grabbed the woman by the arms, but the skin stuck to her hands and peeled off like a pair of gloves. Their fear of flash-over was so great that they hurled bricks on top of the dead woman to put out the flames.

---

22. See Glossary and Chapter VI.

The storm gradually died down as the fires burned out, but no one dared to move. Perhaps each feared he was the sole survivor, and in many instances this was the awful truth. After about five hours people did begin to move around and, miraculously, someone found water. Another picked up a large piece of shell conveniently shaped like a saucer, but Johannsen warned them not to drink as the water would almost certainly be contaminated. Having survived such an ordeal, was it now worth flirting with death to appease a thirst? They washed their faces and bathed their eyes, which were red raw from the burning ash. Frau Johannsen searched for her parents and found them safe under a pile of stones just inside the entrance to the site. At the most only 20 of the 150 had survived.

The Johannsens and the parents set out for Billstedt with perhaps a little more bounce in their step than would have been expected after such an ordeal, but the whole family had survived, and that seemed like a miracle. The little boy clung to Johannsen's hand, but when they met a Red Cross nurse he handed the child over to her.

When describing the behaviour of a large cross-section of human beings under severe stress, antonyms go hand in hand: prudence and folly, courage and frailty, perseverance and apathy. Luck itself also played a part in the struggle for survival, and there seemed to be a callous partiality about the random way the dead lay in the streets like scraps of paper strewn singly and in heaps on the terraces after a football match.

Each of the survivors' stories in this account has been selected to highlight one of these aspects, but many contain others as well. Frau Erika Wilkan's account of the night runs the gamut more than most. She and her husband lived in an apartment at 83 Grevenweg near the Mittelkanal in the district of Hamm, where the early bombing caused uncontrollable fires. Like good citizens the residents of 83 went down into the cellar shelter when the alarm sounded, but less than 30 minutes after the bombs started to drop, smoke was pouring into the cellar.

The Germans had put an immense amount of thought into ARP. The installation of underground exits so that shelters could be evacuated without the need to go above ground appeared to be an excellent idea, but this time it went tragically wrong. In this instance the Wilkans' exit was made impassable by rubble. As in England, clothing was at a premium, so most Germans took with them into their shelters a small case containing a spare change of clothes and a few cherished portable possessions, and Frau Wilkan was no exception. Her husband picked up their case and Erika their blanket, and they led the people up the stairs into the hallway, where they found the door on fire. With much trepidation Herr Wilkan wrenched open the door, only to find the street enveloped in flames, some of them coming from their own building. It would have been easy to panic but they paused to assess their predicament: to remain was suicidal, yet they must have some plan before venturing into the flames. They decided to go towards the Mittelkanal, where they could find temporary shelter in the public toilet by the bridge. They had forgotten that the door had been blown off by a near miss on the 24–25th, but it did mean that they got under cover quickly.

Their refuge consisted of two rooms: one contained three WCs and the other was a small compartment for the attendant. Within a few minutes 80 to 100 people, including three soldiers, had crammed themselves inside. The Wilkans, being among the first arrivals, were pushed further and further back until they were squashed against the wall of the middle WC. At first the air was breathable but the number of people and the heat outside soon made conditions insupportable. Many began screaming "We'll all suffocate," but no one was prepared to leave. Everyone began shouting "Water, water." By chance, the only water left there was in the cistern of the middle WC, and as much to save himself from being crushed to death as for any other reason, Herr Wilkan stood on the seat and dipped towels and handkerchiefs into the cistern. The towels he tore into strips so that as many as possible should have a share. After what seemed like an hour the water ran out and, having been jostled from three sides while trying to maintain his balance, and being compelled to breathe the hotter air near the ceiling, he got down completely exhausted.

The crowd quietened down but it was only a temporary lull, for a phosphorus IB fell in the doorway and the people there were covered with flames. Their screams and the sight of them burning from head to foot brought terror to the stoutest heart. Many fainted and the remainder buried their heads to hide from the gruesome sight. When they felt the tremendous heat others near the doorway realised their peril and ripped off the WC doors, placing them in front of the bomb. They soon realised their folly when the doors too caught fire. This brought a new hazard, for smoke poured into the toilet and the only way out was a mass of flames. As conditions worsened people sank to the ground, moaning and crying, but none dared to face the fire. The clothing of those who had been overcome by smoke began to burn. Herr Wilkan had not yet recovered from his exhaustion, so Erika herself went among them, using her blanket to extinguish the flames.

A shot rang out, then another and another. The moaning stopped and people who had not moved for the past hour raised their heads and stared unbelievingly at the three soldiers lying slumped on top of one another. Long after the echoes had died away the noise still reverberated in the mind. The firestorm, the heat, the struggle to breathe were forced to the back of everyone's mind as they gazed on the tragedy. The fact that three soldiers had chosen to shoot themselves rather than continue to undergo such terrible agony horrified everyone. When the shock began to wear off the trapped people realised that they were in the same hopeless situation which had forced the soldiers to commit such an uncharacteristic act. Their spirits plunged to a lower ebb and they sank down again, crying. Herr Wilkan suddenly noticed that Erika's hair was on fire and he rushed over to her, not caring where he trod, to wrap his arms about her head and put out the flames. They retreated back to the WC and, all inhibitions forgotten, dipped their towel in the lavatory pan and washed their faces. Blessed relief.

As the temperature rose and the oxygen became scarcer and scarcer their hearts began to beat faster and faster and their faces became red and bloated. As often happens to people who live close to one another, the same thought came into their minds simultaneously: "If this is the end then outside cannot be worse than here." Erika got up, wrapped the blanket round herself and, lest she should fall, picked her way very carefully over the bodies between herself and the door. Then, shouting "One, two, three, jump," she leaped through the doorway, with her husband, still clutching the suitcase, immediately behind. Fear lent speed to their tired limbs and they reached the canal with only their shoes burnt. Totally exhausted, they sank to the ground and had it not been for the people in the canal exhorting them to hand over their blankets so that they could wet them they might not have survived. Their example was followed by between 15 and 20 people from the toilet who were still conscious enough to comprehend that someone had braved the firestorm. Even in their affliction they found time to thank the Wilkans for their help and, particularly, for giving them courage.

As the fires burned themselves out and the storm gradually abated, the howling of the wind, the roaring of the flames and the crackling of the fires faded away. Then everyday noises like the lapping of the canal water on the banks brought them some small solace. Their minds would have liked to dismiss it all as a nightmare but the pain would not be denied; every time they blinked it was agony, their mouths and throats were parched. By the middle of the morning the people in the canal were becoming exhausted. They had hoped that they would be rescued by boat long ago. After the hot, dry summer the canals were low and most of the swimmers could not reach the top of the bank, and others were too fat to lift their own weight. Together the Wilkans pulled out about 20 of them, including a woman who was pregnant. The need for drinking water was urgent. They found an iron bar and, taking it in turns, tried to force open a fire hydrant, but all their efforts were futile and they sank down, completely spent. Every fibre of their bodies ached with fatigue and they felt too weak to get up again without help. Neither the hunger gnawing at their stomachs nor throats too dry to cry out for water could persuade them to move.

However, when the *Kleinalarm* sounded[23] just before 11 o'clock, the memory of the night's ordeal revitalised them. They struggled to their feet and, looking neither right nor left, just concentrated on putting one foot in front of the other as they staggered towards Horn. Walking down the autobahn, they reached an army post and were given first aid, but the soldiers had problems of their own and had no means to help them further. The Wilkans, with only the determination to get away from the stricken city urging them on, made pitiably slow progress. Their bodies, dehydrated by the heat, refused to supply the fluid needed to wash the dust and grime off their eyeballs and allow the eyelids to work smoothly, and now they were almost blind. Along the way a group of nuns took them in and attended to them with such sincerity and Christianity that they began to feel like human beings again. After a short rest they plodded on once more.

At Barsbüttel a family called Wilmer put them up for the night, and here too they were made to feel that their comfort was the primary concern. They certainly needed love and tenderness, for they were both temporarily blind, and in addition Herr Wilkan had pains in the chest and liver, the result of breathing the smoke and phosphorus-laden air near the ceiling of the toilet. On the Friday afternoon they set out for Erika's parents' home, where they hoped to convalesce for a few weeks. We shall meet them again.

The most significant thing that can be deduced from the various reports of that night is the fact that there was no certain way of survival. The canals were described as havens of refuge in the Police President's report: "Numbers jumped into the canals and waterways and remained swimming or standing up to their necks in water for hours until the heat should die down. Even these suffered burns on their heads. They were obliged to wet their faces constantly or they perished in the heat. The firestorm swept over the water with its heat and its showers of sparks so that even thick wooden posts and bollards burned down to the level of the water. Some of these unfortunate people

23. The Americans made a feint at Kiel and Hamburg before turning south to Kassel.

were drowned. Many jumped out of windows into the water or the streets and lost their lives." Some is too modest a word; there are no exact figures, but the numbers can be counted in hundreds. Nor was exhaustion the only hazard; probably one third of the corpses taken from the canals had their skulls crushed in, killed by falling masonry, planks and beams as the walls of the houses near the canals crashed down into the water.

In the house shelters many died because they did not evacuate early enough; to them the fire outside seemed the greater of the two evils. Some who braved the fires found sanctuary, yet thousands succumbed to the fierce heat. Because of the extremely high temperature some died of hyperthermia and others suffocated. Many were burned to a cinder by the flames, or were blinded by sparks and became so demoralised that they sat down in the street to await an inevitable death. Those on the streets were driven from pillar to post, the situation changing so rapidly that what one minute seemed to be a haven became almost instantaneously a death trap.

We left Sergeant-Major Schmidt reassuring the people that everything was under control. Almost as if to prove him a liar, the firefighters came into the shelter to ask for help because the fires were getting out of control. Schmidt went out into the street, to find that at that time the house was not dangerously on fire. When he returned to the bunker he was surrounded by people asking him questions all at the same time. This had its virtues because he was able to answer the questions, many of which were embarrassing, in general terms. However, 20 minutes later a member of the Fire Service came into the shelter and said that in his opinion the fire was now so large that evacuation should be delayed no longer. Schmidt gave the order and the first group of people left in a calm and orderly fashion. The fireman remained in the street and pointed out the best escape route, towards Nagelsweg.

When some of the more timorous reached the street the flames and heat evaporated the remnants of their courage. As they tried to push their way back into the shelter Schmidt was compelled on several occasions to use force to keep them out. Since the balance between fear of the unknown and the dread of being trapped in the bunker was so fine, Schmidt knew that unless a steady exodus could be maintained panic could easily result. All this took time, and with conditions on the streets varying by the minute, in the later stages the best escape route seemed to be down Spaldingstrasse towards Heidenkampsweg. Schmidt made a final check to make sure no one was hiding in the cellar, and then tried to catch up with the others, but the wind proved too strong. It was curious how several people huddled together seemed to make better progress. Schmidt first tried the cellar of the public house on the corner of Spaldingstrasse and Hammerbrookstrasse, but the flames seemed to be following him and, having caught his breath, he ventured out again into the storm. Another strange feature of the firestorm was the fact that the gale would change direction by fully 180°.

Schmidt was not the only person trying to find some secure place of refuge. It was fatal to stay on the street for any length of time: the heat was intolerable and everywhere there was the danger of flames, burning timbers and falling masonry. Nor was there much relief in the doorways: the heat there was unbearable with the door closed, the sparks unbearable with it open. Schmidt made a dash down the road to Spaldingstrasse Sportsplatz, hoping to find a way out, but the *Luftwaffe* barracks there was a blazing cauldron and retreat was the only possible course. The wind was so strong that it whipped his helmet off and, before he could even raise his hand, whirled it well beyond his reach. He slipped back into his last refuge to catch his breath again.

After an unsuccessful attempt to get to the railway crossing at Norderstrasse and Hammerbrook he realised that he was fast becoming exhausted; a permanent refuge had become essential. He remembered that close by his own shelter was one at No 150A with an iron door and several rooms. Just as he arrived there he met a group of people leaving, and he warned them that conditions on the street were impossible. In turn they said it could not be worse than in the shelter, but they were back within three minutes. Conditions in the first room were certainly ghastly, and the moaning and whimpering of the women and children were demoralising. He searched the room for water, but the only water he could find was in a lavatory pan and so he had to dip his handkerchief in that. He held it to his face and dampened his lips. Feeling slightly revived, he decided to explore the other rooms in the bunker, reasoning that conditions there could not be worse. In one of the rooms he found a barrel of water and soaked his uniform in it. The release of tension as the wet clothing brought relief to his parched skin made him succumb to his exhaustion and he lay down like the others. It was so hot that it hurt to breathe, and soon he found himself coughing and groaning like everybody else. Hour after hour they lay there, too demoralised even to pray that the heat would subside.

Gradually he came out of his stupor, and when he started to move around another man came and joined him. They looked at their watches and were astonished to find that it was ten o'clock in the morning. By then the exits were blocked, so their immediate need was to find a tool to help them prise their way out. They were so weak that only the will to survive and each man's determination not to be the first to yield made them persevere. They found a hammer and had to take it in turns to pound against the hot bricks until they had made a hole large enough to crawl through and escape into the open. The noise of their exertions had aroused the other people in the room (four men, three women and four children), so they pushed them out before making their own escape. The air outside was much better and as they paused to view the devastation they discussed their next move. Schmidt was aware that everyone was in urgent need of succour, so by mutual consent they trudged their way to Hammerbrook Bridge, which they believed to represent their best hope of rescue. They sat there patiently until half past one and, just as they were thinking they must move on, a group of soldiers came along in a boat, searching the canal for survivors. In spite of their sore throats they managed to make enough noise to attract the soldiers' attention. They were taken to the nearest first aid station and then sent to St Georg's hospital for further treatment. All of them were suffering from carbon monoxide poisoning and hyperthermia, and were lucky to be alive. Partial blindness from the hot ash proved to be only temporary, but it was more than a month before Schmidt was considered fit to return to duty.

Truth, it is claimed, is stranger than fiction, and on this night in Hamburg the adage would seem to be beyond question. Schmidt's exploits after he was separated from his group took place near Berliner Tor; Erika Wilkan and her husband survived the night by the Mittelkanal a quarter of a mile further east; Johannsen outlived the storm buried on a building site to the north of Hamm. Between them lay Hirtenstrasse, where two separate accounts so closely corroborate one another that, because collusion was impossible, their authenticity has to be accepted.

Sergeant-Major Schäfer had been in lodgings at 31 Hirtenstrasse with his wife and 15-week-old child. On the night of the 24–25th a bomb had hit the house but the people in the cellar had survived. Schäfer had managed to get rooms at No 46 and had spent the day of the 27th salvaging what remained of his furniture. The sound of flak bursting overhead gave the first warning that Hirtenstrasse was in danger again, and within minutes a shower of incendiaries fell on the rooftops and in the street. Seconds later HE thundered down and the house shook right down to the foundations, one bomb being so close that the upper storeys of No 46 collapsed. The Sergeant-Major tried in vain to get volunteers to go out with him to assess the damage and attempt to put out the fires. Nothing daunted, he opened the cellar door. Flames leapt towards him but, undeterred, he jumped through them, only to find himself baulked by his own furniture stacked in the doorway. He returned to the cellar, where he found some gardening tools. Armed with a hoe – it had the longest shaft – he ventured out again and managed to push the furniture out of the way without getting burned himself. From the doorway he could see that the majority of the houses were on fire, Nos 46 and 48 down to ground level. The whistle of falling bombs, the crunch as they hit buildings, the detonations as they exploded: the cacophony of the raid was all around him. Without warning No 48 collapsed before his eyes, but not before he was able to hurl himself indoors away from the direct force of the blast.

Back in the cellar, although shaken by his narrow escape, he was so keyed up by everything that had happened during the last half hour that he had become completely aware. He could sense the opposite feelings of panic and apathy in the cellar, and he it was who heard the cries from No 48 and wielded the axe to break down the wall between. The inhabitants pushed their way into No 46 and smoke and dust poured in with them. The look of terror on the faces of these new arrivals brought fear even to the apathetic. At that point the lights went out. People threw themselves on the floor and the Sergeant-Major had to yell at the top of his voice to make himself heard. He warned them that the cellar might collapse at any minute and that their best hope of survival was to make a dash for Ohlendorff Park.[24] Not even the men took the slightest notice, so he grabbed hold of the two people nearest the cellar exit and, despite their struggles, dragged them up the stairs, frog-marched them through the flaming doorway to the corner of the street by Ohlendorffstrasse and pointed them in the direction of the park. He made the trip several times and dragged out some 25 women and children. Once he was struck on the foot by an incendiary but he ignored the pain. Ultimately, after a non-stop harangue, he managed to get all the others out. His wife, who had sat stoically nursing the baby, then handed it to him and they rushed out into the street. They were less than 100 yards away from the house when it was hit by a bomb and demolished. At the same time the route to the park was blocked by fallen masonry, so they ran straight ahead towards the main road, Hammer Landstrasse. The wind was increasing in strength with every stride they took and Schäfer had to cling tightly to the baby to prevent it being torn from his arms. Some of the women, bowled over by the wind, fell to the ground screaming and pleading for help, but he was too concerned for the baby's life to pay them any heed. He noticed a warehouse and office that was not yet on fire and

24. Now called Thorls Park.

he forced his way in. As it was the only house in the street not burning, it could be only a temporary refuge, but it would give them a chance to regain their breath.

His own plight did not lessen his gallantry. Three times he ran out into the street to rescue women who could not battle against the storm, tearing off their burning clothing. As he made a fourth attempt he was thrown to the ground by blast from a bomb and fell onto an IB, burning his right hand. Because of the excruciating pain he lapsed into unconsciousness. His wife implored the watching men to go and rescue him and, having witnessed his bravery, three of them ran out and dragged him to safety. A woman came forward voluntarily and gave him a drink of her precious water, whereupon he revived quickly and, ignoring his burns, started looking for some means of escape. With the help of a soldier he broke down a locked door and finally found an exit which led through a coal cellar to the park. Meanwhile, the warehouse had caught fire and the wall abutting the neighbouring house had collapsed and buried the people sheltering in the adjacent room. Because of the fierce heat and flames, Schäfer and the soldier were able to rescue only one man from the shambles.

The people from the other rooms had gathered together in the cellar and were all evacuated successfully. The dash to the park was not without incident: the storm winds were problem enough, but then out of the sky came a shower of phosphorus bombs and some of the women's clothing was set on fire. Fortunately the water tank in the park still contained some water and after being immersed they all survived, though many had ugly burns. After two hours of constant bombardment by sparks, supplemented by waves of flames, the houses round the park eventually caught fire and the heat, which had previously been merely unbearable, now became impossible. Schäfer's guardian angel, who must have been working overtime that night, now took a hand again. The Sergeant-Major and his flock fled from the park down Horstwesselstrasse, where they found a single house not yet on fire. They went through it into Schwarze Strasse, where, two hours later, they were picked up by a transport truck and taken to Bergedorf.

Hans Brunswig recounts the story of a *Brandmeister* who was in charge of a cellar at 38 Hirtenstrasse, where an HE bomb flung the front door into the hallway. The *Brandmeister*, who was on the cellar steps, was hurled back into it and the people within were thrown about by the blast. The shelter became so hot and the air so unbreatheable that the only hope of survival lay in flight to the nearby park, but to many the initial dash through the burning entrance was too great a challenge. Subsequently, 38 charred bodies were recovered from the cellar.

A few blocks away Herr Verleiah had a similar experience. When he looked outside houses on both sides of the street were burning and both HE and IBs were falling with regularity. He went back into the cellar, where he was pinned down for at least 45 minutes as load after load of HE fell in the vicinity; one bomb exploded near the emergency exit and the door caved in. It was time for action, as smoke was flooding into the cellar, making the air impossible to breathe, the hall was ablaze and burning timbers from the rooms above were falling into it. Yet a glance outside sent cold shivers down the spine. The firestorm was raging: sparks driven along by the fearsome wind came pouring in as if they were seeking to get out of the stampede, waves of flame roared past, and the cellar seemed like a haven to everyone except Verleiah. As if he had had a premonition, he cajoled, bullied and even kicked those lying on the floor to try to get them to leave for Hammer Park. In this way he induced 17 people to go with him.

Although bombs were still falling they were not the major problem. Nor was the blizzard of sparks, nor even the hurricane wind, which at times stopped them in their tracks as it made its headlong dash to Landwehr. The biggest threat to survival were the flames which suddenly leapt out of the buildings on either side, forcing the fugitives to jump to one side, only for flames from the other side to reach out and send them screaming back. It was a nightmare flight and when they reached the park they sank down exhausted. Verleiah did not know the fate of the others but the house was burned to the ground.

Following an RAF attack on October 24–25, 1940, the Lombard railway bridge had been closed for 12 hours. The tracks connected the *Hauptbahnof* (the main station) with Altona and the local district lines between Berliner Tor and Sternschanze used the same route.[25] The damage was not extensive but three UXBs[26] held up the repair work, since it was feared they might have been LDs.[27] Bomb disposal squads were rushed in to deal with them, and traffic across the road bridge was also restricted. After this it was decided to camouflage the bridges and the main railway station.

Hamburg's first major effort at camouflage would have been a tourist attraction in peacetime, with its fir-lined avenues and dimly lit streets. Built on the frozen lake, it sank with the first thaw. Early in 1941 it was rebuilt on a more elaborate scale in the hope that it would prove more durable. The whole area of the Binnen Alster, nearly 300,000 square yards, was covered over and disguised as streets. On the Alster itself the Lombard bridge was simulated, and an imitation *Hauptbahnhof* completed the camouflage. It took tons of wooden posts, stakes and battens to make the base. Thousands of yards of rush matting and netting were used to cover it and hundreds of bales of straw were placed in rows to look like streets lined with houses or shops, casting shadows in the sunlight to create more realism when viewed from the air. The whole area was painted and beautifully coloured, and it was certainly an impressive sight from the ground. In July 1941, much to the chagrin of the German Air Command, the British Press published "before and after" photographs of the area. During the raid of November 9–10, 1941, the main station was hit again, and it is doubtful if the camouflage served any good purpose.[28] The police had pointed out the dangers if it caught fire, but as no one could envisage an attack large enough for the fires to get so out of hand that the surrounding buildings would be endangered, particularly with a plentiful supply of water so near, their warnings fell on deaf ears. However, the impossible did happen on July 27–28. The camouflage, bone dry after the hot summer and below-average rainfall, caught fire and within minutes the whole of the structure was burning. The blaze, encouraged by the wind, threw tongues of flame outwards from the perimeter, first to lick the adjacent buildings and then to devour them. Damage was extensive all around the Binnen Alster; whether it would have been as widespread if the camouflage had not been there is a moot point. It was not in an area of concentrated bombing and much of it might have escaped serious damage; it is certain that many of those who perished would have had a chance to flee. The Ack-Ack battery, sited on a raft in the middle of the lake, received a hit from an 8,000-pounder and sank.

---

25. They still do today.
26. Unexploded bombs.
27. Delayed-action bombs.
28. The RAF had switched to area and night bombardment.

It is interesting to compare the effectiveness of underground shelters and surface bunkers in the same areas on the 27–28th. Under normal circumstances the underground shelters would appear to have been the safer. The decision to turn them into tunnel systems would seem to have given them many advantages, notably the possibility of evacuation without surfacing and having to contend with falling bombs and shrapnel from AA guns. Surface shelters, on the other hand, were always at the mercy of bombs, particularly the heavier HE. An incident of the 27–28th south of the river in Eichenstrasse (Wilhelmsburg) illustrates the point (see photograph on page XXIX). A near-miss by a 1,000-pounder blew a hole in the side of the surface bunker wall, killing 23 of the 35 occupants. A total figure of 100 deaths in surface shelters is quoted for the night, and this includes an instance in Dietrichstrasse, Wandsbek, where people crowded into the shelter even though it was not yet completed. Incendiary bombs fell on the structure near an entrance, and the scaffolding, including that round the doorway, a storage shed and a cement mixer caught fire. The entrance was blocked by flames which shot into the bunker, and 41 out of the 110 people inside died from burns or suffocation as smoke and phosphorus fumes filled the shelter. The total figure of 100 seems to be exceptionally low when more than 1,141 tons of HE were dropped.

The two factors which seem to have tipped the scales against the cellars and underground shelters on this night were the enormously high temperatures created by the firestorm fires, and the fact that the surface bunkers were set apart from surrounding buildings and so were not vulnerable to fire spreading from adjacent properties. The enormous heat seems to have turned the cellars and underground shelters into crematoria. The exits and emergency exits were surrounded by fires; steel doors, specially installed as a safety precaution, became red-hot or jammed; ceilings, weakened by excessive heat, collapsed under the weight of falling masonry; and even when they were not actually invaded by fire, many rooms were made untenable by smoke and fumes. The problem of heat was the common factor between the two types. In the surface bunker it was only essential to maintain calm and quiet to save as much oxygen as possible, whereas, as Herr Bey's report clearly illustrates, the additional hazards of being underground demanded evacuation for survival.

We left Herr Bey lighting candles in his shelter in Frankenstrasse, with HE and incendiaries falling all around. The light quelled the rising panic, but then began to enhance the pessimistic mood of the moment. On this occasion its sheer inadequacy seemed to echo everyone's feelings of presentiment, and the flames seemed to go out momentarily as the bombs exploded and hearts missed a beat.

The intensity of the bombing in Hammerbrook was having a dramatic effect outside too. The whole area was ablaze within minutes and already there were many people on the streets looking for alternative shelter. Only the desperate would venture out in such conditions, and dozens forced their way past the guards at Bey's shelter without being checked for phosphorus, many with their clothes on fire and others naked after ripping them off to avoid getting burnt. The people inside the shelter crowded closer together as the light from the fires, streaming through the doorway, swamped the candlelight and made them shade their eyes. Then the ventilating system broke down. If the failure of the light was used to good psychological advantage, the inability of the ventilators to cope with the demands made of them in the extreme conditions had the opposite effect. As the shelter grew hotter so the danger of hysteria grew also. Those few stories of this night which have relatively happy endings all have a common factor: the warden inspired confidence. Although the chances of getting the ventilators to work again were very remote, Bey instructed a team of men to repair them in order to show the people that he was trying to do something to combat the problem and also that he could offer some hope of improvement if his men managed to get them working again. Bey sent out one of his aides, Herr Engel, with a group of men to try to get through to the precinct HQ, but because of the firestorm they could get no further than Hammerbrookstrasse. The battle against heat and the storm winds had exhausted the patrol, so Bey set out himself to try a different route. However, a wet blanket and metal helmet were insufficient protection and he too was forced to turn back. Conditions on Heidenkampsweg were just as bad as those on Hammerbrookstrasse, perhaps even worse because the buildings were crumbling and the rubble was red-hot.

At 0120 hours it was the turn of the Stirling crews to drop their cargoes into the inferno, and to the near-hysterical victims below, the aircraft seemed to be down at rooftop level. Had the crews known that they were striking fear into the hearts of the people below it would have been no consolation, for they had problems of their own. They were even nearer to the flak than the Wellingtons,[29] and the light bomber squadrons used them as flak screens. They were literally between two fires, showered with incendiaries from above and the obvious choice of the gunners on the ground.

Hammerbrook was under siege from falling bombs, and one HE which exploded in Frankenstrasse hard by Bey's shelter made the firefighters realise that they were risking their lives to no good purpose. The fires had been out of control for some time, and the house opposite on the canal side of the street was doomed. Some of them searched it to make sure no one was still inside, and they did find a woman unconscious in the doorway. In the shelter she received first aid, though she really needed urgent hospitalisation. The firefighters also found some water in the house and they brought this much needed commodity out with them. The shortage of drinking water was a constant problem for the wardens. While ARP instructions warned people to take plenty of drinking water with them into the shelter, there were four imponderables. How much was "plenty"? What happened if you were forced to leave your original shelter? Whose responsibility was it to cater for the irresponsible, and how could sufficient be obtained when, after the 24–25th, drinking water was rationed?

Bey's first objective was to get his charges to Heidenkampsweg, where they could at least find temporary sanctuary in the Hochwasser Bassin. Having failed to find a safe way out on the surface he decided to explore the connecting passages to find an underground route through to Heidenkampsweg. Of course his own shelter had an emergency exit but an early bomb had put paid to any hope of using it and the room on that side of the shelter was unbearably hot and the stench was nauseating. Some of the men wanted to knock a hole in the wall adjoining the emergency exit but Bey counselled them to make only a crack at first. This proved to be a wise precaution, for the cellar on the other side was ablaze and when smoke came pouring through the crack the people in that room had to be evacuated. Next Bey made his way into the adjacent industrial

29. The service ceiling for the Stirling is quoted as 17,000 feet. Most crews would have been very happy to have got within 3,000 feet of this height. The Wellington's ceiling was between 17,000 and 18,000 feet, depending on the variant.

cellar, where he found that there was plenty of room and even a supply of water. More than 700 people had crammed into the bunker at No 38. Though it was grossly overcrowded and for the most part people were lying on top of one another rather than sitting or standing up, the prospect of being able to stretch their legs in the industrial shelter appealed to only a few. The majority, despite the discomfort of their cramped conditions, were too apathetic to move. Those who did make the effort tended to wander back, saying it was hotter in there, which was believed only because no one could think of any other reason why they should return.

Although the fires still raged and conditions on the streets in Hammerbrook were appalling, when the All-clear sounded some people, realising that their only hope of survival lay in flight from their present shelters, ventured out and ran towards the nearest water, in this instance either the Mittelkanal or Hochwasser Bassin. The water was balm to their parched skins but few of them were strong swimmers and as the blizzard of sparks made it imperative to keep their bodies under the protection of the water, this sanctuary could only be temporary. They had to keep some strength in reserve to climb the steep canal bank and also to run the gauntlet of the flying sparks, burning ash and sheets of flame as they sought a new refuge. Perhaps some of them worked in the area because they ran directly to the industrial shelter, theoretically the most secure in the area. The new arrivals offered no new threat because there was plenty of room in the shelter, but the overall situation remained critical. The urgent need was to find a safe place of refuge.

While Engel made another attempt to get outside help by swimming to the bridge in Heidenkampsweg, Bey made a final effort to find somewhere underground. The last option was the cellar of No 40, but this too was hopeless. In fact he met people from there wandering aimlessly through the passages, completely bewildered and in an advanced stage of exhaustion. The ceiling in this part of the industrial cellar, weakened by the great heat, was on the point of collapsing beneath the weight of the fallen masonry. If Bey had not found them they would assuredly have died. Bey was beginning to suffer from his exertions in the extreme conditions: his uniform was soaked with sweat and the amount of smoke he had taken into his lungs had left him with an excruciating headache. When Engel returned without help he knew he must go out himself immediately because his strength was draining away, and only by using all his willpower could he force his muscles to obey. On Frankenstrasse he saw a major in Fire Service uniform and brought him to the shelter to look at conditions for himself. This officer had several men with him and they began to organise the evacuation. The feeling of relief at being in contact with someone from the world outside was a tonic to Bey, but the people in the shelters were almost past caring. Those in Bey's own shelter knew the main door was almost red-hot and jammed tightly shut, and they had been told that the stairway was glowing hot. They also knew that the emergency exit had been blocked at the beginning of the raid and, ignorant of Bey's efforts, had lost all hope.

Bey picked out some he knew to have confidence in him and persuaded them to follow him on the understanding that he would lead the way. As he stepped out into the open Nos 42 and 44 collapsed and he disappeared in a cloud of soot and hot ash. For a moment he thought it was the end, but then found that he could move his arms and legs. He scrambled up on his hands and knees and finally got to his feet. He had been hit by falling masonry but would only have a few bruises to show to support the story of his narrow escape. His group had vanished inside with an alacrity which they had not displayed for many hours. He rounded them up again and berated them while in fact fully appreciating the reasons for their fears. A man from the Fire Service went first and, clinging tenaciously to each other, they made a chain all the way down Frankenstrasse, along Heidenkampsweg, over the bridge and on to Storton Park. Some had to be ejected forcibly from the cellar and one woman kept trying to force her way back in. Bey eventually had to take her on one side and warn her that if she did not behave she would have more than one reason to remember that night.

The Fire Service patrol were prepared for all emergencies, even providing clothing for the naked. It was one thing to dash through the streets naked at night, goaded along by falling bombs and flames, but even in the midst of such unparalleled destruction the normal proprieties obtained once again when the danger was past.

The tarmacadam on the road had been softened by the heat and those carrying the unconscious found progress very difficult, for the extra weight caused them to sink into it as if it were mud. Bey stayed until everyone was out and then searched all the rooms to make sure they were empty. Everywhere the ceilings were sagging and it seemed that the bunkers would cave in at any moment. When he arrived at the park, physically exhausted but mentally exhilarated, he found some of the people sitting, some lying and some standing or walking around. But all of them were safe and their expressions showed that they were beginning to realise it.

The fact that many police stations, fire stations, ARP posts and control centres were damaged or destroyed could not be attributed to bad organisation, but rather to concentrated bombing. In all, 76 were destroyed. The Police Presidency was an early victim on the 24–25th, when it had to be evacuated with some urgency. A principal weakness was the heavy reliance on telecommunications. The Fire Service probably suffered more than the other services in this respect, even though their HQ at Berliner Tor, while surrounded by fire, was never in real peril. The administrative centres around Billhorner Brückenstrasse, similarly beset, were not so fortunate and two of them had to be evacuated.

Herr Scheer was a police protection leader, and when the sirens sounded he sent three groups of men to patrol the station area. When, after 10 minutes, the first bombs fell in Rothenburgsort, some of them struck the station itself. The alternation of HE and IB allowed the fires to get a hold and in a very short time Scheer was ordered by his superiors to supervise the evacuation of the buildings. The obvious choice of refuge was the *Hauptbunker* near Billhorner Brückenstrasse and everyone was urged to go there as quickly as possible. The telephone girls picked up their handbags and dashed out of the exchange. Sheer noticed that they were all wearing thin summer dresses, so he stopped them before they reached the outer door and made each of them take a blanket, soak it and then wrap it around herself before he would allow her to leave. By the time Scheer had made sure that everyone was out of the station the firestorm was already raging in this area. The fires had compelled many occupants of underground shelters to face the inhospitable streets, so that when Sheer arrived at the *Hauptbunker* hundreds of people were trying to fight their way in. They had completely lost control and were thinking solely of their own survival. What shocked Scheer most was the fact that the men were behaving so badly, crowding the women out of the way and pushing so violently that children were in danger of being trampled to death. Asserting his authority, he managed to restore some semblance of calm, and when he called for the children to be passed over the heads of the crowd the men were made conscious of their irresponsible behaviour. However, there were still some who were trying to fight their way in and Scheer expended much energy restraining them. Before entering the bunker himself he went round to the other entrance and was horrified to find people already lying dead only yards away from safety. The sweltering conditions added to his exhaustion and, without warning, his knees buckled and he found the ground spinning towards him as he fell down unconscious, completely spent. He was dragged inside and after a short rest and a drink of water he soon recovered.

When at last the storm sounded as if it was dying down Scheer ventured outside, where he found corpses scattered along the streets on both sides of the main road. Again he was horrified as he saw bodies lying outside the surface bunker at 24 Billhorner Bergedamm, like people caught in the desert without water and too weak to crawl the extra few yards to an oasis. His grief was all the more intense because he himself had suffered a terrible premonition of doom just before his earlier collapse.

Few Westerners, unless they lived in the East End of London during the Blitz, can have the slightest idea of the conditions in Hamburg on the 27–28th. The cinema has often used the forest fire theme and shown spectacular sequences, the most significant being the illustration of spontaneous combustion as flames flash over from one tree to the next. Asthmatics know the dread of being unable to suck breath into the lungs, but although this is very frightening it causes little physical pain. In the firestorm it actually hurt to breathe; the air was hot rather than merely warm, and it was drawn in down a parched throat into lungs which were straining for oxygen but being fed smoke and often phosphorus fumes. At a time when the brain required richly oxygenated blood to help it perform the clearest thinking, it was receiving an increasingly polluted supply. As conditions worsened so the ability of the individual to deal with them decreased.

Erika Wilkan, Schäfer and Verleiah proved that people with strong characters could, given the slightest chance, beat the odds. Others, like Scheer, were a credit to their training and position of authority, remaining calm in adversity. The incidents described here were in the main success stories, and there were many instances in which people who were trapped or needed guidance, like ARP warden Bey, were rescued by men from the Fire Service. When they realised that the fires were completely out of control the firemen went round in groups helping the distressed and rescuing people. In this manner they were responsible for saving thousands of lives. A local ARP centre in Harburg received a message saying that more than 3,000 people were trapped in the Baustrasse *Hochbunker*, which was surrounded by fire. They were suffocating and beginning to panic, and help was urgently required. A rescue team was sent and once the people realised they were in contact with the outside world again they calmed down and were subsequently rescued.

To the majority of the citizens the cellars seemed safer than outside, particularly during the raid. By then, especially in the heavily bombed areas, it was either too late or the firestorm had already begun, bringing with it a new set of dangers. Parks and open spaces offered the best chance of survival, and the canals also seemed like havens, but there was no certain formula for survival. When on September 10, 1943, the first official total of deaths (26,409) was published, the majority were said to have perished on the streets and the view that they were worse death traps than the cellars would seem to have been justified. Apart from the storm-force wind, which exhausted the people, and flying sparks and hot ash, which set clothing alight, "fire whirls" swept them off their feet, wrenched suitcases and packages out of their grasp and tore children from their mothers' arms. The extreme instability in the lower air, generated by the intense heat of the incendiary fires, caused violent fire whirls, which were powerful enough to tear off roofs and gables, rip doors off their hinges, pick up hoardings and carry them along, and even uproot trees, twisting them out of the ground and stripping their branches of leaves. The fugitives seemed particularly vulnerable at corners, where winds, crashing head-on wherever two main streets met, produced the mechanical force which created the fire whirls. At the corner of Grüner Deich and Heidenkampsweg 25 people perished, and the photograph on page XXII shows how between 25 and 30 people were caught in a pocket of fire where Camperstrasse, Bullerdeich and Heidenkampsweg meet.

The photograph on page XXIII shows how even a fireman who knew the area like the palm of his hand was caught by a fire whirl. In the areas where the heaviest bombing had taken place the roads were so cratered and rubble-strewn that they became impassable for cars. The Fire Service HQ needed information more up to date than the fragments reaching them from patrols sent out hours previously. Where distances were involved the bicycle seemed the logical conveyance, since it could negotiate the rutted streets and was light enough to lift over the rubble. Ordered out, this unfortunate survived a bare half mile before the flames claimed him at the junction of Ausschläger Weg and Hammer Deich. The bicycle tyres, the leather on the saddle and the rubber on his gas mask were totally consumed, and of the man himself there were only charred remains.

Three questions need to be answered. Was the number of survivors from the streets greater than is generally assumed? Why were so many caught in the open? Why was the death rate on the 27–28th out of all proportion to that of the other night raids?

The answer to the first question is, I believe, yes. The Police President stated:[30] "Many of these refugees even then lost their lives." Many is the important word, but his following sentences enumerating the various ways that people met their death on the streets tend to dwarf the original statement. To remain on the streets for any length of time was certainly courting disaster, and this is probably how the confusion arose. Phrases like "few survived" and "there to die" could have referred to those who did not find refuge quickly. The experiences of Schmidt, Bey and, to a certain extent, Schäfer proved that they survived because they realised that to remain exposed to the firestorm was folly. Scheer offers proof[31] that a crowd of people were panicking to get into the *Hochbunker* at Billhorner Brückenstrasse and that fear had made them into an unruly mob. It was some time after the alarm had sounded, so undoubtedly their burning bunkers had forced them onto the streets. Brunswig says that firemen rescued thousands from burning shelters, and he records how at 0130 hours people came crowding into the Fire Service shelter at Berliner Tor, some of them soaking wet after swimming the canal. He also quotes other instances of people being led to safety. The

30. An official report by the Police President (Major H. Kehrl) on the *Katastrophe*, the German name for the Firestorm raid.
31. The conditions described in Scheer's story above.

Rothenburgsort II area was as heavily bombed as nearby Hammerbrook, so thousands were in need of help. The leader of the Fire Service in District IV, who had quickly realised that his men were wasting their time trying to extinguish the fires, had a moment of inspiration. Retreating with his men and machines to the wharf at Billhafen, he ordered them to man the hoses and make an umbrella of water for the fugitives to escape beneath. This umbrella provided protection from the two most dangerous and inhibiting hazards, fire and heat. Other firemen in his squad went into the shelters and brought the people out to safety. The force of the water kept the flames away and kept their clothing wet as it fell. By this means they rescued between 3,000 and 5,000 people. There were some casualties but in all instances they were individuals who scorned the help offered them. The telephone girls and the women and children in the shelter of Firewatch 6 in Reginenstrasse were rescued in this manner.

The overall picture is not necessarily one of people jumping out of the frying pan into the fire, but it does leave the second question unanswered. Undoubtedly the difference between the 27–28th and the other raids was the ferocity of the firestorm, and particularly the fact that it evolved in a short space of time. Fires developed at an alarming rate because of the hurricane winds. There were firestorms on the 24–25th and the 29–30th but the winds increased gradually and temperatures were never so high. As Dr Umglaube, a physicist serving as a news specialist with the Fire Service, put it: "On the one hand it was like fires in open fields, on the other like a fire in a furnace." People living near the canals jumped in to escape from the heat. People away from water who tried to flee from the fires had to search for open spaces and, as the winds were being sucked into the centre, they were battling against the storm. That, together with the excessive heat, sapped their strength and they sank down exhausted. By then they were completely demoralised and lacked the will to rise again. Gigantic waves of flames rooftop high, blizzards of sparks too painful to penetrate, and the ever-present risk of clothing being set alight drove others into the side streets, where eventually they became lost. Hemmed in by fire, they were petrified with fear. Sergeant-Major Dietrich's report of July 24–25 illustrates this quandary and highlights the difference in intensity between the two nights. He and his squad of men concentrated on rescuing people caught in the streets. Dietrich stated that he was astonished at how deep his men were able to penetrate into the fire mass. There they found people huddled together in groups of up to twenty. Surrounded by fire, totally bewildered and not knowing which way to turn, they readily followed his men through the flames to safety. He rescued several groups all in the same predicament. Many of them had been on the street for 30 minutes to an hour. If on July 27–28 they had been exposed to the heat of the firestorm for 30 minutes few of them would have survived.

Although thousands perished on the streets, thousands more were rescued, so the assertion that the streets were probably worse death traps than the cellars may not be true. The authorities were too occupied counting and attempting to identify the dead to give much thought to those who survived. Also, as the numbers grew they became so appalled by the tragedy that they naturally forgot the reason why the fugitives were on the streets. Again at that time many of the cellars lying beneath the tons of rubble had not yet yielded up their dead. Later, when they did, the total was so staggering that the authorities did not stop to consider that if no one had challenged the storm, there might easily have been three times as many entombed. Even today the memory of the carnage on the streets, the horror of the cellars and the numbing totals of more than 50,000 dead and 47,000 injured seem to prohibit any discussion of comparative figures. Statistics apart, no one in his right mind would have risked the burning hell outside unless the chances of survival in the shelter were very bleak indeed. It can therefore be safely assumed that the vast majority who died on the streets would most likely have perished if they had stayed where they were.

Some of the answers to the second question partially answer the third, but the startling difference between the second night raid and the others lay in the intensity of heat. It either forced the people out of their shelters and into equally inhospitable conditions, or caused their deaths by suffocation and hyperthermia if they remained in their cellars. The stronger (hurricane) winds brought an abundance of oxygen which, over a wide area, encouraged the fires to burn with uncontrollable ferocity. After the attacks Dr Umglaube carried out a scientific investigation, studying the weather charts for the period. His conclusion – that the firestorm was caused by freak atmospheric conditions – was made a military secret, although the Police President used Umglaube's work when composing his report. An article written for the newspaper *Hamburger Abendblatt* for January 23, 1949, said: "There is still a secret buried behind the fire walls and the clouds of smoke concerning the air raids of 1943 . . . the weight, type and proportion of high explosives to incendiaries were similar. . . . It was the fault of the weather. Some would say that was the same for both days; hot and humid, with no cloud. These people . . . had no idea of the prevailing meteorological conditions."

# Chapter VI

# The Firestorm Phenomenon

THE SECOND of the night attacks in the *Gomorrah* raids, on July 27–28, produced a new phenomenon, what Hans Brunswig called an "atmospheric firestorm". Herr Brunswig has made an exhaustive study of this night in Hamburg and his writings are known and accepted universally because he speaks with first-hand knowledge. As chief engineer on duty at Fire Services headquarters, he was an eyewitness. Indeed, part of his work was to assess the damage and report on conditions in general. After a distinguished career in the German Fire Service he returned to Hamburg in 1963 as Chief of the Fire Service. In the period 1949 to 1963 he had six works published, and the Hamburg Firestorm had never been far from his thoughts. Much that was in the official reports had not sat well with him, and his new appointment allowed him easy access to all the existing records, including those of his own department. His latest book, *Feuersturm über Hamburg*, gives details of every air raid on Hamburg, and the *Gomorrah* attacks receive special attention. I have talked with experts at the British Meteorological Office and the Fire Research Station, and have verified the facts wherever possible, but Herr Brunswig is the main source of my information.

The phenomena of firestorms are well known, having been collated from the histories of large city fires such as those at Hamburg (1842) and Chicago (1871). Briefly, a firestorm comes about as a result of small fires combining; the air above the fires is heated, its density is lowered, the air rises and cooler surface air is sucked in. In its turn the new air is heated and replaced. As the inrushing winds become stronger the abundance of oxygen acts like a bellows and temperatures in excess of 600°C (1,112°F) are reached.

Meteorology also plays its part at the outset, but the developing firestorm quickly produces conditions which transcend all normal rules. A steep lapse rate[1] up to medium heights is a common factor in firestorms, and it has been suggested that the absence of one during the Great Fire of London (1666) may have been the single factor that kept it less intense than those of Hamburg and Chicago in the 19th century.

Wind is one of the most important agents in the spread of fire, and in a conflagration the extent of the damage can be directly related to the strength of the wind. In general, fires tend to remain contained unless influenced by external factors, while the presence of an initial ground wind will spread a fire downwind and not laterally. In Tokyo (March 9, 1945) a fire started by a mass incendiary raid swept across the city in a huge wave of flames driven by a 25 mph wind, but, as in London (1666), there was no updrive and so no firestorm developed. In Hamburg (1842) and Chicago (1871) the initial ground winds (20–30 mph) drove the fires before them with such intensity and

1. Temperature gradient.

ferocity that in Chicago the flames actually leapt the river. The wind drove the flames onto new kindling, the temperatures rocketed, and the fires, encouraged by an ever-increasing supply of oxygen, gorged themselves until there was nothing left to consume. In both cities the wind was estimated to have average speeds in excess of 65 mph; on the Beaufort Scale this is "storm force," so the term "firestorm" was used to describe these occurrences.

Local features can affect winds, the North American Chinook and the European Föhn being good examples. Two RAF raids in which topography played a dominant part come to mind. The first was at Wüppertal (May 29–30, 1943), where the updraught from the heat of the incendiary fires caused the wind to rush down into the valley and drove the fires from one end of the town to the other. The second was at Pforzheim (February 24, 1945), where the fires sucked the air through a deep railway cutting. The effect was so intense that winds soon reached storm force.

In contrast, thermal firestorms are formed in conditions of complete calm. Each conflagration has its own individual characteristics but thermal firestorms have three features in common: conditions of calm; a stationary column of convectional air; and an almost complete burn-out within the boundaries of the fire. Krefeld (June 21–22, 1943) and Dresden (April 13–14, 1945) fall neatly into this category, as do the raids on Hamburg during the nights of July 24–25 and 29–30. The still conditions have two main effects: first, the winds are drawn in from all sides and so prevent the fires from spreading outwards; second, the fires develop a strong vertical updraught which in its turn creates an effect like a chimney with open flues at the bottom, acting in a similar manner to the bellows instanced above. The stationary column of air is important because without it the stovepipe effect which accentuates the flue-like action of the inrushing air would not be created. The strength of the updraught increases relative to the temperature, and as the wind grows stronger so the cycle repeats itself until there is nothing left to burn (**Figs 5–8**).

The damage from radiating heat should not be underestimated, particularly in view of the high temperatures involved. All flammable materials, including liquids and gases, will burst into flames when heated to "flash point".[2] One Hamburg eyewitness, recounting his experiences while trapped in a bomb crater, said that he saw women's clothing suddenly burst into flames as they were fleeing ahead of the fires. He swore that this was caused by extreme heat and not by flying sparks. In wartime the intense heat of incendiary fires often caused gables, doors and window frames – in Hamburg's case bone dry after an unusually hot summer – to burst into flames, helping the numerous small fires to combine into two or three large conflagrations.

What then were the differences between these thermal raids[3] and that of July 27–28? The real answer is there were very few differences: the mechanics, the abundance of kindling, the concentration of the attack, and the bomb load (the proportion of incendiary bombs to high explosive) were almost identical. But while the features were similar the intensity was incomparable. The stovepipe or chimney effect is the clue, and because this came about as a result of freak meteorological conditions the firestorm of the 27–28th has been classified as "atmospheric".

2. Technically used only in relation to liquids; the equivalent term for materials is "spontaneous combustion".
3. Kassel, Dresden, Hamburg July 24–25 and Hamburg July 29–30.

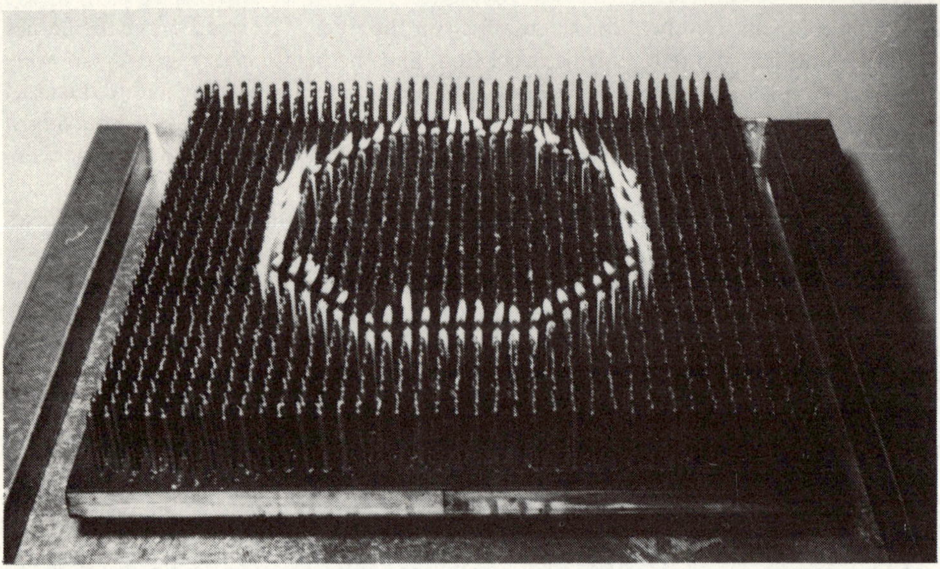

Fig 5

Fig 6

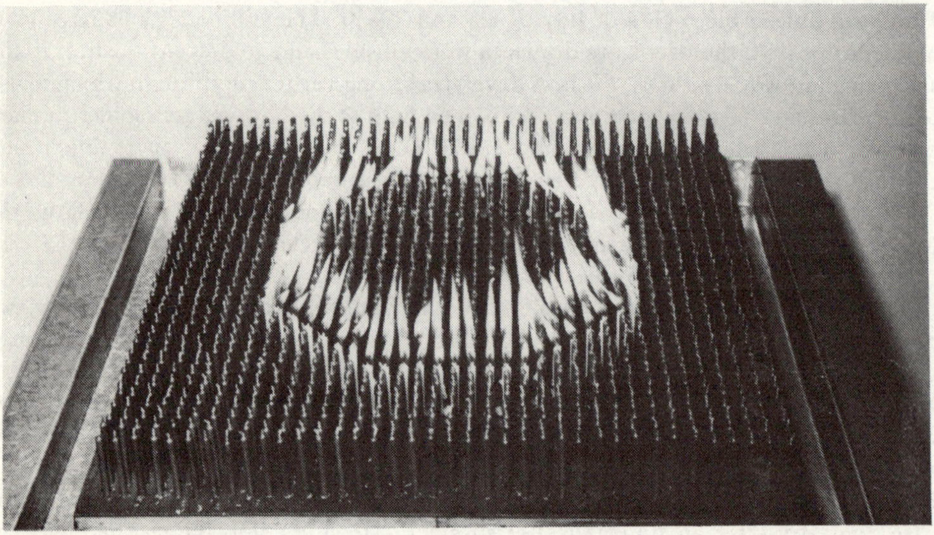

The Hamburg Fire Department carried out an experiment to show how a firestorm develops in the absence of a ground wind. 1,444 candles were set out in a 20-inch square. Next, an octagon of 400 candles was marked out in the centre of the square, and the 64 candles forming its perimeter were lit. In less than a minute the flames had reached four inches high, with a decided tilt towards the centre (**Fig 5**). After a further 20 seconds, when almost half of the candles had ignited, the flames reached a height of 12 to 16 inches and were forming a cone over the centre of the octagon (**Fig 6**). A minute later all the candles inside the octagon were alight and smoke was rising to 4 feet (**Fig 7**). To simulate the stovepipe effect over the firestorm area a flue, height 20 inches, was held over the burning candles **(Fig 8)**. This accelerated the updraught to such an extent the flames leapt out of the to the flue and the heat could be at a height of more than 6 None of the candles outside octagon were set on fire. (*H Brunswig*)

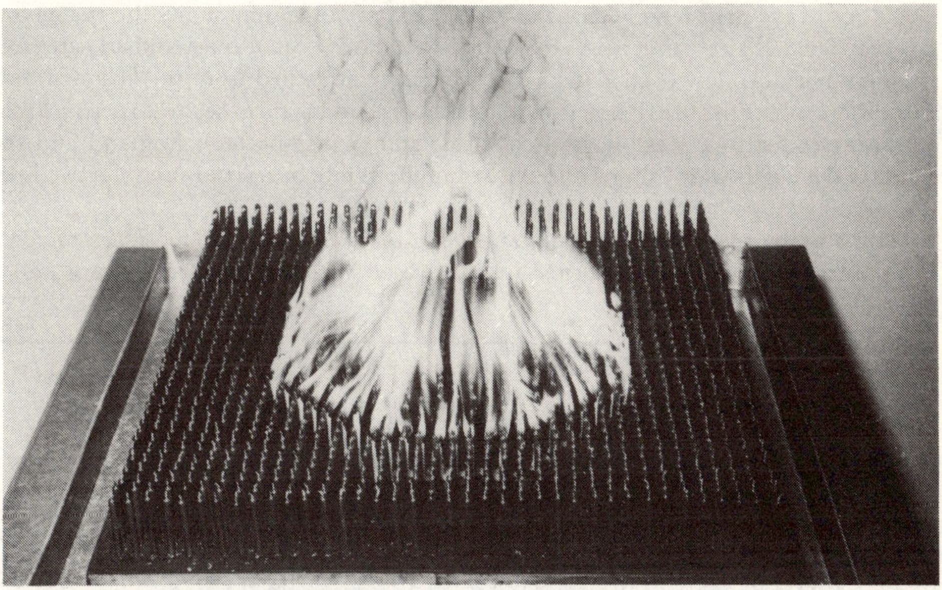

Fig 7

Fig 8

A study of the British and German weather charts at the time shows the customary low over Iceland stretching north-eastwards to the Norwegian coast and an extensive although not deep low over Russia. High pressure stretched from the Caspian Sea, along the whole of the Mediterranean to the Azores, having three separate peaks. From here it extended in a ridge north-eastwards, embracing southern England and the whole of the north-west European seaboard to the White Sea, separating the two lows (**Fig 9**).

With a pressure of only 1015 millibars along the German coastline, it resembled a huge col.[4] Summer thunderstorms are associated with cols, and Hamburg had a

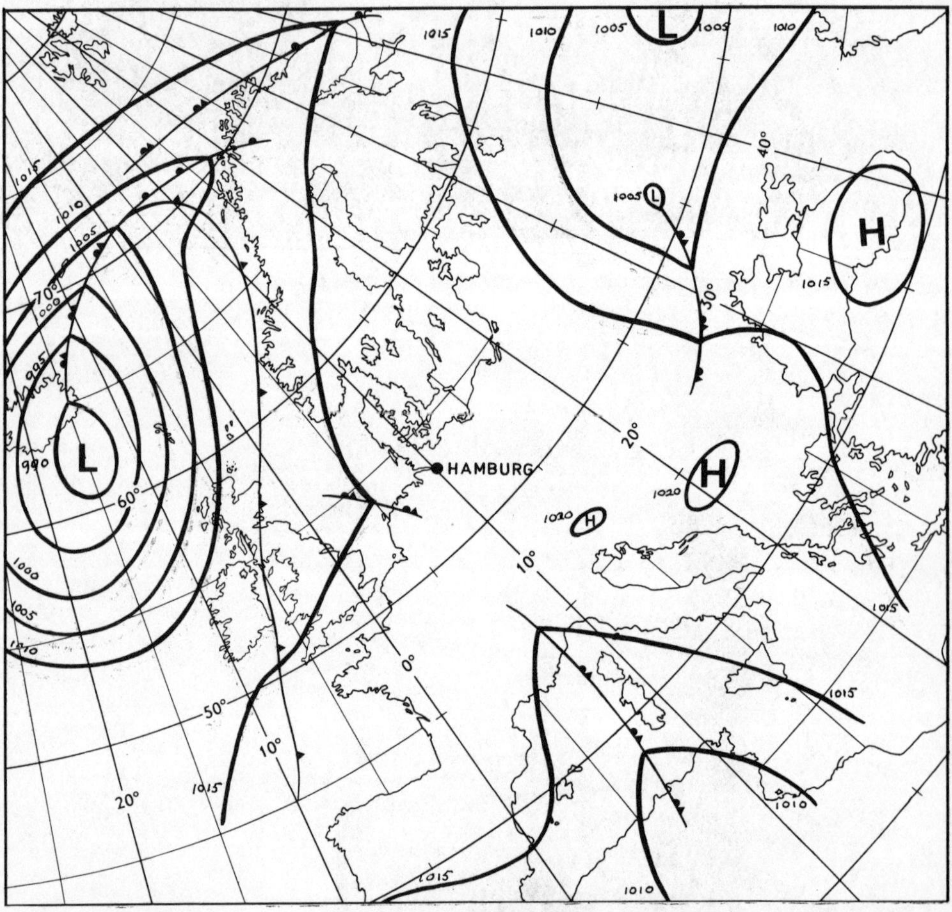


**Figure 9:** An approximation of the weather map of Europe for the night of July 27, 1943, compiled from British and German records. Because of the war neither side had complete knowledge of conditions; they also drew up their charts at different times.

4. A col is the meeting place of two anticyclones. It is an area of very light winds but also one in which the air mixes because the winds are going in opposite directions. In summer this mixing of air often leads to thunderstorms.

thunderstorm on July 22 and another on August 2–3. The high persisted, with pressure remaining almost constant, and on the 27th, after eight days, it still showed no signs of breaking up. With clear skies and day temperatures in the upper eighties Fahrenheit, Hamburg was enjoying a fantastic spell of summer weather. In Hamburg the average noon temperature in summer is a mere 63°F. By sheer coincidence the 0500 GMT temperature outside the city was 63°F, with an inversion up to 1,300 feet, where the temperature was 84°F (**Fig 10**). The night had been as warm as a normal summer day. A layer of smoke and haze, formed by the still glowing embers from the night raid of the 24–25th, lay over the city, trapped by the inversion. Without a cloud in the sky above, the scene was set for a hot, sultry day, and so it turned out. Towns do not in general radiate heat as readily as the open country, and "heat islands" are formed, sometimes as much as 20°F higher than the surrounding districts. With the radiation being further

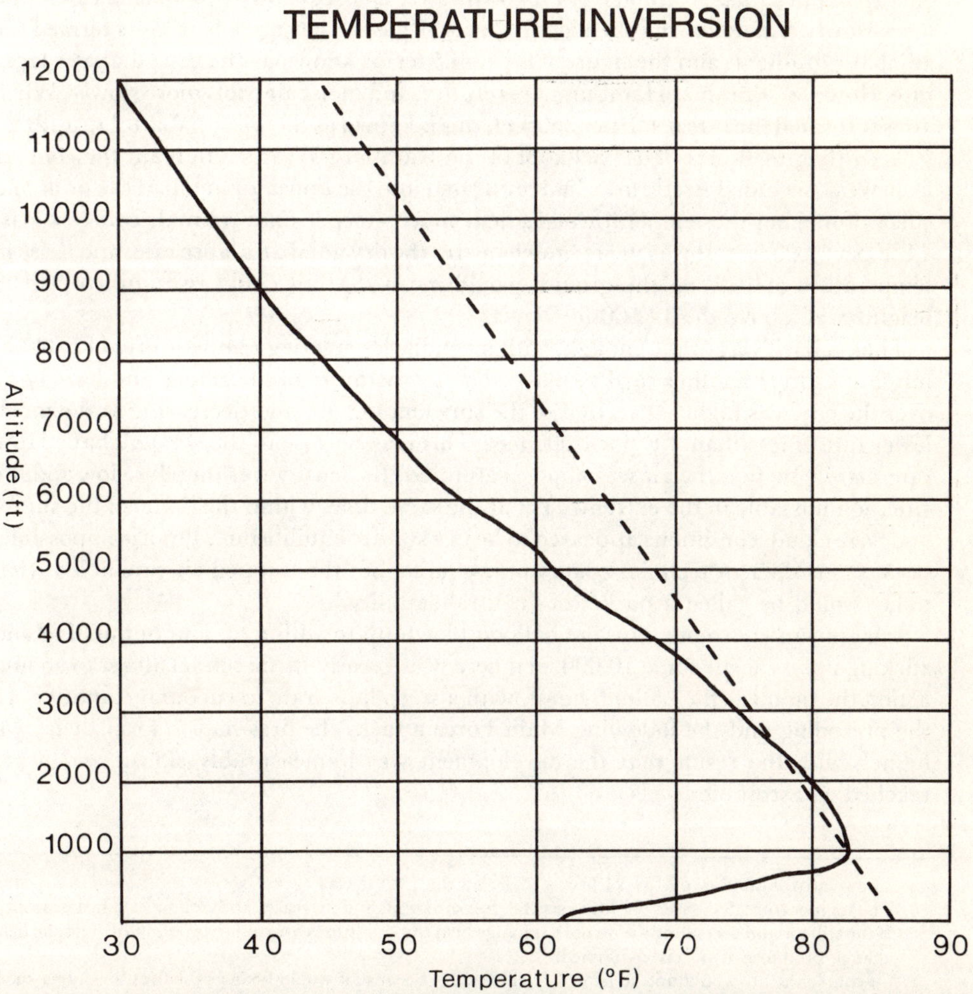


**Figure 10:** The unusually strong temperature gradient at 0500 hours, July 27, 1943. The broken line shows the dry adiabatic lapse rate. Once the hot air has broken the inversion it will rise unrestricted at least until the dry adiabatic line cuts the actual temperature line.

inhibited by the smoke and haze, the temperature in Hamburg must have been near the 100°F mark.

Another unusual feature of the day was the low relative humidity. Being near the sea Hamburg normally has a high humidity, averaging 78% in July, whereas on the 27th it was a mere 30%, and probably even lower in the heart of the city. This, and the drying-out effect of the long spell of arid weather, was a major factor in the initial growth of the firestorm.[5]

Before considering why the atmosphere was thought to be abnormal and how and why the "once in ten years" conditions guaranteed a firestorm if a raid took place, some knowledge of how air behaves is essential. Normally, still air has a temperature gradient of approximately 1°F per 300 feet of height.[6] Rising air has to push the stationary air out of the way, and if the conditions are assumed to be adiabatic,[7] the energy required has to come from its own store. Consequently the molecules vibrate more slowly and, following the kinetic theory of gases, the air cools. This is termed the adiabatic gradient, and the figure 1°F per 185 feet is known as the dry adiabatic lapse rate. However, the air at Hamburg is rarely dry, and moist air cools more slowly. When air is saturated the rate is 1°F per 360 feet; this is known as the wet adiabatic lapse rate.

According to Professor H. Seilkopf of the Hamburg Weather Bureau, the cold air from weak occluded Arctic lows had infiltrated into the upper air and had the profound effect of making the temperature gradient much steeper than normal, being at least 4.8°F per 1,000 feet. It was in fact much nearer the dry adiabatic lapse rate, and a rise in temperature of 10°F on the ground would mean that air could rise unrestricted to heights well above the 12,500 feet level.

That in itself was tragic enough, with incendiarics creating temperatures of 1,000°F, but fate had yet another card to play.[8] The temperature of the smoke and haze lying over the city was higher than that of the surrounding air, and decreasing at the much lower rate of less than 3°F per 1,000 feet. This is very close to the wet adiabatic lapse rate, signifying that the air was almost saturated. Its density was therefore low and the situation unstable in the extreme. Yet at the same time, within the limits of the smoke and haze cloud, conditions appeared to be in a state of equilibrium. Proof is impossible, because insufficient technical data are available, but the trapped air resembled what today would be called a pocket of "neutral stability".

Imagine an enormous sausage balloon blown up to within an iota of bursting and sticking up in the air some 10,000 feet; here was a ready-made funnel all set to go into action the moment the balloon burst, with a steep lapse rate to encourage updrive. In the preceding and the following Main Force attacks the fires had to form their own funnel, with the result that the development was immeasurably slower and never reached catastrophic levels.

---

5. The relative humidity on the 24th was 62%; on the 29th it was 52%.
6. The temperature decreases 1°F for every 300 feet of ascent, and increases at the same rate in a descent.
7. If the still air and ascending air do not exchange heat the conditions are said to be adiabatic and the heat change produced is purely dynamical.
8. Of course the air would not be heated to this extent because it would be over the fires for only a short period of time, and then only a thin layer would be heated to any extent, for air is a poor conductor of heat. However, the water in the lake, the inland stretches of the river and the numerous canals would be affected, evaporation would take place, and the rising air would contain water vapour.

To summarise: a pocket of warm, unstable air over the city to 10,000 feet, cold air above and all around with a steep vertical gradient, and calm conditions at ground level produced a gigantic facsimile of a furnace with a tall chimney, just waiting for a match. The final link in this chain of improbabilities was perhaps the most predictable: Hamburg was destined to suffer a second large night attack at the earliest possible date. The link was forged at 0055 hours on the 28th, when the first TIs fell in the Ohlsdorf district of the city.

What happened after that was incomprehensible. Professor C.H.V. Ebert of New York says: "In less than one hour the fires in the core area had merged to form a concentrated mass conflagration that burned with increasing intensity for several hours. A gigantic convectional system began to develop. . . ."[9] Professor Seilkopf, at the Hamburg Seewarte meteorological station about four miles west of the Alster, observed the rapid development of the smoke cloud over the firestorm area. It looked like a cumulo-nimbus rising eventually to 30,000 feet, where the typical anvil head began to form, thus confirming the reports of Bomber Command crews.

The concentrated bombing, in particular the IBs, produced a superheated ground layer which, in combination with the violent updraught, "set in motion a true heat cyclone that measured 1.5 to 2 miles in diameter with a column of air rising to a height of 3 miles".[10]

No fire can prosper without an abundant supply of inflammable material. Two extracts from the Police President's report will show how and why there was no lack of kindling. "As a result of HE bombs and land mines, roofs were laid bare in large numbers, windows and doors were blown in and smashed and the Self Protection Service was driven into the cellars. The incendiary bombs of all kinds then dropped in great concentration found ample food amongst the destruction already caused. More HE bombs and land mines drove the Self Protection personnel who, despite the complete failure of the municipal water supply, had hurried out to fight the fires, back again into the shelters. This constantly alternating dropping of HE bombs, land mines and incendiary bombs made possible an almost unimpeded spread of fires. . . . Urban building conditions in the affected area may assist or delay the formation of firestorms, as may the nature, extent and size of the original individual fires. In Hamburg the firestorms originated in densely built-up and thickly populated areas where, therefore, by reason of the type of building and the densely massed houses, conditions were favourable for the development of firestorms. In the affected areas in Hamburg there were mostly large blocks of flats in narrow streets with numerous houses behind them, with terraces (inner courtyards) etc. These courtyards became in a very short time cauldrons of fire which were literally man-traps. The narrow streets became fire-locks through which the tall flames were driven. . . ."

That the narrow streets were a major factor in the fire development on the night of the 27–28th is a myth, though it was true on the 24–25th, when the fires were concentrated in the old part of the town. On the night of the Firestorm the centre of the conflagration was in the modern, residential districts, where the streets were much

9. Article in *Weatherwise*, April 1963: *The meteorological factor in the Hamburg Firestorm*.
10. United States Strategic Bombing Survey. The figures are untypically conservative. The generally accepted figures are three miles in diameter and five and a half miles high.

wider.[11] They were also longer and straighter, allowing the winds to reach the core of the cyclone more quickly and encouraging the updraught. When cyclones develop in open spaces the winds are drawn to the centre in a precise, anticlockwise direction. The tall buildings, many of them more than six storeys high, prevented this from happening and forced the masses of air into the streets and courtyards.

One important effect of the strong winds was to make the fires prosper, and isolated fires joined together until they became huge conflagrations. In their turn they united and became a single fire covering an area of 4½ square miles. Two other factors were necessary for the fires to unite at such a fantastic rate. First, the enormous heat from the IBs and the fires made spontaneous combustion quite common. Second, the hurricane winds picked up the burning material and carried it along, forming walls of fire travelling at speeds of 100 mph.

The winds, being sucked into the vortex with ever-increasing volume, crashed head-on wherever two main streets met, forming fire whirls (described above). The swirling air disgorged sparks and blazing logs into the houses through the gaps in the walls where the doors and windows had been plucked out or laid bare by the HE. In this manner, with each spark driven on by the wind, new fires were started.

The firestorm began in single streets about 20 minutes after the first bombs fell, chiefly in the south of Hamm, where the IB fires had raised the ground temperature much more than the 5°F needed to burst the balloon. Although Hammerbrook was heavily hit during the first phase of the attack the firestorm developed more slowly there. Between 0100 hours and 0115 hours HE and incendiary bombs started fires in the buildings on the corner of Berliner Tor and Beim Strohhause, and these burned vigorously but showed no tendency to spread. Hamburger stalls were a regular feature in the city, as they still are today, and the one on this corner had caught fire. It had been burning for over half an hour before it was suddenly torn asunder, lifted up in great pieces and carried down Berliner Tor in the direction of Borgfelder Strasse. Fire whirls also occur when a large amount of heat is being generated in small sheltered areas like the terraces and courtyards of the flats.

An interesting instance, vividly described, occurred in the Eilbek area, where again the hurricane winds were slow to develop but came with equal suddenness. A fireman was spreading out his hoses: ". . . the wind at first seemed quite normal but within a couple of minutes was definitely a gale and then a storm. I was opposite Fette, the wood trader, and dashed in there to get out of the wind. I was sheltering under a scaffolding when, to my amazement, large timbers [beams for roofing], sheets of plywood, laths and even wooden planks were lifted up like matchsticks and remained swirling in the air over the fire. Then, just as suddenly, both large and small pieces were swirling at a furious speed down Vogelweide. In an instant the firestorm became a whirlwind. . . ."[12]

In the same area, at the corner of Eilbektal and Kleiststrasse, where a fire engine was taking on water from the Eilbekkanal, the driver found that the firestorm reached him so quickly and so powerfully that he was forced to abandon the vehicle and seek shelter under the bridge. The move saved his life, for the fire engine was burnt out. A report by

11. Main roads were 15–20 yards wide, and some of them, like Beim Strohhause at Berliner Tor, had a grass verge lined with trees and a service road on both sides in addition to the footpaths.
12. *Feuersturm über Hamburg*.

*Oberstleutnant* Dr R. Schubert, an engineer in the Fire Service, said that at 0300 hours the entire way from Berliner Tor to Wandsbek Chaussee was a sheet of flames. This was in stark contrast to his earlier report at 0200 hours, when he said that to the south as yet only the roofs were burning, to the north the fires were isolated, and the streets were everywhere deserted. During that hour the whole situation had changed dramatically.

Confirmation of Schubert's second report came from a sergeant-major of the Fire Service. Around 3 o'clock he was in a car travelling down Hammer Weg when he noticed people lying in the street. Alighting to go and help them, he suddenly saw a tremendous sheet of flame travelling down the main road. The driver of the car skidded it round and escaped down a side road. The sergeant-major tried to escape by running before the flames. He said: "There was no smoke in the street, only flames and flying sparks blowing about like thick snowflakes. The hurricane was a firestorm." As he ran he noticed people on their own and in groups, completely bewildered, absolutely unaware that they were stumbling over other people lying on the ground, and often treading on them. He ran until he was exhausted and threw himself to the ground.

The incendiaries and the HE bombs concentrated in the districts to the south-east of the Alster, together with the fires which they began, trapped thousands of people in the underground shelters, in many of which conditions were critical. Already great numbers had been forced out into the open, and unless they jumped into the canals or found shelter from the fire quickly they were doomed. In the south of Hamm only those who fled early had any real chance of escape. In Hammerbrook, Grasbrook, Rothenburgsort and Borgfelder the 15 minutes between the last bombs falling and the firestorm taking command offered the fugitives a short breathing space to find a new place of refuge. To remain on the streets in these areas after 2 o'clock was to commit suicide. The winds showed no mercy to the unfortunates caught on the streets. They had to lean right over while trying to make progress against the storm, and then without warning they were slapped on the back and knocked down as two winds met. The buildings, grabbing at the coat-tails of the hurricane, caused violent eddies and the victims were swirled around and, as they put out their arms to prevent themselves from falling, their belongings were snatched from their grasp and whisked away. The whirlwind tore children from their mothers' arms and sucked them into the cauldron. The storm reached its height around 3 o'clock. Previously only in the areas near the centre of the storm had the fires been a major hazard, but now the hurricane winds whipped the small fires on the outskirts into a frenzy, and the scenes of horror were re-enacted from Eilbek in the north to the Elbe in the south, from the banks of the Alster as far east as Horn.

Even had there been any escape routes it was impossible to stand up, the air was too hot to breathe and the people were in shock for any of a dozen reasons. Perhaps a near-miss by a bomb had made them aware of their peril and started the adrenalin flowing, but when they became exhausted it drained away and they realised the hopelessness of their predicament. Then they sank down in despair, there to die of hyperthermia or to be burnt to a cinder.

The survivor from Hammer Weg, quoted above, went on to describe the scene around him: people lying in the street too exhausted to respond when he called to them, others already dead. Some sat there unmoving, apparently resigned to their fate. "The heat was unbearable, so hot that my protective glasses broke." Here was a man facing almost certain death, yet he thought: "They [the glasses] are very scarce." "Instinctively I threw myself down. From time to time my clothing started to burn and I had to put out the flames. The wind was so strong and the heat so intense that I had to suck oxygen directly from the pavement. It burnt my nose and throat and my knees blistered even through my clothing. The crisis lasted for an hour to an hour and a half." As the storm began to blow itself out breathing became easier and he found that he could move. Death lay all around him: bodies in groups, some in piles, others strewn about. After the howling of the wind, the roaring of the fire and the shrieks of terror, everything suddenly seemed quiet. No one moved. He was perhaps the only survivor.

Another eyewitness, Herr Dehler, worked for the water company as an engineer. His duty on the 27th was to report on damage to water pipes. His patrol took him to the south-east corner of Hamm, where a storm was raging and approaching from a southerly direction. In the dark, and perhaps with one eye on the advancing storm, he drove into a deep bomb crater at the corner of Ausschläger Weg and Süderstrasse and was trapped. "The heat was intense. At first I remained in the car with the windows open, but sparks kept blowing in and setting my clothes alight. With the windows closed the heat was unbearable. I decided to get out." (In this he was probably wise: the photograph on page XXIII portrays a mother, father and child sitting in the front of a car, where they presumably died of suffocation.) "But I found the door would not open, nor would the window wind down. I had to break the window and crawl through. The crater was beginning to fill with water so I soaked my clothing. The heat was unbearable. I tried to crawl out of the crater but the sparks and the wind drove me back." The buildings were collapsing and the debris kept falling into the crater. He had to cling close to the sides to protect himself. Amidst the clamour he suddenly realised that he could distinguish moaning. He was not alone in the crater. He searched around and found a youth who, having crawled into a burst water pipe for protection, was now in danger of drowning, being unable to free himself. The officer could just reach the boy by thrusting out his helmet and hanging onto the strap. In this manner he was able to pull him out. By now the crater was becoming a haven for people fleeing before the fire. Some of the incautious "threw themselves in head-first and broke their skulls on the broken pipe sections; others drowned in the water. From time to time I peeped over the rim and saw the street covered with bodies; there were people running, and their clothes suddenly burst into flames. The air was terribly hot. I felt about to suffocate; my lips, mouth and throat were completely dry. I became dizzy and breathing became difficult. I must have been in the crater at least an hour."

One of the significant features of the story is the fact that, between relating each incident, came the recurring thought: "The heat was unbearable." His story was confirmed on the 29th, when Civil Defence men came into the area to lay out and count the dead. In the crater and all around there were estimated to be 400 corpses, mostly people who had been sheltering in a school at the corner of Süderstrasse and Ausschläger. Compelled to leave their shelter, they had probably tried to find refuge in the neighbouring Südkanal.

After 3 o'clock it became almost impossible to travel through the streets in or on motorised vehicles. Near Hammer Weg Dr Schubert was forced to park in a side street. His van did have a puncture but conditions were so bad that he did not dare to change the wheel until the heat died down.

The crisis lasted until 0430 hours, when the wind began to abate, but the heat was still unbearable and the air an agony to breathe. Most of the survivors were content to stay where they were, happy to be alive but fearing that they might be sole survivors. Fortunate indeed was a family with no one to mourn. By 6 o'clock the storm had blown itself out and the fires were dying down; the danger of their spreading was over. It was estimated that two billion[13] tons of air were drawn into the inferno. A twenty-fifth of this amount would have sufficed to burn everything within range, and the remainder served only to make it burn hotter and more furiously. Some measure of the force of the updraught can be gauged from the fact that lighter objects such as letters were swept up to the top of the smoke cloud like hailstones and disgorged into fields miles from the city centre. The freak conditions caused violent electrical storms in the surrounding districts, followed by torrential rain. Within the firestorm area there was scarcely a building which did not show some scars from the holocaust. A detailed survey of the small, densely populated area of Hammerbrook (140 acres), one of the heavily damaged regions enveloped by the firestorm, showed that out of a pre-attack population of more than 27,000, less than a hundred remained. Undoubtedly the bulk of the 27,000 were refugees, but thousands had perished. Even after the war, when bulldozers were levelling the ground for redevelopment, arms and legs were unearthed daily.

At six o'clock in the morning of the 27th the early trams were trundling down the streets, the milkmen clinking empty bottles as they exchanged them for full ones, the postmen rattling letter-boxes, delivering the early mail. Twenty-four hours later this part of the city was dead. The smoke cloud over Hamburg was so thick that the sun was unable to shine through. Frau Lahaine's young daughter looked at the sky and said to a neighbour: "The RAF came last night and shot out the sun." Every effort was being made in the northern suburbs to keep some semblance of life going, but it was a well nigh impossible task. The inhabitants were without water, gas or electricity, there was a scarcity of food and, above all, everyone felt a foreboding of impending doom. It seemed to the citizens that the RAF were destroying Hamburg to a premeditated plan: first the south-west, next the south-east and east; Barmbek and the north-east must be next on the agenda.

In his report the Police President said that people who had no reason to stay in Hamburg were encouraged to leave. This is not strictly true. Many people like Frau Lahaine would have liked to go, but they were turned down by the authorities because they "still had a roof over their heads". No one prevented them from leaving but they had to provide their own means of transport. The authorities did have problems: after the attack of the 27–28th the survivors fled the town in droves. An estimated 50,000 went by boat, the number who travelled by road was never known, and over 625 trains, many of them specials, transported the vast majority of the estimated 900,000 refugees. Many were sent to Bavaria, where they joined evacuees from other badly damaged German cities and were later followed by thousands more as Bomber Command wreaked havoc in all the important towns the length and breadth of Germany. Bavaria became known as "the air raid shelter of the Reich".

From the demolished district of Hamm came an endless stream of refugees, some

13. The English meaning of a million millions (the second power of a million) is used here, not a thousand million, as in the USA and some other countries.

with children in their arms, all in the last stages of exhaustion. It was pitiful to see them trudging along, oblivious of everything and stumbling over anything in their path, even corpses, as they made their way to the west in the hope of finding a conveyance to take them away from the doomed city. They had but a single word on their lips: "Water". The two main assembly areas for the fugitives were the Stadtpark in the north and the Moorweide to the west of the Alster. Field kitchens were set up in both places and, in addition, sanitary facilities were provided at Moorweide. The mass flight from the city continued all through the 29th. People who during the 28th had salvaged what few belongings they could find packed them onto barrows (see photograph on page XXVI), prams, bicycles, horses and carts, vans, lorries and cars.

Most of the 28th was spent in searching for survivors in the stricken area, and those who were still conscious were begging for water. It needed a strong stomach to look on the thousands of dead lying singly or in heaps in the streets, some fully clothed, others naked, their light clothing either consumed so quickly by the flames that their bodies were blistered rather than burnt, or torn off in terror when first set on fire. Nearby lay corpses, their faces with agony written all over them and mouths agape with the final shriek forced from them by a pain-wracked body. Just yards away were piles of ashes which only hours before had been human beings, sacrificed to a doctrine which demanded the murder of millions of innocents.

Smoke still rose from the glowing embers within the shells that once were houses and all around the unmistakable odour of burning flesh assailed the nostrils. From time to time a wall here or a floor there would crash down to break the silence. Hundreds of men in boats were searching the canals for survivors. There were bodies floating everywhere but seemingly all were dead. Callous as it may seem, to check so many they had to resort to poking the bodies with poles to see if there was any spark of life left in them.

The elation at Bomber Command HQ when the PRU reports were studied was unbounded. The photographs had been taken when more than half the city was obscured by smoke or shadow, but it was evident that enormous damage had been caused. St Georg and Billwerder showed up well on the prints. The report[14] said: "In St Georg, particularly, scarcely a building escaped unscathed, and in both that district and Billwerder damage to commercial and industrial property was on a phenomenal scale." Then came a list of priority targets known to have been hit, including the Tiefstack gas depot and Unterelbe electricity works. The main station and Holstenstrasse station (there were others unknown to the RAF), the railway power station at Altona and two tram depots were also extensively damaged. It was stressed that this was all additional damage. Post-war, when the damage list was updated, it covered more than 10 pages of foolscap.

Herr Brunswig points out that because the devastation to the east of the Alster was so enormous and the number of dead so unbelievable, the fact that the damage extended to the west to Altona, north into Barmbek and south of the Elbe is often overlooked. Here the winds, while perhaps not reaching storm force, were nevertheless strong enough to whip small fires into large, uncontrollable ones.

Several reports from firms in the dock area prove that they had little opportunity to

14. Immediate interpretation report K1639 (PRO AIR 24/257).

while away the night. The German American Petroleum Company, with several factories and wharfs in the dock area, sent in a damage report for each of them. At 0130 hours bombs dropped in the wood yards around the works started fires which proved difficult to contain. In general the damage was similar to that of July 24–25, but in addition cranes were hit, a crane bridge was damaged and a pontoon bridge sunk. A barge filled with wood and moored on the opposite bank was set on fire, broke its moorings and floated towards their docks, endangering shipping; the fire took 2½ hours to extinguish. Another of their factories, a storage depot at Billwerder Steindamm, was hit by HE and incendiaries. This report was dated August 6, 1943, and went on to say that there was still no trace of the six men from their fire protection service thought to have been killed during the raid. Work at the depot was still impossible at that point.

Deutschewerft, on the other hand, were happy to report very little further damage, though the American attacks had given them some nasty headaches. General Electric, one of their subsidiaries, had received fresh bombing, but the damage would not hinder production. Two code-named projects were down to 5% of normal production in the one case and 25% in the other, whether because of previous damage or absenteeism is not clear. Several floating docks were sunk.

The *Wehrmacht*, who had been at work since July 25 clearing the streets in Altona of hundreds of tons of rubble, were moved to the new area of devastation. It was a slow and arduous job, most of which had to be done by hand. Bulldozers, although a fairly common feature of the American countryside, had not at the beginning of the war made any real impact on this side of the Atlantic. In Hamburg they were as scarce as "Rooms to Let" signs. The Fire Service were undoubtedly the busiest people in Hamburg: fire brigades from outside had to be organised, water was a major problem, and equipment that had not been completely destroyed had to be extricated from the stricken area and repaired. To add to their troubles, the authorities were convinced that the RAF would make at least one more attack.

Coke, which kept bursting into flames, seems to have been one of the Fire Service's recurring headaches. Hermann Bauermeister, makers of machinery, had been bombed on July 24–25, when IBs had started a fire in a coke bunker. The firm's own ARP squad had been able to put out all the fires in the factory except for one in the machine shop. They ran out of water and had to ask the Fire Service for help. At about 1.30 p.m. a machine arrived and sprayed the coke bunker for 4½ hours without stopping. On Monday morning it burst into flames again, and the fire engine came and gave it a five-hour soaking. Then, on the 27th, the Service put in a voluntary appearance and gave the still steaming coke another soaking.

The *Selbsthilfedienst* (Self-help Service) got little rest: they had to lay out, count and, if possible, identify the corpses, all the time being pestered by a throng of relatives who wandered among the dead searching for lost loved ones. Their grief seemed to make them impervious to the scenes of horror as they looked only for a particular face. They were a broken-hearted crowd who spoke only in whispers lest they disturb the awful silence in this place of death. To find relatives dead was perhaps worse than not finding them, since while they were missing there was still hope.

The report sent in by Police President Major Kehrl to the Reich representatives on July 29 gives the following figures: killed 20,000, injured 6,000 and missing and homeless 330,000. The report contained a rider: "This is a rough estimate – must figure on higher casualties." It certainly was a rough figure. As yet no attempt had been made to open the thousands of house cellars buried beneath the rubble. In fact it was impossible to begin excavations until the middle of August, when the bricks had finally cooled enough to handle.

# Chapter VII

# Mosquitoes

THE Mosquito was one of the outstanding aircraft of World War II and certainly the most versatile. It served with distinction in all the British Air Commands at home and overseas, and a special variant was built for the Royal Navy. It was also used by the USAAF. Although it cannot be claimed the Mosquito had a significant role in the *Gomorrah* attacks it did play an important part during Hamburg's 10-day ordeal. 8 Group had almost all the Mosquitoes which operated in Bomber Command, although Bennett did lend a squadron of them to 5 Group for low-level marking during 1944–5. In July 1943 there were three squadrons and a flight in 8 Group. More significant than its title suggests, that flight will reappear later in the narrative. 109 Squadron was a founder member of the Pathfinder Force, and its Mosquitoes were equipped with *Oboe*, the most accurate blind bombing device of World War II. Because of teething troubles the Squadron lay dormant during PFF's first three operational months, but in the New Year of 1943 it led a small group of bombers into the heart of the Ruhr. The Lancasters released their bombs when they reached flares dropped by the Mosquitoes; this was the first *Wanganui*[1] of the war. Several attacks, all over cloud, followed, and they were so accurate that Hitler flew into a rage when told about them. He refused to believe the facts, insisting that the reports about the cloud must be untrue or, conversely, that someone was transmitting signals from the ground below.

On March 5, 1943, the Squadron ground-marked (*Musical Parramatta*)[2] Essen and the Krupp works received its first real taste of aerial bombardment. Some 66 acres within the huge complex lay devastated, in addition to more than 230 acres in the surrounding districts. It was a major breakthrough. The next four months saw more and more Ruhr towns wrecked, always with *Oboe* pinpointing the target. Nor did the smaller Ruhr towns escape Bomber Command's attention: 130 acres of Bochum were wrecked on June 12, and two nights later the centre of Oberhausen lay in ruins after 203 heavies had bombed the town through cloud, using 109 Squadron's *Wanganui* flares as markers. One of the most successful raids of this period took place on May 29–30, when the small town of Wuppertal-Barmen was attacked. The target was only two miles long and barely a mile wide yet 90% of the Barmen area was devastated and 50% of the Elberfeld half also lay in ruins. However, in this instance *Oboe* cannot take all of the credit. The first reds went down two minutes late and then there was an 18-minute gap as a result of a failure in the special equipment. During that time Backers-up from 83 and 156 Squadrons kept the target marked with a plentiful supply of greens. Great

---

1. See Glossary and Appendix IV.
2. The adjective *Musical* was added to *Parramatta* and *Wanganui* when *Oboe* aircraft dropped the primary markers.

credit must go to the 44 crews of the first wave who were carrying incendiaries; they lit such a huge fire that the German decoys, hopefully lit as a diversion, paled into insignificance. Nor can the remainder of the force be excluded; they stoked the fires so efficiently that the air, rushing down from the hills to replace the strong updraught caused by the intense heat from the raging fires, reached storm force. This was a major factor in the town's destruction.

Cologne, although not in the Ruhr, was not neglected. The Rhineland capital did not come into the firing line until the later stages of what has subsequently become known as the First Battle of the Ruhr, but towards the end of June three raids made it into one of the most damaged cities of the Reich. The important railway centre of Aachen, also an outsider, was severely damaged in the last raid of the series, on July 13. One of the features of 109 Squadron's introduction into the front line was their remarkably low loss rate, only two crews having failed to return from all their operations to date in 8 Group. It was remarkable because they had to fly straight and level for ten minutes on the run-up to the target.

During all this excitement two major changes had taken place in the Command. Previously Harris had had to rely on Coastal Command for information on the weather over the target, and much of the photo-reconnaissance had to be "requested" too. No 521 Squadron, which had been flying Bomber Command's *Pampa*s[3] since its formation on August 1, 1942, was disbanded on March 31, 1943, and the following day 1409 Flight was formed at Oakington under the command of Bennett. Its first operational flight in 8 Group took place on April 2, when the west coast of France came under the scrutiny of F/Lt P. Cunliffe-Lister. That night the Main Force attacked St Nazaire.

The idea behind a *Pampa* flight was to find out weather conditions over the target and on the proposed bomber route. A certain amount of deception was necessary, otherwise the Germans would have been able to guess the target from the *Pampa* operation. During the war the weather over the Continent was a German secret, and even though Bomber Command had Pathfinder *Wanganui* flares to help them bomb through cloud, this type of attack was rarely as good as a *Newhaven* or *Parramatta*. Thus knowledge of weather conditions at the target was essential if the best method of marking was to be employed, for accurate marking was useless if the markers could not be seen. Just as important were the conditions upwind, which indicated the weather that the Main Force crews would experience some hours later. Cloud on the route could be a problem for bomber crews, for they might have to fly through or round it. Nor was it sufficient to log its presence: base and height had also to be noted. If the *Pampa* crew suspected that icing might take place in the cloud they were expected to fly through it to seek confirmation. The position of fronts was of great interest to Met and navigators alike, since a change of wind direction usually occurs when crossing a front. The height of condensation trails was important: night fighter pilots loved them and happily flew along them in the knowledge that a victim was dead ahead. Contrails were more reliable than AI and a boon to *Cat's Eyes* night fighters. On the Nuremberg raid of March 30–31, 1944, contrails stretching backwards for miles plotted the bombers' planned routes, which were ridiculous enough even without being given away in this manner.[4] In fact contrails were important to the *Pampa* crew. Fw190 and Me109 pilots

3. Code name for Met Flight operations.
4. The Nuremberg raid was probably the worst planned of the entire war.

also knew their significance, and although the Mosquito could in some respects out-manoeuvre the Focke-Wulf, the latter was certainly faster than the Mosquito at heights above 22,000 feet. The Met Flight Mosquitoes were unarmed, so flight was the only defence when intercepted. Courage was not enough: skill and complete knowledge of the aircraft's manoeuvrability were essential for survival, and so most pilots and navigators were usually "tour-expired".

The second important change took place on June 1, 1943, when 2 Group, with the exception of 105 and 139 Squadrons, was transferred from Bomber Command to the Tactical Air Force. These two Squadrons had been operating Mosquitoes since the 1,000-bomber raid on Cologne (May 30–31, 1942). On that occasion two crews took off to bomb the city as the motley procession of twin- and four-engined bombers trundled its way home. Three more took off at noon to disquiet the fire services, and a sixth, flown by S/Ldr R.J. Channer, did a low-level photo-reconnaissance of the city in the late afternoon. With 380 mph on the ASI Channer noticed that people did not look up until the Mosquito had passed them. Low-level attacks were their *métier*, and the daylight sortie to Jena on May 25, 1943, ranks as one of the outstanding raids of the war. It was as brilliantly executed as the daylight attack on the MAN works at Augsburg by 12 Lancasters on April 17, 1942. On that raid 7 Lancasters were shot down, whereas during the Jena attack only 1 of the 14 Mosquitoes crashed over Germany due to enemy action. Two crews collided while avoiding flak and two more crashed in England. Both 105 and 139 Squadrons took part in this raid, which was the Mosquitoes' last in 2 Group. A week later they took up their duties in 8 Group.

In retrospect, the introduction of Mosquito bombers into 8 Group was of great significance. Both squadrons flew high-level "nuisance raids" until June 24–25, when Duisburg was the target. 105 Squadron pilots then took a crash course on how to fly the *Oboe* beam and the Squadron became the second *Oboe* unit. 139 Squadron continued in its high-level nuisance role with no assistance until November 12, 1943, when 627 Squadron was formed. Phrases like "feeling the Mosquito's sting" became commonplace in the ORBs. At the end of July 1943 Air Vice-Marshal D.C.T. Bennett's fertile brain was devising methods of drawing the night fighters away from the bomber stream. Using the Mosquito's speed, 139 Squadron could risk drawing the night fighters onto themselves and yet maintain their low loss rate. Thus, in addition to nuisance bombing, spoof marking (route and target) and *Windowing* (both genuine and spoof) became part of their duties.

F/Lt G.H. Hatton's *Pampa* on July 24 heralded the beginning of the *Gomorrah* raids. His route was Base – 56°00N 07°00E – Frederickivaak – Verdingborg – Base. His duties were to measure the base and height of the cloud on the Danish coast and to observe weather conditions in general in the Baltic. His report read: "Baltic generally clear, isolated cumulus to 18,000 feet; strato-cumulus North Sea to 20 miles inside the Danish coast; stratus 10/10ths between 2,000 and 2,700 feet." Harris was happy with the report, and routes and zero hour were confirmed and no "C" notices were necessary.

No 139 Squadron had 13 crews operating during the night of the 24–25th: four to Duisburg, three to Kiel, three to Bremen, where the reception committee was all primed to receive the wayward bombers, and three to Lübeck. The crews on Lübeck used the PFF Hamburg route-marker TIs to check their position. With so much activity to the west the searchlights and flak were on the alert and gave the Mosquitoes a hot reception. On their return W/Cdr R.W. Reynolds and F/Lt E.B. Sismore stayed over Hamburg to "watch the fun" and were still back at base by 0335 hours, long before the first Main Force bombers. "Spectacular" was their summary, and such an assessment from so experienced a crew spoke volumes.

1409 Flight flew weather sorties for the Eighth Air Force also, and the Flight's ORB (PRO AIR 29/867) for July 25 reads:

**0755** F/O A.F. Pethick. Sylt – Heligoland – 53°40N 05°30E. Early *Pampa* for *Pinetrees*,[5] measured the high and low cloud in Heligoland Bight.

**1140** Second *Pampa* F/O C.L.H. Dennis. No cloud except a bank of 4–6/10ths strato-cumulus 55°00N 07°00E.

**1650** *Pampa* to Sylt – Flensburg – Kiel – Hamburg – Cuxhaven – Base. F/Sgt F. Clayton. He reported on the smoke at Kiel and Hamburg after the USAAF attack.

There was moderate smoke at Kiel, but at Hamburg it went up to 20,000 feet, with dense oil smoke in the southern part (perhaps from the smoke screen). Flak was heavy at both targets but, probably because of their recent practice, more accurate at Hamburg. After leaving the German coast Clayton discovered a heavy coolant leak in the starboard engine. The engine had to be shut down and as it drove the electrics careful thought was needed to make sure that the essential information was received at HQ. Two W/T messages were passed and a QDM[6] received before the power gave out. Clayton brought the Mosquito down safely on the one engine and made a perfect landing at 1650 hours, one and a half hours after his original ETA. It was his report that finally tipped the scales in favour of Essen.

Nos 105 and 109 Squadrons had been on standby all morning and eventually the order came through: "Ops tonight." There were several famous Mosquitoes on parade: LR500, 503, 504; DK331; DZ433.[7] The attack, a *Musical Parramatta*, was carried out by 705 medium and heavy bombers and 33 Mosquitoes; 16 of the latter were in a marker role: 12 (two as Reserves) from 109 Squadron and 4 (one as Reserve) from 105 Squadron, on their first marking duty. Eleven of the Mosquitoes successfully marked the target with TI reds (the Reserves were not called). The technique for a *Musical Parramatta* differed from that for an ordinary *Parramatta* in that the Backers-up dropped their contrasting markers on primary markers throughout the attack. This was because the *Oboe* Mosquitoes dropped their markers at intervals, whereas the H2S primary markers were all dropped at the beginning of a raid, before zero hour. On this night 19 Lancasters, 5 Stirlings and 9 Halifaxes were acting in the role of Backers-up and were dropping green TIs. Most of these crews had the dual role of route marking with yellow TIs, using H2S. The attack was a resounding success. Several factors contributed, not the least being the fact that red TIs were burning throughout the raid and could be seen clearly. *Oboe* was ground-controlled from England, with two stations for each aircraft, one advising the pilot and the other the navigator. On this night three pairs of stations

5. Code name for USAAF HQ.
6. Magnetic bearing to base.
7. LR503 was perhaps the most famous of all Mosquitoes. Heroine of 213 operations, she was flown to Canada after the war to go on exhibition. Sadly, on reaching Calgary Airport she inexplicably dived into the ground and was destroyed.

were operating simultaneously for the first time on a major raid. The timing of the marker crews was exemplary. Apart from the superior accuracy of *Oboe* marking, the big advantage of having primary markers burning throughout a raid was that creep-back was minimised because the almost impossible task of estimating the MPI of the markers was eliminated.

The Krupp works are in the centre of Essen and daylight photographs showed that 110 of the 190 workshops in the complex had been damaged or destroyed. Damage to the town was severe, particularly in the area adjacent to the factory, and fires were still burning two days later. Baron Gustav Krupp was so appalled when he saw his vast empire in ruins that he had a heart attack from which he never fully recovered. Fifteen of the 28 departments in the works never exceeded 50% of their previous peak production. *Window* was used again and played its part in the success.[8]

Although 43 aircraft suffered flak damage, Happy Valley[9] did not live up to its reputation. The defences were completely disorganised and the numerous guns were reduced to putting up a barrage while the beams of the countless searchlights groped aimlessly across the sky, hoping by chance to light on a victim. Only 24 bombers were missing for a loss rate of 3.4%, which compared favourably with the 5.4% average of recent raids. The ORS report said that (according to the evidence of the night cameras) of the 604 crews who claimed to have bombed the target, 368 were plotted within three miles of the aiming point. The town was shrouded in industrial haze – Essen's saviour before the formation of the Pathfinders – but the TIs could be seen clearly. Later crews reported smoke at 22,000 feet and flames to a great height. Of the many explosions reported one was described as enormous and the fires could be seen for 150 miles.

No 139 Squadron put up 13 Mosquitoes; four went ahead of the Main Force and dropped *Window* over Essen before bombing, and six went to Hamburg to stoke the fires and drive the citizens into the shelters. They reported fires burning north and south of the river, the Americans having added to the general confusion. The remaining three went to Cologne, hoping to confuse the fighter defences. Gelsenkirchen was the target for four *Oboe* crews flying *Overture* sorties.

Hatton of 1409 Flight was the early riser on the 26th, being airborne at 0425 hours; his duty was a *Pampa* for *Pinetrees*. His message to base reported cloud in the Heligoland area, with high cirrus to the east. On the return journey Hatton came down to sea level (at Sylt), where the Mosquito's performance at full bore was as good as that of the Fw190. At 0525 hours F/O B. C. Becker and Sgt P.H. Harvey made a second sortie for *Pinetrees* to Heligoland Bight, and by now the cloud had given way to haze, which was good news for the Americans.

Having operated on consecutive nights the Main Force had a stand-down but, as ever, the Mosquitoes were airborne. No 139 Squadron sent six aircraft to Hamburg, where the fires were still burning. F/O P.F. Denny, for reasons unstated, dropped his cargo on the fires at Harburg, which was still burning from the American daylight attack.

On the 27th 1409 Flight had an easy day, F/O T.E. Dodwell flying their only sortie.

---

8. Gavin Lyall's account of *Window* in *War in the Air* would appear to have been for this night rather than the 24th, because no British aircraft crossed the enemy coast west of Hamburg on that night and so could not have been in the vicinity of Amsterdam. The accuracy of the account is not in question, only the date.
9. The Ruhr Valley.

Airborne at 1140 hours he flew Texel – Osnabruck – Hamburg – Cuxhaven – Base, checking on conditions of cloud and smoke at Hamburg for Bomber Command HQ. It was his report which made Bennett decide on a *Parramatta* rather than a *Newhaven* attack. Duisburg and Hamburg were 139 Squadron's targets. Happy Valley claimed another victim: F/O E. Snider, whose navigator was S/Ldr K.G. Price, the Station Navigation Officer, failed to return. The four crews who went to Hamburg found the city a blazing inferno. The idea behind sending Mosquitoes to the Main Force target some two hours after the heavy bombers had left was to hinder the fire service, but on this night the Hamburg Fire Service had been impotent for some time.

On Wednesday the 28th the Main Force was stood down, so it was left to 139 Squadron to carry the war to the enemy. Predictably, it was sent to Hamburg and the fires, which were still burning, pinpointed the target for the four crews. To keep the Ruhr ground defences on the alert three crews attacked Düsseldorf, where F/Sgt T.D.N. Campbell was coned for five minutes with the German AA gunners pumping up shells into the cone the whole time. Fortunately, flak takes some 20 seconds to get to 30,000 feet, so the manoeuvrability of the Mosquito enabled it to be in another part of the sky when the flak arrived, but the searchlights always held on like leeches once they had a victim.

For 1409 Flight July 29 opened with a pre-dawn *Pampa* for *Pinetrees*. Pethick was airborne at 0235 hours, his route taking him to 54°00N 04°30E – Amrum Island – 54°40N 04°00E – Base. His report said that there was patchy strato-cumulus over the sea; over Denmark there were two layers of 4–5/10ths cloud: cirrus at 25,000 feet and alto-cumulus at 12,000 feet. The Americans said "Thank you" and sent their bombers to Wesemünde and Kiel, where they dropped leaflets as well as bombs.

That evening 139 Squadron was given a new role. Four crews were sent to drop spoof route markers in the hope that the TIs would draw some of the night fighters away from the Main Force, an early indication that the *Cat's Eye* method was causing concern at Bomber Command HQ. P/O I.A. Isfeld had to make an early return because the supercharger and the radiator flaps on his Mosquito were unservicable. The crews first made their way to Hamburg, where they *Windowed* the target and then went round again to drop their bombs. Then they flew to 53°33N 07°33E, where they dropped their spoof markers, one crew being detailed to circle the area backing up the markers at three-minute intervals. F/Sgt V.J.C. Miles completed the round trip but did not drop his TIs because his ASI became unserviceable. The four crews who went to Düsseldorf were agreeably surprised, the ground defences having apparently been given the night off. Felixstowe – 51°40N 02°10E – Flamborough Head – 52°30N 02°30E – Base was the route taken by F/O Dennis of 1409 Flight on the morning of the 30th to check the haze and coastal fog forming over the North Sea.

After the "good show" of the 26–27th 105 and 109 Squadrons had done little more than sit back and preen their feathers, but the 30th saw them back in the front line, marking Remscheid for 273 bombers. Six crews were scheduled to mark the target, with 3 crews in reserve, but when P/O R.E. Leigh returned early with a defective ASI the 2 Reserves from 105 Squadron were called and both marked the target, a bonus for the Backers-up and Main Force. It was in fact a significant factor in the raid because, owing to a change of wind, the Stirlings were late on target. The marking initially was not as good as at Essen, but once again the advantages of *Musical* marking were demonstrated: this inaccuracy, small by marking standards, was corrected when the later primary reds fell close to the aiming point.[10] Excellent marking is useless unless it is followed by concentrated bombing, but the Main Force turned in what was perhaps Bomber Command's finest piece of bombing to date; in fact it was rarely excelled even in 1944 or 1945. Of the 228 crews who claimed to have bombed the target, 191 (83.7%) were within three miles of the aiming point.

The town was virtually destroyed and the huge fires, with smoke rising from the centre to 10,000 feet, were completely out of control. Twenty-four hours later the fire services had made little impression on them. A study of the PR photographs showed that in the central districts around the railway station devastation was so complete that roads and foundations of buildings were almost indistinguishable. The defences at the target were only slight; Remscheid, one of the smaller Ruhr towns, was not heavily defended and this undoubtedly contributed to the accurate bombing. Flak from Düsseldorf and Cologne, both near the prescribed route, more than made up for the comparatively easy bombing run. *Window* was used again and the loss rate, 5.5%, would seem to indicate that the ground defences were overcoming the problems. Curiously, it also served to prove that, as had been predicted by Command, "The *Window* which protects *you* is not so much that which you drop yourself as that which is already in the air dropped by an aircraft ahead. To obtain full advantage, it is therefore necessary to fly in a concentrated stream along the ordered route."[11] The Stirlings, late on target, had probably failed to gain full *Window* protection and suffered accordingly. A study of the loss rate by type of aircraft makes the point abundantly clear:

| **Mosquitoes** | **Lancasters** | **Halifaxes** | **Stirlings** | **Total** |
|---|---|---|---|---|
| 0/9 | 2/82 (2.44%) | 5/95 (5.26%) | 8/87 (9.2%) | 15/273 (5.49%) |

An interesting tailpiece is provided by Frau Erika Wilkan, whose experiences on the night of *Die Katastrophe* have been recorded earlier. After an arduous journey from Hamburg she and her husband arrived at Remscheid on the Friday afternoon. Having recounted the events of the 27–28th in Hamburg she had no difficulty in persuading her parents to take shelter when the sirens sounded. It was a wise decision, for four HE bombs fell in the vicinity.

A three-hour flight on July 31 by F/O Becker of 1409 Flight to measure cloud in the English Channel and the Western Approaches[12] began with an unusual experience: after five minutes Becker had to return to base because the undercarriage of DZ388 would not lock up. A quick dash to the reserve Mosquito and within 30 minutes he was airborne again. The Main Force, on standby for Hamburg, was eventually cancelled, but crews went mining, laying their eggs in the approaches to Lorient harbour, which the Germans were using as a submarine base.

Because the previous night thunderstorms at bases had caused the cancellation of operations, on the morning of the 2nd F/Sgt Clayton flew a long-range *Pampa* to the west, testing the cloud. He encountered heavy rain over Wales, with cloud tops already up to 10,000 feet by noon. In the early evening it was Hatton's turn to have problems.

---

10. With non-*Musical* marking the original errors tended to be magnified as the MPI shifted.
11. See Appendix I.
12. Testing the weather for the *Gardeners*.

He took off at 1815 hours and almost immediately the constant-speed unit of the starboard motor went unserviceable, compelling him to stop the engine. Having made a masterly single-engined landing he switched to LR509 and 30 minutes later was on the runway ready to take off. His route was Texel – Harderwijk – Oldenburg – 54°20N 06°15E – 54°20N 04°00E – Base. His report was not encouraging: various layers of cloud, alto-stratus and alto-cumulus, with tops varying from 18,000 to 25,000 feet and one enormous cloud mushrooming up to 31,000 feet. Much of this cloud was over the North Sea along the bombers' route, and his money was on a "scrub". He was not alone in this belief, for the majority of the bomber crews were betting the same way. For Hatton it was a day to remember, six Typhoons pursuing him for part of the return journey.

The first of five Mosquitoes of 139 Squadron took off from Wyton at 2346 hours on August 2. Their duties were similar to those of July 29: to *Window*, bomb and drop spoof route markers. As with the Main Force, the elements proved too much and – with the exception of F/Lt R.A.V. Crampton, who made an early return because of a defective supercharger – the crews dropped on last-resort targets in the Hamburg region.

Duisburg was the Ruhr target for five Mosquitoes. Local thunderstorms were encountered on the route, causing two crews to turn back, one because of icing, the other because the bumpy conditions were too much for the navigator's stomach. Above the cumulo-nimbus visibility was excellent. Once again the defences were described as negligible.

Fighter Command sent intruders to Germany and occupied Europe most nights when flying was possible and more particularly when Bomber Command was operating. By July 1943 many of the intruder squadrons were operating in Mosquitoes. It was on the night of the 24–25th that F/Lt E.R.F. Cooke and F/Sgt F.M. Ellacott of 25 Squadron shot down their first enemy aircraft since re-equipping with the Mosquito. Three aircraft from the Squadron were detailed for bomber support work, their duty to patrol Westerland aerodrome on Sylt. After being airborne for an hour they were recalled, but Cooke did not hear the recall. The crew arrived over Sylt at 2330 hours and, to their delight, found the aerodrome lights on. Even more gratifying, an aircraft, later identified as a Ju88, was gathering speed down the runway before taking off. Cooke dived in pursuit and by the time the Junkers had gained 1,500 feet he was 600 yards away on its tail. He opened fire and the Junkers made for the nearest cloud with the port engine ablaze. The cloud was not thick enough to hide the glow of the fire and at 200 yards Cooke executed the *coup de grâce*; the Junkers spun to port and crashed into the sea. The Germans on the ground appeared unaware that anything untoward had happened because the aerodrome lights remained on. Cooke patiently completed his patrol, which was something of a let-down after such a promising start. The Squadron was up the other nights, but apart from making a nuisance of themselves the crews had no successes.

No 418 Squadron put up seven Mosquitoes on July 25 for bomber support; Venlo, Gilze Rijen and Deelen were their targets. The captains were F/O H.A. Hoar, F/Sgt H.I. Hay, F/O J.R.F. Johnson, F/Sgt C.D. Ball, F/Lt D.C.S. McDonald, F/O F.W. Hallwood and F/Lt M.W. Beveridge. The crews found little or no activity at the aerodromes and no enemy aircraft were seen. So, after completing their patrols, they left their calling cards (2 × 500-pounders) on the runways. It was a bad night for the Squadron:

two Mosquitoes were damaged and one missing. It was one of those tragedies which happened all too frequently, and this one could easily have been avoided. On the one hand was a trigger-happy convoy, unaware that British aircraft would be flying in the vicinity, and on the other a stupid route which took the Mosquitoes over the convoy. Presumably Naval and Fighter Commands had exchanged confidences, but then the information had not been passed on to the convoy and 418 Squadron obviously had not been warned about it.

Hoar was the first to take off and he encountered the convoy "off Manston", which was the RAF's way of saying off the East Kent coast. The Mosquitoes flew low over the sea to keep from being detected by the German GCI, so they were an easy prey for the Navy gunners. After he was hit in the starboard wing Hoar pushed the throttles through the gate and, showing admirable constraint, waited until he was clear of the convoy before jettisoning his bombs. He then made a dogleg round the convoy and returned to base.

Hay and Johnson had already taken off before Hoar returned, so they too were engaged. Johnson, who took off a minute later than Hay, saw firing ahead of him and, from the position of the flashes, realised that it must be a convoy. He was at least partially prepared when he too was fired on, but even so his Mosquito was damaged. It was assumed that the firing which Johnson observed was directed at the unsuspecting Hay, who was missing.

No 605 Squadron was also operating intruder patrols, and during the 10 days of *Gomorrah* this unit experienced varying fortunes. In the early hours of July 25 F/Lt C.F. Knowles and P/O A.R. Eagling arrived over Soesterburg and found two aircraft in the circuit preparing to land. He selected his mark but when he opened fire the ground defences came to life. The searchlights picked him up and although he was by now less than 100 yards from the bomber the ground gunner opened up. Nothing daunted, he pressed home the attack, scoring strikes on the port engine and fuselage. The enemy aircraft turned to port and was instantly recognised as a Do217.[13] Knowles too turned to port in readiness for a second attack, but although the German pilot made a valiant effort to keep the Dornier airborne it eventually crashed. In the meantime, the other aircraft had landed and the aerodrome lights were switched off.

Five minutes later, at 0225 hours, S/Ldr A.W. Mack and F/Sgt W. Harrison, on patrol at Eindhoven, saw an aircraft approaching, displaying red and white recognition lights. At 200 yards the Squadron Leader told his navigator it was a Do217 and pressed the firing button, but nothing happened. The enemy pilot went on to land, completely unaware of how close to death he had been. Undismayed, the crew circled around and at 0230 hours their patience was rewarded when a second Dornier came in to land. Mack took up the same position and this time his guns fired. The ground defences opened up immediately and forced the Squadron Leader to take evasive action. He certainly damaged the Dornier but was much too busy dodging lead to see if it managed to land without crashing. The aerodrome lights were doused so Mack climbed to 3,000 feet, made a run across the aerodrome dropping 2 × 500-pounders, and so back to base and a cheerful debriefing.

Barrage balloons were part of Fighter Command, so it seems incredible that 605

13. The Dorniers were probably returning from minelaying sorties in British waters.

Squadron should have had so much trouble with them. On the 26th the Squadron was informed that they would be flying at 1,500 feet, yet at 4,000 feet W/Cdr C.D. Tomalin suddenly found himself flying among balloon cables. The lines to Group got very hot, but even then the balloons continued to be a hazard. On July 28 another Mosquito pilot found himself caught among the balloons, and to add insult to injury he was engaged by a battery of searchlights, whose blinding light did nothing to ease the situation. The IFF was on and the letter of the day was flashed, and still the searchlights were not doused.

The ORB[14] for July 29 reads: "An intruder's dream come true." When F/O A.G. Woods arrived over Lüneburg there were between 10 and 15 aircraft orbiting the aerodrome, all with their lights on. The dust and smoke from the Hamburg fires were blamed for the poor visibility over the aerodrome and, in some measure, for Woods not taking full advantage of the golden opportunity. Two aircraft had landed by the time he was in position to attack. Suddenly he found himself so close to his prey that he had to pull away without firing or he would have rammed the fighter. He was getting more used to the conditions by now, however, and on his next run his shells were striking home when the ground loomed up ahead and he had to pull hard on the stick to avoid crashing. Next time round he opened up at 600 yards and, firing all the time, closed to 150 yards before the fighter, an Me110, burst into flames and crashed. As he raced across the aerodrome he met another Messerschmitt head-on, but although his guns were blazing as he flashed past he apparently did little or no damage to the enemy. He then climbed away to get his breath back. It had all been so hectic that he needed a quiet journey back to base to get the sequence of events clear in his mind.

14. PRO AIR 27/2090.

# Chapter VIII

# Barmbek Burns

AFTER a Wednesday when only 16 Main Force crews were on the Battle Order[1] (mining in the Frisians), July 29 lived up to expectations: a maximum effort and the bets were odds on Hamburg. The people of Hamburg too were convinced that their tribulations were not over and the mass flight from the city continued throughout the day. Anything and everything with wheels was used to transport what few remaining goods they had managed to salvage. Moorweide, an open park to the west of the Alster, opposite Damptor station, was the jumping-off place for thousands. To facilitate the exodus by road, clearing the main thoroughfares around the park became the top priority. Both the inhabitants and the authorities believed that the RAF was systematically destroying Hamburg area by area, working in an anti-clockwise direction and also avoiding the Jewish and wealthy districts. As Harris said afterwards, "If only we could have been so accurate."

However, when the Americans attacked Kiel in the afternoon of the 29th the *Luftschutzabteilung* (Air Raid Defence Division) decided that the night force would go to Kiel also. They withdrew some of their units and assembled them outside the city, ready for a dash to the Baltic port. This manoeuvre came as a complete surprise to the Hamburg Fire Service, because earlier it had been agreed by all parties that a third great attack on Hamburg was imminent. Half of the Hamburg force had been given time off to visit their homes, and for many of them it was their first opportunity to find out if they still possessed one. The unattended fires revived and fire engines from other districts had to be sent to these areas. As the sun set people gathered their valuables together and made their way to the shelters hours before the bombers had taken off.[2]

On the stations in England everything went according to routine. At briefing Command produced another surprise: in addition to *Window*, *Zephyrs* and Recenterers, spoof route-marker yellows were to be dropped by Mosquitoes at 53°33N 07°33E. The hope was that, because on the two previous attacks yellows had been used as route markers, they would draw the fighters away from the Main Force route-marker reds, which were to be augmented by a red flare. This was 139 Squadron's first direct spoof and during the following months this role was to become one of its chief functions, though in many different guises. The need for spoof markers also shows how quickly the night fighters had adapted themselves to the new conditions imposed by *Window*, and the respect in which Command held the newly introduced *Wilde Sau*.

Zero hour was 0045 hours and so take-off was earlier than on the previous nights.

---

1. Seven Mosquitoes of 139 Squadron were also operating.
2. During the German raids on London people went down into the Underground every night and stayed there until morning, irrespective of whether there was a raid or not.

## NIGHT OPERATIONS July 29–30 & 30–31

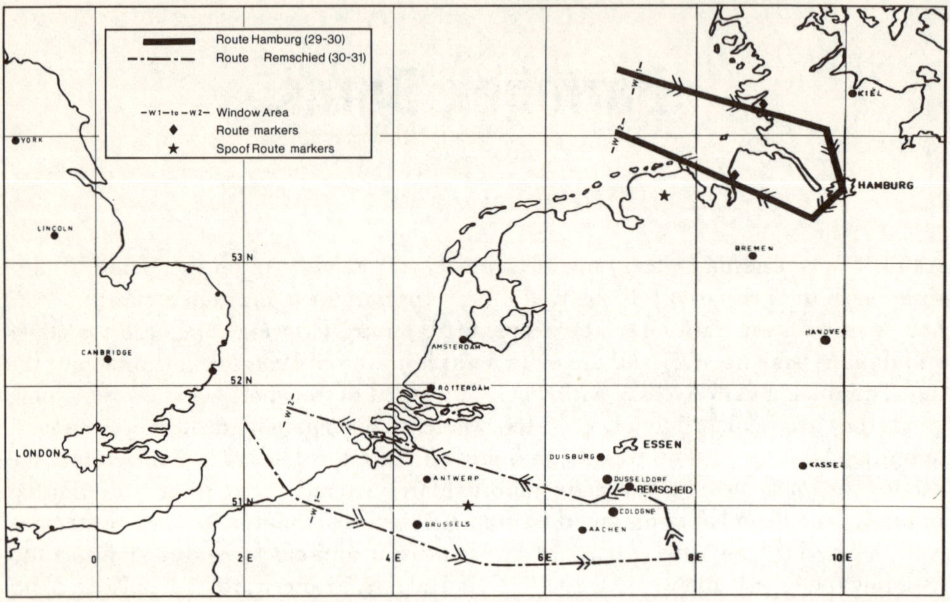


Two aircraft crashed on take-off. Sgt E.W.A. Clarke of 50 Squadron, stationed at Skellingthorpe, swung as he took off and his Lancaster crashed into a hangar, burst into flames and was completely burnt out; the crew managed to scramble clear. They were taken to sick quarters, where they were treated for shock, slight burns and abrasions. At Grimsby F/Sgt C.A Cox also swung on take-off, the undercarriage collapsed and the Lancaster came to a halt at the intersection of the runways. No one was hurt. Cox was however not very popular, because there were 11 Lancasters behind him ready to take off and they had to be cancelled. To have screwed "your their courage to the sticking place" for nothing was bad enough, but the two previous attacks on Hamburg had produced so few casualties that most of the crews were furious at missing an easy trip. It was a completely wasted evening. Nor was he very popular later when the 13 crews returning from Hamburg had to be diverted to Binbrook, Blyton and Lindholme because the runway had not been cleared in time. Cox's bomb load included an LD,[3] which armourers hated. The recent accident at Graveley had been caused by one, so routine precautions had to be taken before any effort was made to move the aircraft. Consequently Cox was not popular with the armourers either.

Three crews were seen to be shot down over the sea on the outward route, one as far south as Heligoland. There would seem to be little excuse for being so far south of track because *Gee* was working very well, even over the target. However, the gunners must have given a good account of themselves since the fighter was seen to crash at the same time. There was no evidence that the spoof route markers were successful but plenty to support the theory that the night fighters were using route markers to contact the bomber stream. Six attacks on bombers were made near the reds: F/Sgt E.L. Pickles

3. A bomb armed with a long-delay fuse.

and Sgt F.E.S. Parker before reaching the enemy coast, P/O E.F.G. Mills, Sgt C.R. Hilton, Sgt P. Jennings and F/Sgt P.R. Raggett immediately after crossing it. At 0027 hours, some 20 miles short of the enemy coast, Pickles was "accurately engaged without warning by an unseen enemy aircraft."[4] "Without warning" seems to be carrying the British idea of fair play too far, yet the phrase is not uncommon in combat reports. The attack closely resembled Elder's, reported earlier,[5] in that the flight engineer, Sgt A.H. Marshall, and the mid-upper, Sgt O.H. Mackie, appear to have been dispensing *Window*. They were both killed.[6] The tail gunner, Sgt W.L. Porcher, was wounded in the face, the upper arm and both hands, so the Lancaster was virtually defenceless against a second attack. Pickles took violent evasive action and lost the fighter, the bomb load was jettisoned and he asked for a direct course to Grimsby (base). The damage to the Lancaster was extensive rather than vital. Pickles had to be diverted to Binbrook because Cox's aircraft was still blocking the runways at Grimsby, but he landed there safely. Mills and Hilton only had brushes with the enemy, although Sgt J. Moran, the rear gunner in Hilton's crew, claimed to have damaged the Ju88 which attacked them.

Jennings of 158 Squadron had just crossed over the red route markers at Wesselmünde and his navigator had scarcely had time to pat himself on the back when suddenly he had to grab onto everything as the Halifax did a violent dive to starboard. Jennings had "heard" an aircraft in close proximity and overreacted, throwing the Halifax on its back. However, after his initial panic he proved his airmanship by performing a rudder stall and gaining control of the aircraft at 8,000 feet; he also kept his head when all the engines cut during these unusual gyrations. Looking down he saw a small town, and after jettisoning his bombs live on the unsuspecting people below he turned for base.

Several aircraft had more than one encounter and there were two instances of this on the outward route, "Y" of 35 Squadron and "Z" of 57 Squadron. Raggett of 35 Squadron had crossed the enemy coast just north of track when Sgt D.S. Wood, the rear gunner, saw a twin-engined fighter slightly to starboard below. There were indications on *Monica* so the gunners were expecting trouble. Wood ordered "Corkscrew" but Raggett did not hear the order clearly and took no immediate action. The enemy opened fire just before Wood, who had realised that Raggett was not taking any action, shouted the order again. The captain dived to port, losing almost 2,000 feet, but in those few seconds between the first order and Raggett's eventual reaction the starboard mainplane had been hit in the area of the No 4 tank. The enemy aircraft did not appear to make any attempt to follow the Halifax's manoeuvre, so Raggett pressed on to the target. He was on his bombing run when the Halifax was coned, and at the same time Wood identified an Me110 at 400 yards sporting red and green lights on the wingtips. As Raggett dived to port to escape the searchlights Wood opened up on the Messerschmitt, which, having crossed to the starboard quarter, suddenly burst into flames and was seen to crash by the bomb-aimer, F/O S.A. Baldwin, still lying in his bombing position in the nose.

---

4. From Operations Record Book (PRO AIR 27/796).
5. Pages 73–75.
6. Elder's engineer was only wounded.

On the 27–28th Parker had been caught off track and only lightning reactions and accurate shooting by Wharton, his rear gunner, had saved the Lancaster from twice being engaged by the enemy. There was understandably some apprehension among the crew on the 29th after those experiences. The tension heightened as they approached the enemy coast and it was almost a relief when at 0031, a minute after Raggett's first encounter, Wharton reported a twin-engined aircraft with a yellow light in the nose overtaking their Lancaster. He ordered Parker to turn to starboard and dive, and immediately opened fire on the fighter. Now that it was nearer, he identified it as a Ju88. Wharton was a little puzzled by the light in the nose because previously this tactic had been confined to the target area, but the puzzle was quickly solved: the moment he engaged the Junkers, tracer came pouring towards the Lancaster from the port quarter. Immediately afterwards the Junkers switched off the nose light and dived away without firing, disappearing into the dark sky. Wharton was now free to swing his turret to port, where there was a second Ju88 on the port quarter down 400 yards away. He pressed the trigger as soon as his guns came into line and extended the burst when he realised his shells were striking home. The starboard engine burst into flames and seconds later the Junkers blew up into two pieces which fell into the sea; first round to the Lancaster, which suffered no damage. Parker climbed back to 20,000 feet and had just settled onto his new course from the red markers when Wharton warned him to be ready to dive to port, "Junkers 88 port quarter down at 600 yards". As soon as Wharton had the Junkers in his sight he called "Now, Skipper, go," and opened up. Perhaps it was the first Junkers again, because the German pilot showed the same reluctance to "mix it", diving away without firing. Then, as Parker started his run-up to the target a searchlight on the port side seemed to be signalling, so he ordered Wharton to be on the look-out. Through the glare Wharton spotted a single-engined fighter coming up to attack from the port quarter down, about 500 yards away. He opened up immediately with the order "Go port, Skipper, Me109, dive." As the enemy came nearer he noticed that its navigation lights were on and that it also had a yellow identification light on the belly. So far all the fighting had taken place below the Lancaster and the mid-upper gunner, Sgt Read, had had no opportunity to fire. Now as the Messerschmitt came level with the Lancaster, he was able to get a slice of the action. Once again the enemy did not like the odds, switching off his navigation lights as if in submission and climbing away to port without firing. He showed his respect for the Ack-Ack too, for he left the identity light burning.

The cloud on the route was mostly below the bombers, giving them no problems, and was left behind long before the German coast. From Wesselburen on the coast the route took the bombers eastwards to the last turning point before the target, which was the southern tip of the lake, close to Plon. The coastline and the lake would have shown up clearly on the H2S screens, so the *Zephyr* crews should have obtained a good wind. Hamburg itself was clear of cloud but hazy. Visibility was good but the smoke from the fires of the 27–28th was noted by most crews, almost as if they were making excuses just in case one should be needed. However, the TIs could be seen clearly.

The attack was opened at Z−8 by F/Lt M.R. Chick, who reported seeing a second group of yellows go down. The timing of the Blind Markers was excellent but their accuracy left a lot to be desired, as they were scattered over a wide area, principally to the east of Hamburg, the MPI being 2–3 miles from the aiming point. The first greens went down at Z+2 and they were all in the eastern sector, east-south-east of the target and well placed if the original yellows had been accurate. The Main Force also bombed to the east of the Alster but short of the greens, and by Z+7 substantial fires were burning three miles east-north-east of the aiming point. At 0057 the first of three enormous explosions was reported by many crews; one was as far as 80 miles away. Crews on target at 0100 hours reported that the fires were taking hold and from then on Backers-up and Recenterers had a thankless job. British crews enjoyed bombing fires (as did their German counterparts), which is why decoy fire sites were so successful. During the Hamburg raids, however, the decoy sites were poorly patronised, as also were the decoy TIs put up by the enemy; the real fires were so huge that no one could be deceived.

The German radio transmissions between ground and fighter were monitored in England and much valuable information on how the enemy was combatting *Window* was gleaned from these conversations. The *Wilde Sau* operating in the target area were co-operating with the searchlight batteries, which had been strengthened for this purpose, and when they had a victim in their beams they informed the fighter. Until the fighter arrived the Ack-Ack batteries took the opportunity to fire at something they could see,[7] a welcome change from the boring task of firing a barrage. Two such calls were made, one at 0033 hours and the other at 0048. The later victim was probably W/O J. Finding of 83 Squadron, who was well and truly held by the searchlights for four minutes. During that eternity the AA guns had been pouring flak into the cone and had scored several hits on the Lancaster. As Finding dived to starboard in another effort to get out of the limelight, tracer shells were seen coming from the port quarter. The mid-upper gunner, Sgt J.A.P. Logan, was partly protected by the fuselage from the searchlights' glare and was the first to spot an Me109 closing fast from the port quarter. He ordered "Dive port, go, go" and opened fire. The captain could not comply with the order immediately because he was already diving to starboard. He wrenched the controls over and the Lancaster slowly responded. During those vital seconds the rear gunner, Sgt C.R.D. Everard, who could see nothing of the fighter because of the glare from the searchlights, had a brilliant idea: he turned his ringsight full on (sunshine procedure) and saw the Me109 a mere 250 yards away. Although Logan had been scoring hits his two guns were not a sufficient deterrent, but Everard's extra weight and accuracy tilted the odds and the enemy pilot broke away to port, climbing hard as if to show that he too was well aware of the danger from the Ack-Ack guns. The searchlights were obviously co-operating with the *Wilde Sau* and not with the flak, because shortly after the Me109 broke away the searchlights were doused. Fortunately the enemy did not make a second attack, because both turrets were out of action. In addition, the fuselage was riddled with small holes and a flak shell had torn a two-foot hole in the port wing.

Six aircraft were hit by incendiaries from above and one crew from 460 Squadron had a lucky escape when an incendiary pierced the fuselage but did not explode. It just missed the flight engineer, who was standing by the flare chute. Shortly after 0100 hours an enormous explosion, which lit up the inside of aircraft at 19,000 feet, was reported.

---

7. Possibly one of the reasons why the fighters sported a belly light when over flak areas.

F/Lt J.M. Sullivan and S/Ldr W.J. Lewis of 467 Squadron were also intercepted in the target area after releasing their cargoes. Obviously it was better for the fighters to intercept the bombers before they reached the target, and this was the German tactic before the advent of *Window*. The *Wilde Sau* were day fighter (Me109s and Fw190s) units recently formed to help the controlled night fighters, which were hard pressed to cope with Bomber Command's new tactic of concentrating the bombers into waves and pushing them through the controlled areas in a narrow stream in the shortest possible time. The main problem for the ground controllers was to feed the fighters into the bomber stream. The three areas in which this could best be achieved were around the route markers (outward and homeward) and at the target. Because the target area invariably had a searchlight defence this was the most profitable area for the *Wilde Sau*, and both Sullivan and Lewis were soon made aware of the fact. Sullivan, like many Bomber Command pilots, put the nose down when leaving the target to gain speed and "get to Hell out of here" as quickly as possible. There were of course many factors governing the amount of height a pilot was willing to sacrifice for speed. The distance from the target to the coast was an important consideration: a low-flying bomber was in some circumstances more vulnerable, and the height of optimum performance varied from aircraft to aircraft. Sullivan was down to 14,000 feet and was receiving the unwelcome attention of the searchlights as he ran up to the first turning point after the target. When a microphone was switched on he expected to hear the voice of his navigator, Sgt J.A. Wainwright, but it was Sgt A.P. Power, the rear gunner, urgently calling "Corkscrew, Skipper, Me109 dead astern". Then, chiefly for Sgt J. Spurr, the mid-upper gunner, "800 yards up". Although both gunners opened fire the fighter closed rapidly and at 500 yards opened up with cannon and machine-gun fire. However, because of the combat manoeuvre, the shells went harmlessly by under the starboard wing. The fighter next appeared on the starboard up, dived towards the Lancaster and at 300 yards fired two short bursts before breaking away in a climb to starboard. This manoeuvre gave Sullivan's gunners an excellent opportunity to get in good breakaway shots. Nothing daunted, the enemy positioned himself on the starboard beam and, hoping to nullify the Lancaster's evasive action, began a curve-of-pursuit attack. Once again, Power and Spurr opened up first but the enemy came on relentlessly and closed to 300 yards before firing. His aim was poor, though, and the tracer was seen to pass in front of the Lancaster. It then became clear that he had come once too often to the well, when at 200 yards the Messerschmitt burst into flames and, seconds later, fell away, apparently out of control. As it spiralled downwards it left a trail of sparks and smoke. The searchlight crews, who were seemingly working in conjunction with the fighter, followed it as it plunged to earth and exploded. Before it reached the ground the gunners saw the pilot bale out and observed his open parachute silhouetted in the searchlight beam. Cutting through the excited babble, the calm voice of Wainwright announced the new course. Then the crew settled down to the immediate task of getting back to base and assessing the damage. Considering that the Lancaster had been engaged at such close quarters the damage was not extensive: the starboard wing was holed and the starboard outer had been hit, but not seriously. Sullivan was of the opinion that the target area was divided into flak zones and fighter zones.

S/Ldr Lewis was attacked by an Fw190 in the target area just after releasing his bombs. Sgt G.P. Bayliss, the mid-upper gunner, saw the enemy fighter on the starboard quarter 500 yards away. As it came in with cannon and machine guns blazing Lewis made a diving turn to starboard and Bayliss, firing all the time, followed it until it broke away to port. The Lancaster was illuminated by searchlights during the attack and Sgt J. Mallan, the rear gunner, was temporarily blinded and took no part in the action. Bayliss claimed to have damaged the Focke-Wulf and Lewis successfully eluded the searchlights' attentions. Either or both of these considerations may have accounted for the fact that the enemy pilot did not continue the combat. Ten minutes later, as "Y" was approaching the turning point to the coast, Mallan saw an Me109 on the port quarter down climbing to attack. He opened fire as Lewis dived to port and saw his tracer hit the Messerschmitt. When the enemy aircraft drew level with the Lancaster, Bayliss joined in the defence. Once again the searchlights were working in conjunction with the fighter and swung onto the bomber as the fighter closed in to attack. However, the hot reception from the British gunners proved too much for the fighter pilot, who did not open fire. The Messerschmitt fell away in a spiral dive, followed by the searchlights, and disappeared into a thin layer of cloud. Both fighters were claimed as damaged.

The Stirlings of 75 Squadron seem to have caught the attention of the night fighters on the 29–30th. They were accustomed to special treatment from the Ack-Ack but the night fighters did not usually single them out. Perhaps it was because they were flying higher than normal: F/O G. Duncan claimed he was at 14,000 feet, a rare achievement for a Stirling. F/Sgts E. Wilkinson and J. Darney and Sgt P. Hartstein had only brief encounters, the enemy breaking away as soon as the gunners showed they were on the alert. Duncan had just left the target at 0108 hours and was still doing a gentle corkscrew when the mid-upper gunner, P/O S. Strong, sighted a Ju88 on the port beam silhouetted against the searchlight glare. The fighter was 600 yards away when Strong opened fire and ordered a corkscrew to port; the enemy aircraft banked steeply and dived away without firing. Five minutes later Duncan was still playing it safe (corkscrewing) when the rear gunner, P/O J. McCorkindale, sighted a Ju88 on the port quarter 400 yards away. It was probably the same Junkers because it came in with all guns blazing. McCorkindale replied with a long burst and, as the enemy closed from 300 to 200 yards, he saw his tracer entering the Junkers. This forced the German to break off the attack, and as he dived away McCorkindale sent a hail of bullets to speed him on his way. Although the Stirling's mainplane, tailplane and undercarriage doors were hit the damage was widespread rather than extensive or serious. The Junkers was claimed as damaged.

If anyone over the target at 0112 hours had observed the strange antics of F/Lt J.C. Morton's Wellington they might have been forgiven for thinking that the pilot was suffering from lack of oxygen: it appeared to be making a beeline for parts of the sky where the flak was thickest. In truth that was what was happening. Morton had tremendous faith in the Almighty – "God is with us" – and he was a fervent believer in flying straight and level. He was therefore an ideal pilot to accommodate the whims of his guest, Major T. Southgate, a research officer from an anti-aircraft unit.[8] On July

8. I vividly remember a lecture by an equally mad captain who said that Essen was his favourite target because the flak was thicker there and they got the latest types of shells.

24–25 Searby had reported a new type of flak like a Catherine wheel, and other captains had also reported seeing something similar, so the Army sent along one of their experts in the hope that the Germans would be using it again.[9] Here were two men who scorned danger to help their fellow men, for every time Southgate said "Look, over there," Morton steered to the spot. A sortie with Southgate invariably meant staying over the target until the German gunners had completed their repertoire and, if they produced anything novel, waiting for an encore.

Bennett quickly realised that if he sent 139 Squadron Mosquitoes ahead of the heavies to *Window* the target they could help the Pathfinders and the early crews. On the 29th the six crews, who were later to drop the spoof route markers, arrived over Hamburg before the Main Force to drop *Window*. On this occasion the ploy did not work, for Finding was coned and hit by flak before being engaged by a fighter. F/O B.A. St Louis of 405 Squadron said that he was coned by 250–300 searchlights and held by them for the whole of the time he was over Hamburg. Many crews said the searchlight batteries had been strengthened but St Louis was probably handed from one group (of batteries) to another and in all the total was 250. Damage was mainly to the starboard wing and one of the petrol tanks was holed. In addition to Finding and St Louis two other Pathfinders, F/O H.S. McIntyre of 405 Squadron and P/O A. King of 83 Squadron, received flak damage. Both inner engines of McIntyre's Lancaster were hit and the starboard inner burst into flames. The fire subsided when the Graviner button was pressed. McIntyre jettisoned his bombs and took the shortest route back to Gransden Lodge. King also lost an engine and back over Wyton he was advised to go to Wittering, noted for its long runways, because he had no brake pressure. His R/T (ground-to-aircraft) then became unserviceable and nearby Sibson, realising he was in trouble, gave him a green. Sibson was a grass airfield and the runways there were only short, so King, thinking he was at Wittering, suddenly found himself at the end of the runway. He careered straight ahead across a field and into a hedge before the Lancaster came to an abrupt stop. The crew were unhurt but the aircraft was a write-off.

* * * *

Frau Thea Lahaine lived in Stammannstrasse in the district of Winterhüde on the western border of Barmbek. She it was who wanted to leave after the first raid, when her uncle and aunt had been bombed out. She was told that there was no objection to her leaving but that she must go at her own expense, for the state could not find her accommodation when she still had a roof over her head. The food ration was meagre enough but after the first raid food and water had become scarce. A water truck came round twice a day with drinking water, and although it was not strictly rationed the driver limited the amount he would give to each person. On the 28th and 29th there was no food in the shops and the whole area was without gas or electricity. A neighbour had a coal stove, so everyone brought what bits and pieces of food they had left – scraps of meat and vegetables – and these were all put into a large iron pot with portions of fresh water contributed by each family. This stew comprised their main meal for the day.

9. Sgt C.M. Coutlee of 419 Squadron said: "It burst like a smoke ring and enlarged like one, then cascaded into a lily-shaped affair." (ORB) (PRO AIR 27/1822).

Just before midnight the alarm sounded and Thea took her children down to the cellar. The talk for the past two days had all been about the disaster of the 27–28th, and the fear that the area to the north-east would be the focal point of the RAF's next attack was prevalent among her friends. The iron cellar doors, put in by the State, she had always considered a blessing, but if the rumours were to be believed they had proved to be entirely the opposite. The emergency exit to the next-door cellar she had always viewed with misgivings; it was much too small. So, when the Ack-Ack shells began to burst overhead she became tense and frightened. All at once there was a deafening explosion, followed by several thuds on the ceiling above. Plaster fell down on them but the main structure held and the door stood firm against the blast. Her one thought was to save the children; fear was thrust into the back of her mind. She gathered the baby and the little girl in her arms and made her way up the cellar steps. The house had received a direct hit and everywhere was a shambles. Thea did have two pieces of good fortune: the pram was intact and the bucket of water for fire emergencies had not spilled. She poured half of it over the children, who were wrapped in blankets, and the rest over herself. The whole street was alight and incendiaries were lying close together on the footpaths and in the road. Her single thought was that she must get to the Stadt Park. Looking neither to right or left and through slitted eyes, she picked her way through the incendiaries and made a headlong dash with the pram through the fires to the park, successfully ignoring the terror from the skies as falling bombs seemed to dog her heels. At the park she collapsed, mentally exhausted and physically spent, but a group of soldiers came to her rescue and took care of her. On the afternoon of July 30 she started a week-long journey to Bavaria, first by truck and then by train, sleeping rough, sometimes in the open and in pouring rain. Herr Lahaine, along with hundreds of other soldiers from Hamburg, was given special leave from the Russian front. When he could not find his family in Hamburg he paid a visit to his son at Schwargenfeldt[10] before returning east. That was the last the family heard of him. It was just as well that Frau Lahaine fled when she did, because by 0130 hours the whole area around the Stadt Park was a mass of flames.

Herr Brunswig,[11] who extracted much of his information from the Fire Service records, reveals some surprising anomalies on the night of the 29–30th. He writes that at 0023 hours there were a great number of flares over Fühlsbuttel and Barmbek, and at 0040 hours more intense detonations in the neighbourhood of the local command. This is puzzling because Bomber Command aircraft were not carrying flares[12] and 0023 hours was 22 minutes before zero hour, so it is doubtful if there were any bombers over the port at that time.[13] The first TIs were dropped by Chick at 0038 hours and he made no mention of the early bombing which is implied by Herr Brunswig's observation at 0040 hours. The British account says that there was very little bombing south of the Elbe, yet the Germans reported fires at Blohm & Voss and Stulcken, both south of the river, at 0054 hours and confirmed this at 0130 hours, when the report stated that

10. The whole school, teachers and pupils, had been evacuated there in April 1943.
11. *Feuersturm über Hamburg*.
12. This is not strictly true; red flares were dropped as part of the route-marking but this was nowhere near Hamburg.
13. Many crews took a short cut from the reds to the greens, but this was after the target was marked.

"Christmas trees,"[14] HE and incendiaries were dropped in the harbour area. The bomb plot shows only a few photographs in this area, but whoever was responsible caused some headaches. F/Sgt N. Rollett got a photograph of the A/P, and while he is to be congratulated on his accuracy, the question must be asked: "Why was he bombing miles from the centre of the TI pattern?"[15] Also, south of the river to the west of Wilhelmsburg in the dock area at Reihersteig, warehouses and small businesses were set ablaze, but these raging fires attracted only the occasional bomber because they were south of the main conflagration and the track was from north to south through the port. The German report confirms that although the numbers of bombs dropped within the three-mile criteria was probably only the 34% stated in Bomber Command ORS, the bulk of the remainder was concentrated in and around Barmbek, a district which had to date escaped extensive damage. This error was not due to creepback, which was the cause of the poor "three-mile" percentage on the 24–25th, but to marking errors.

Before the inception of Pathfinders concentrated bombing was a pipe dream and few aircraft bombed within three miles of the A/P. A report[16] on bombing errors in 1941 stated that only one in five aircraft got within 75 square miles of the target, and of these only 32% were within three miles of the aiming point. Before the introduction of the Pathfinder Force, even when some measure of concentration was achieved – a good fire started in the target area or a fire started by crews who had been lured to bomb a decoy fire site – only 35% of the photographs plotted were within three miles of the centre of concentration (MPI). After three months of the PFF regime the concentration had increased to 50%.

The Main Force preferred bombing TIs: it relieved the captain of the responsibility of finding the aiming point; the TIs could be seen from a distance, meaning the crew spent a shorter time in the dangerous target area; the risk of collision was lessened as all aircraft were approaching from one direction; and dropping bombs in the right place improved morale. However, although concentration was the immediate result of the introduction of PFF, a new error crept in. "Systematic error"[17] was caused by inaccuracies in the markers. Although few TIs were dropped outside the three-mile area, the centre of the attack moved to the largest concentration of them and the "random error" (limited accuracy of the Main Force crews) was around this point. So, in spite of the welcome increase in concentration, the average number of photographs plotted within three miles of the aiming point increased by only 5% to 37%. H2S was designed as a navigation aid beyond the limits of *Gee* and not as a precision instrument by which to drop marker bombs. The devastating attacks of 1944 and 1945 were due to the greater accuracy of the Main Force, the random error being reduced to 500 yards, and to the systematic error being greatly decreased after the introduction of the Master Bomber and the GPI.[18] The former selected the best-placed TIs, the latter allowed the marker crews to take evasive action yet still make an accurate run to the aiming point.

It was the widespread marking by the Blind Markers and the difficulties of establishing a concentrated MPI which resulted in Barmbek becoming the centre of a huge

14. German name for TIs.
15. There were one or two yellows in the vicinity but Main Force crews were instructed to bomb greens.
16. The Butt Report.
17. The *Oboe* systematic error was always small.
18. Ground position indicator.

conflagration which covered 24 square miles. For Bomber Command it proved to be a fortunate error, for by the morning of the 30th another huge portion of Hamburg lay in ruins. Barmbek was mainly a residential area but the number of dead and injured was small in comparison with the previous raid because most of the inhabitants had fled the district. That in itself produced a new problem, since the incendiaries were left to do their worst. The Fire Service on their own were powerless to deal with the numbers of incendiaries dropped, even if they had not been widely dispersed, so most of the fires were allowed to spread unchecked.

Herr Schirmer of 95 Hamburgstrasse in the district of Barmbek had a fabulous night. He was alone in the house when the siren sounded at two minutes to midnight. He checked to see he had everything he needed in his air-raid shelter. Time dragged by and from time to time he peeped out of the door to see if anything was happening. The guns were firing and the constant drone of the bombers overhead roused his curiosity. As he looked out for the umpteenth time, he noticed the street was as bright as day. He rushed outside to find incendiaries burning along the whole length of Hamburgstrasse, roughly 16 feet apart. As he was completely helpless he returned to the shelter. Loneliness, or more particularly having no one with whom he could talk over his predicament, drove him out again. The fires were taking hold: the houses directly opposite had started to burn and those diagonally opposite on the corner of Richardstrasse were on fire from top to bottom, as also were some on Hamburgstrasse itself. Having lived through the firestorm of the 27–28th, he was certain that the howling wind was stronger than the last time he was outside. Common sense told him to go into the bunker but the progress of the fires held him spellbound in the doorway. Suddenly, the whole building shook and he fell down the steps into the cellar. Shaken but nothing daunted, he just had to find out what had happened, so he dashed outside again. A large HE bomb had exploded in the air shaft of the Karstadt building on the other side of the road and the display windows were ablaze.

Karstadt's Stores was one of the largest shops in Hamburg and by far the biggest on Hamburgstrasse. It boasted two air-raid shelters, one for the public and a "private" one for staff, relations and, in particular, the Luftwaffe. The public shelter took upwards of 700 people while the private one could comfortably house a thousand. To help the AA battery sited on the Alster searchlights were located on the roof of Karstadt's. In February 1943 the fire department had pointed out that the wooden shed which housed the generator for the searchlights was a fire hazard. It was near one of the main exits to Rönnhaidstrasse and if it caught fire it could endanger the storeys above, particularly if the store windows broke. The reply was firm but undiplomatic: it was the most convenient place to take the power cable to the roof, and there the generator and shed would remain.

Once outside poor Schirmer knew it was safer inside, but even then his curiosity got the upper hand. When he looked at his watch he could hardly believe it was only an hour since the siren had sounded. So much had happened in the meantime. At about 0110 hours he was back on the stairs again when, as if on cue, a second bomb hit the store. Some ten minutes later he noticed a group of about 30 people leaving the store and hurrying down the street in his direction, having come from Karstadt's main shelter. One of the group was an injured member of Karstadt's Fire Service and in his opinion the store was doomed. They stood around watching the fire as if mesmerised.

All at once there was a dull crash and seconds later a shower of sparks and a cloud of dust shot into the air. The far wall of the Karstadt building had collapsed onto Rönnhaidstrasse, and the searchlights had probably crashed down at the same time.

It is time to leave Schirmer and his companions, who still had a long night ahead of them, and return to the men who were causing the mayhem.

* * * *

Students of Bomber Command tactics and practices know that each aircraft found its own way to the target and back to base. Yet many people in Britain, and even on the Continent, think that some effort was made to fly in formation, with a Squadron Leader in the van. The British, untrained in this type of flying, found it very difficult to maintain any semblance of formation in daylight, except in very small numbers, and even then collisions occurred with monotonous regularity. Yet because crews on the same station took off at minute intervals, several aircraft of the same squadron were invariably flying close to one another. This accounts for the apparent anomaly of several aircraft from one squadron being intercepted while other squadrons had trouble-free sorties. On July 24–25, of the 49 interceptions and 7 actual combats, 3 of the crews involved were from 51 Squadron; on the 27–28th, of 82 interceptions and 15 combats, 2 of the crews were from 106 Squadron and another 2 from 207 Squadron. The point was vividly illustrated on the 29–30th, as the number of interception grew to 94 and the combats to 22:4 Squadrons (49, 83, 102 and 467) each had 2 interceptions, 57 and 90 Squadrons had 3 each, while 75 Squadron had 4. In sharp contrast, on August 2–3, when because of adverse weather conditions crews did not maintain any semblance of a stream and the timing was poor, there were 49 interceptions and 11 combats, yet in only 2 cases were crews from the same squadron involved.

It would seem that some German fighters, chiefly Ju88s, had been briefed to fly at Stirling height, for in addition to the 4 bombers of 75 Squadron, 3 Stirlings of 90 Squadron were intercepted, Mills and Hilton on the outward route and P/O W. Day on the homeward route. Day reported seeing yellow and green TIs, but the yellows must have died out before he bombed at 0058 hours, so presumably he saw them as he approached the target. Perhaps he mentioned the yellows because he knew he would not have seen them had he bombed at the correct time, between 0102 and 0110 hours. However, his report confirmed the evidence that the bombing of the first wave was concentrated, as already, only 13 minutes after zero hour, the smoke was rising to 14,000 feet. His was one of several crews who reported seeing a large orange explosion at 0055 hours.

The Stirling, having struggled valiantly up to 14,000 feet, was given a little respite as Day lost height on the way to the enemy coast, and he was down to 8,000 feet when he crossed it. Shortly after, the Stirling was intercepted by a twin-engined enemy aircraft. F/Sgt C.A. Mitchinson, the rear gunner, ordered his captain to corkscrew and sat patiently waiting until the fighter had closed to 400 yards. A two-second burst was all that was required, and the fighter seemed to stop in its tracks as Mitchinson's bullets ploughed their way through the nose. After bursting into flames it broke into three pieces before crashing into the sea. The kill was confirmed by Sgt P.A. James and Sgt

T.M.B. Fitzsimmons, and also by Day, who turned the Stirling to port to watch the crash.

In exactly the same way as the night fighters were drawn like moths to the Pathfinder TI candles route-marking the way to the target, so they assembled round those on the homeward route. There were searchlights all round, weaving aimlessly across the sky in the hope of lighting up a bomber. Sgt A. Kularatue had just informed his navigator that they were over the route markers when the voice of Sgt A.J. Stapleton in the mid-upper turret cut through the congratulations: "Corkscrew port, go, go, go. Ju88, starboard quarter, moving to port astern." Although the mid-upper turret was firing and P/O J.M. Filmer added his weight to the defence, the Junkers followed the manoeuvre and closed to 100 yards. However, realising his aim was poor, he let discretion take over from temerity and broke away to starboard, accelerating out of the field of Filmer's gunfire. Stapleton continued firing and the anxious spectators confirmed his claim to have hit the Junkers. The fighter pilot circled round the nose of the bomber contemplating a head-on attack and trying to remember whether Halifaxes had nose guns. Then he flashed past without firing on a reciprocal course to port and disappeared into the night, either to assess the damage to his aircraft or to seek out a less alert crew.

Eight minutes later (0140 hours), just after leaving the enemy coast, Filmer saw a single-engined aircraft on the port quarter up, at about 800 yards distance and diving from the dark part of the sky. At the same time *Monica*, which had previously ignored the presence of the Ju88, gave out warning pips and Kularatue immediately dived to starboard. Almost simultaneously Filmer ordered "Corkscrew, dive port," but just too late to stop his captain's reflex action. Finding's Lancaster had been caught in the same predicament minutes earlier, and similarly the Halifax suffered the indignity of having cannon shells rip into her, tearing holes in the fuselage, damaging the starboard flap and puncturing the tyre on the tailwheel. Filmer was firing at a dark speck approaching too fast for comfort when suddenly his guns jammed in quick succession in first position stoppages. It all happened so swiftly that Stapleton's turret had not yet had time to rotate, nor had he picked up the fighter. Filmer gave him a rough angle and told him to fire "whether he could see the bastard or not," and the mid-upper gunner opened fire in the hope that he might at least frighten the enemy. The rear gunner recocked his guns with feverish haste, all the time watching the fighter closing in. By now the Halifax had responded to the frantic tug to port, and the fighter flashed by, never to reappear. The whole action had taken only a few seconds but it was some time before pulses returned to normal after two encounters so close together. The initial lack of response by the Halifax had resulted in the first burst of cannon fire damaging the bomber, but the eventual turn to port had taken the fighter pilot by surprise and left him unable to counter the manoeuvre. Just when he had been sensing a kill he had found himself exposed to a broadside from Filmer's and Stapleton's guns.

F/Lt O.F. Grime had just passed the red markers on the homeward route when Sgt A. Bruce, the rear gunner, saw an Fw190 on the port beam 500 yards away. The enemy did not attack in the first instance but took up a position on the starboard quarter up. Had Grime taken evasive action instantly by diving to port the fighter would have been in an ideal position to attack. As it was, when he dived down on the Lancaster, Grime did a diving turn to starboard and the fighter went streaking by without having had time to take aim. Bruce, admirably supported by Sgt A. Barker, forced him to break away down on the port beam. Grime then went into a corkscrew and the gunners watched the Focke-Wulf as it made a climbing turn to renew the combat from the port quarter. Bruce kept his captain informed of the enemy's position and warned him to be ready to dive to port. In the tradition of 5 Group gunners Bruce and Barker fired first on both occasions, giving the fighter no chance to get near the bomber without flying through a stream of bullets. Again the enemy was forced to break off the engagement, and he finally decided that enough was enough.[19]

Although on this night many crews took a short cut from the route markers at Wesselburen directly to Hamburg, in general on the outward route the bomber stream maintained a good concentration. However, on the homeward route the stream seemed to spread and crews became individuals rather than working as a team. Naturally, survival was always uppermost in the airmen's minds, and thoughts on how it was to be best achieved varied with the individual. Private routes home were not uncommon, and Parker's excursion down the Elbe has been recorded.

On the 29th Sgt C.H. Storer and Sgt K. Hewson took a route much nearer to the Mosquitoes' spoof route markers than to the reds dropped for their benefit. Like Parker, they were both intercepted. Storer was well south of track, and at best he was going to have to brave the flak from Wilhelmshaven and Bremerhaven, and once out of the *Window* canopy he was risking interception by controlled night fighters. In fact, the twin-engined night fighter which intercepted the Lancaster was probably a *Zahme Sau* acting in a freelance role. When he made his first attack he had a white identification light in the nose. The fighter appeared on the port quarter but moved to starboard before diving towards the bomber. As Storer made a diving turn to starboard the gunners, Sgts C. Frankish and M.J. Martin, fired long, accurate bursts and the enemy broke away. When the fighter made a second pass at the bomber the gunners noticed that the identification light had been switched off. Both Frankish and Martin claimed to have hit the fighter during the first skirmish but admitted that their aim was not as good during the second attack. However, it was accurate enough to force the enemy to break off the engagement without opening fire, and the crew were left to enjoy a few moments' peace before they ran the gauntlet of the flak batteries waiting for them on the coast.

The ground defences at Bremen must have cursed the fighter that intercepted Sgt Hewson. The Sergeant was even further off track than Storer, some 10 miles south-west to be precise, and the Halifax was almost in range of the batteries surrounding the port. 76 Squadron, it would seem, had assigned the task of dispensing *Window* to the mid-upper gunners. Elder's mid-upper had been killed near the flare chute on July 27, the same evening Sgt Troake had to fight off the enemy with only one gunner, and there were other instances which support the supposition.[20] In this case the mid-upper gunner was wasting his time because the Halifax was so far off track that the *Window* was helping neither his own crew nor any of the others. A single peak on the

19. This combat is credited to Sgt C.W. Barnett in the ORB. The aircraft letters were "O" and "Q". The combat report was in fact made out by F/Lt Grime and his gunners.
20. Troake learned his lesson. On August 2–3, when he was intercepted again, it was P/O G.H. Potter, his mid-upper, who did the firing.

Although this corner building was hit by incendiaries early in the raid, the fires did not spread to all floors until the storm-force winds blew flying sparks into the lower levels.

Flames being sucked into the street by the firestorm wind. *(IWM)*

**(Below) Fire enveloping a block of houses opposite the Firewatch HQ, Berliner Tor. Flames from the first storey shot out of the windows almost horizontally and burned the paint of the HQ windows 100 feet away. The house on the left is not yet burning. (Right) 90 minutes later the house on the left is burning on all floors, with flames shooting out of the roof.** *(Hans Brunswig)*

XIX

**Burnt-out cars, defoliated trees and gutted or demolished factories. Note that the chimney stack survived.** *(IWM).*

**A tree torn out by the roots during the firestorm.** *(Hans Brunswig)*

Two women who, although they had battled their way to the open spaces and escaped from the fires, were too spent to survive their ordeal. *(IWM)*

A group of people lying dead in the street. Exhausted by the storm-force winds and the intense heat, they sank to the ground, never to rise again. Uprooted telegraph poles and lamp post bear witness to the strength of the wind. *(IWM)*

**(Right and below) The charred bodies of people caught in the open during the firestorm.**
*(IWM [upper] and Hans Brunswig [lower])*

**A man, his wife and child, stranded in the firestorm when their van broke down, were overcome by the intense heat and perished.** *(Hans Brunswig)*

**The remains of a dispatch rider caught in a fire whirl. Note that the saddle, tyres and even the rubber on the pedals of his bicycle were devoured by the flames.** *(Hans Brunswig)*

**The district of Hammerbrook was demolished in the firestorm. This photograph shows Hammerbrookstrasse from the centre of the street, looking north.** *(Erik Verg)*

**This photograph was taken after the roads had been cleared of rubble from the point where Hammerbrookstrasse joined Suderstrasse.** *(Erik Verg)*

Wendenstrasse (above) and Gotenstrasse (below), side streets of Hammerbrookstrasse. The roadway of Gotenstrasse has not yet been cleared. *(Studio Schmidt-Luchs)*

**Bombed-out inhabitants gather their few remaining possessions and flee the city.**
*(Studio Schmidt-Luchs)*

Opening up the house shelters. This did not take place until mid-August, when the rubble had cooled. *(IWM)*

A common sight: a body at the entrance of a cellar. *(IWM)*

The body of a woman found in a cellar shelter. Death was due to hyperthermia and/or possibly carbon monoxide poisoning. *(Hans Brunswig)*

Two women who perished on a stone staircase. *(Hans Brunswig)*

This *splittersichere* (splinter-proof) air-raid shelter in Eichenstrasse was hit by a 1,000-pounder. Some 23 of the 35 occupants were killed. *(Hans Brunswig)*

Public air-raid shelter at Moorweide, which was one of the main stopping-off places for people trying to leave Hamburg. *(Erik Verg)*

**Aerial photograph of the devastated area to the east and south-east of Berliner Tor. In the bottom right-hand corner is Hammer Park, a refuge from the horrors of the firestorm for many local inhabitants.**

**The mangled remains of a bomber shot down over Hamburg during the** *Gomorrah* **attacks.** *(IWM)*

N

A *Gee* **set.** *(Mike Symons)*

**H2S set, showing navigator's table and instrument panel.** *(Author)*

*Würzburg*'s screen was just what the searchlights and gun batteries enjoyed, but when a second blip appeared on the screens, quickly followed by the sound of cannon and machine-gun fire as the fighter came in from astern with guns blazing, they dared not fire for fear of hitting it. Sgt A.W. Davis, the rear gunner, ordered a corkscrew to starboard and waited until the enemy had closed to 800 yards before returning fire. The fighter pilot was a bad shot, and his aim was so wild that he might have accidentally hit Storer. The turn to starboard in the combat manoeuvre took the Halifax clear of Bremen, and the ground defences at that moment would have gladly settled for the fighter had it not disappeared from their screens at the same time.

Undoubtedly the most novel route home was taken by F/O J.D. Woods of 61 Squadron. He was intercepted by a Ju88 at 0125 hours west of Hanover, according to the 5 Group report. It seems incomprehensible that anyone would do a cross-country run over the Reich when the enemy was on the alert.[21] Parker could claim he was getting out to the comparative safety of the North Sea as quickly as possible; Storer and Hewson could say they considered the route markers a homing beacon for night fighters; but this Lancaster was so far off track it is unbelievable. *Gee* was working well over the target, whereas the signals would have been jammed out of sight at Hanover, which in any case was the limit of its range without jamming. Even if all the navigational aids were unserviceable the Met winds were accurate enough on the 29th to get an aircraft from A to B without too much trouble. Fortunately, as in Parker's case, Woods' gunners proved more than equal to the occasion. The first indications that the Germans were interested in the bomber came when three searchlights indicated the Lancaster's track. If the gunners needed any inducement to be on the alert the searchlights would certainly have provided it. Almost immediately a Junkers appeared on the port quarter and the rear gunner, Sgt E. Perry, ordered "Dive port, dive." Woods' left arm dragged down hard as he pushed the column forward, and the fighter pilot's reactions were too slow. By the time he had pressed the triggers the Lancaster was no longer in his sights and the shells went harmlessly past. Not so with Perry, whose lead poured into the Junkers. Three bursts were enough to set it on fire. Sgts J. Kyte, the mid-upper, and W.E. Green, the Wop, saw it burst into flames and dive towards the ground, out of control.

P/O L. Gospel, F/O H. Coates and F/O W. Smyk, in addition to Lewis and Kularatue, were intercepted in the vicinity of the enemy coast. Gospel had been coned for only two or three seconds when the rear gunner, Sgt A. Huntingford, saw a Ju88 coming in to attack the Lancaster from the port quarter up. He ordered a dive to port and opened fire on the enemy, who continued diving to starboard without firing and was not seen again. Huntingford claimed to have damaged the Junkers. Coates was in the same area when his bomb-aimer, Sgt L. Underwood, manning the front turret, saw a fighter silhouetted against the searchlights 800 yards away. The enemy turned in to attack and Coates did a diving turn to port. As the fighter closed, Underwood identified it as an Fw190. He opened fire and the Focke-Wulf roared past underneath the Lancaster without firing, perhaps stunned at seeing bullets streaming towards him

21. It was the 5 Group report that gave his position as west of Hanover. To be charitable, the combat report reads: ". . . 25N 09°10E". 52°25N would have put him west of Hanover, 53°25N would have put him on track.

from the Lancaster's nose. Smyk of 300 Squadron could see the surf breaking on the shore when suddenly *Monica* started bleating and he prepared to take evasive action. As the cannon and machine-gun tracer came streaming towards the Wellington he turned to port and the rear gunner, F/Sgt E. Drozdzynski, opened fire. The enemy passed below the Wimpey without doing any damage. The fighter, an Me210, made a climbing attack from the starboard quarter but Drozdzynski opened fire early and the Messerschmitt broke away without firing. Smyk dived down to 16,000 feet to gain speed and put as much distance as possible between the enemy coast and the Wellington in the shortest possible time.

Chick, having remained an uncomfortably long time over the target taking notes, finally decided to make his way home. Over the North Sea at 54°00N 08°00E, well clear of the enemy coast, he was intercepted by a twin-engined aircraft believed to have been a Ju88. Chick was still at 17,000 feet and the German was looking for victims at 16,000. Sgt A. Ellwood, the rear gunner, saw the Junkers on the starboard quarter down, making a climbing attack, and ordered a diving turn to starboard. He opened up with an accurate burst of gunfire as soon as Chick began the combat manoeuvre and forced the enemy to break away to port under the Lancaster without firing. An alert crew was not the type of prey he was seeking.

If the latitudes and longitudes given in the combat reports are correct there were two more interceptions over the sea on the homeward route. Sgt R. Ellis was at 54°20N 06°50E "... just after leaving the coast..."[22] when *Monica* gave out a warning, putting the crew on the alert. As Sgt J. Buchanan, the rear gunner, searched the night sky *Monica* got more and more excited, so to appease her Ellis started a corkscrew. At that moment Buchanan saw a Ju88 making a diving attack from the port quarter fine. When he opened fire with a two-second burst the enemy immediately broke off the attack.

It could easily have been the same Ju88 which attacked P/O G. Judd if the co-ordinates, 54°16N 06°45E, are correct, but the description of the combat tends to give the lie to the alleged position of the Stirling even though the time supports it. "Shortly after leaving the target..." the rear gunner, P/O K. Banks, saw a Ju88 on the starboard quarter some 800 yards away. The enemy aircraft had "a white light in the nose" and "dropped a flare" just before making his attack. When the enemy had closed to 400 yards Banks opened up and the fighter continued to dive to port. Judd had made a tight turn to starboard on his gunner's instruction. If the German pilot was as truthful as Banks his report would have read: "No damage sustained, no damage claimed." The Stirlings were scheduled to bomb between 0102 and 0110 hours, so by 0154 hours Judd should have cleared the enemy coast. Some night fighters operating against *Gardeners* mounted a downwards-pointing light in the nose so that the pilot could see instantly how close he was to the sea. Dropping a flare was not a common practice unless the fighter was working in co-operation with someone else. If an attack was successfully repelled there was always jubilation, but, whether over land or sea, Judd's crew had endured a minute of fear.

Surprisingly, considering the size of the force on operational duty, the number of incidents at bases was small, only two serious crashes being reported. The first, described earlier, involved P/O King of 83 Squadron. The second came after F/Lt G.

22. "Just" in this instance was almost 60 miles.

Bould of 15 Squadron had returned from Germany with the starboard inner engine of his Stirling out of action. As he was making his approach to land at Coltishall the port inner cut and the Flight Lieutenant was forced to make a crash-landing. The crew escaped unhurt. From a force of 777 bombers 27 failed to return; 43 were damaged, 23 by flak and 6 by fighters.

* * * *

In Hamburg news of the raid kept filtering through to the Fire Service HQ at Berliner Tor. Just after 0100 hours the ARP HQ withstood a fierce bombardment when about 50 HEs fell in the vicinity. Even closer were the IBs, which fell like rain on the building, though they were extinguished before they could do any lasting damage. The firewatch at Wandsbek was not so fortunate: it received a direct hit and 25 people were buried in the air-raid shelter. Although 11 managed to free themselves, ten of the others had died before the rescuers could get to them, and shortly after being rescued the eleventh, a fireman, died of his injuries. Fortunate indeed were the 2,000 people sheltering in the *Hochbunker* on the corner of Wielandstrasse and Schellingstrasse. Finished as recently as May 1943, the eight-storey building was proclaimed to be bomb-proof, but on this night an HE pierced the wall high up on the seventh floor. The two women in the room behind the wall were killed by the blast, but though the other shelterers were near hysteria as the building shook to its foundations, the walls and ceilings held firm.

At 0118 hours heavy bombing in the eastern districts added to the confusion. The pre-raid plan to station the fire engines in zones had long since been abandoned; the fires were so widespread that no fire service could possibly cope. There were 120 fires in a triangular area of 2.3 square miles around Barmbek, the main centre of the conflagration, and 30 large fires in the bordering zones. A detachment of 10 engines could deal with only 20 houses at the same time, but the main problem was to maintain the water supply, which had in most cases to be brought from some distance. Besides being a thankless task, it was also highly dangerous when the bombers were overhead; early in the raid a fire engine received a direct hit and the eight crew members were killed. There were rumours that whole blocks of houses had been blown up to prevent the "fire waltzes" of the 27th from recurring and to create fire breaks, but devastation was so complete that it was impossible to tell whether this plan had been carried out. Such an action would have to have been kept secret from a public already overwrought after their sufferings at the hands of the bombers.

Barmbek was not entirely residential. To the west, close by the gasworks in Osterbekstrasse, was a factory area. The gasworks itself was extensively damaged and many works in the area were hit. Whole workshops were completely burnt out by fires which raged uncontrolled. Across the road on the far side of the canal and stretching to Jarrestrasse, the engineering works of Kamp-Nagel AG, employing 1,500 people, were badly damaged by HE and fire. Over half the factory was burnt out or destroyed and much of the remainder seriously damaged, and a large part of the machinery was a complete write-off. They were specialists in cranes, grabs and similar heavy machinery, and had made over half the cranes in Hamburg. It was almost a month before production began again, and then only after transferring some of the machinery to a factory commandeered for the purpose. By the New Year of 1944 the company was producing only 20% of its former output; a year later, in January 1945, the figure was still only 60%. Both the Treton works in the area were badly damaged. Repairs to the larger factory, employing more than 1,000 workers, took six weeks. Hochbahn power station in Hellbrookstrasse was badly damaged and took weeks to repair; Norddeutsche & Gummiwerke and Conrad Scheltz, makers of conveyor bands and belts for machines, took five and six weeks respectively. One of the plums of the night was the destruction of Hamburgische Schiffbau-Versuchsanstalt, who were engaged in submarine design and experimental work.

After the All-clear at 0208 hours the news came pouring in as the wardens went out and assessed the damage. As well as the early bombing south of the river there had been scattered bombing outside the marked area to the west and south of the Alster. In the vicinity of Grindelallee someone had started a large blaze, while to the south of the Binnen-Alster there was an area of raging fires. Besenbinderhof was aflame, and the *Rathaus* (town hall) market place was impassable. Jungfernstieg and Neuerwall had been heavily damaged on the 24–25th but the new fires still found plenty of fuel. The Bourse itself was burnt out. To the west the fires in Altona, started early in the attack, were keeping the ARP busy, though conditions here, in contrast with those of the night of the first raid, were never out of control. Due east of the Alster, much nearer to the MPI of the greens, a belt of fire stretched northwards 1¾ miles from Hartwicusstrasse in the south, along the whole length of Hofweg, Schillingstrasse[23] and Dorotheenstrasse to the Stadt Park. From there it split into two, one wave going northwards along Alsterdorfer Strasse, the other eastwards to Barmbek.

The Karstradt fire proved to be the most tragic of the night. Life and death were separated by only a few yards. We left Schirmer with a group of people who had fled the building, believing it to be doomed. At about 0140 hours this group decided it was time to put some distance between themselves and the Karstadt building and advised Schirmer to do the same, but he decided to stay for the time being. As if to keep him from getting lonely another group of people came out of the store. They were looking for a new refuge and were delighted when Schirmer offered them the use of his shelter. Five minutes later the whole cellar shook when the front of the store collapsed into Hamburgstrasse. Schirmer jumped to his feet but his new-found friends persuaded him to stay in the bunker. After an interminable ten minutes his curiosity got the upper hand and, on the pretext of wanting to visit his neighbours at No 99, he went back to the street again, where he discovered that the Karstadt wall on Desenissstrasse had also collapsed, sealing off the store's bunker entrance.

After a short chat with the people at No 99 he went back to see how his guests were faring. On the way he noticed that the Karstadt fires had already engulfed the house directly behind his own. This new development worried him, so he went up to the second floor to get a better look at the situation. The wind, which was increasing in strength all the time, was rapidly spreading the fires, and just before 3 o'clock they leapt across the road and Schirmer could see a fire developing in the second storey of No 97. Although the fire was not visible at street level the urgency in his voice persuaded his friends there to join him in his shelter. There were now 35 people in the cellar and

23. Now part of Winterhuder Weg.

Schirmer believed it was only a question of time before No 95 too would catch fire, so they discussed their predicament and decided to go to Wagnerstrasse station before the situation got out of hand. One big factor in favour of flight was that there was no longer any danger from falling bombs: the All-clear had sounded an hour before at 0208. Schirmer brought down the last of his water supply into the cellar and they wet their clothing and towels and blankets to cover their heads.

It was about 0330 hours when they finally left the house, which up to that moment had not caught fire. The most direct way to Wagnerstrasse was past the Karstadt building and down Hamburgstrasse. The wind was now so strong that it was difficult to walk against it; sparks and burning timbers carried by the wind were also a hazard. As the group approached a confectioner's the heat from the burning sweets was so intense that they were forced to cross to the other side of the street. As on the night of the 27th, in their haste to get away people had discarded suitcases and handbags in order to save their lives. The journey between No 95 and Wagnerstrasse station took six or seven minutes, and in that short time the blankets and towels had become completely dry. Conditions at the station were bearable and considerably cooler than in Hamburgstrasse.

Inactivity combined with curiosity finally overcame prudence, and at 0430 hours Schirmer could be seen picking his way back down Hamburgstrasse towards his home. The sweet shop was almost completely burnt out but it was still too hot to pass except on the far pavement. Karstadt's had also burned to the ground and was just a mass of glowing embers. Nos 97 and 99 were mere shells but his own house was only half burnt, one side having apparently escaped the fire completely. As the fires burned themselves out the wind gradually abated, and when Schirmer strolled back to the station the sun was trying pitifully to pierce the gloom.

Around 0730 a woman in a very agitated state came to the station begging for help. Her parents had gone to the Karstadt shelter and although the All-clear had sounded more than five hours ago they had not yet returned. Schirmer and several other men went to Karstadt's. The entrance doors to the shelter in Rönnhaidstrasse were still hot but this was the only possible way in. So, armed with a hose, Schirmer forced his way down the stairs. The air was very hot and scarcely breathable. At the bottom of the stairs men and women were lying on top of each other. Some of them were whimpering, too exhausted even to cry. Almost all of them had burns and, seeing no prospect of escaping, had become apathetic. With difficulty some were persuaded to go up the stairs, but the whole operation was taking too long and the rescuers were rapidly becoming as exhausted as the victims. Visions of ambulances to ferry them to safety brought no response, so Schirmer and his friends had to resort to bullying. Hitting and kicking them revived their will to survive and eventually 26 people were rescued. As Schirmer ran through the rooms looking for survivors he realised that a stack of coal in the bunker was alight and the safety doors were still red-hot. Rescued and rescuers trudged their way wearily to Wagnerstrasse. At about 0815 hours two trucks stopped at the station and everyone was given a drink of water. The injured were loaded into the trucks and taken to the nearest hospital to get their wounds treated. Later in the day, at around 10 o'clock, rescue teams broke into other rooms in the public shelter at Karstadt and found a total of 370 people dead from carbon monoxide poisoning caused by the burning coal and coke. In the private bunker there were no fatalities; about 1,200 people had been sheltering there and they had waited patiently until their rescuers reached them.

The law of diminishing returns was beginning to operate. Many bombs fell in the already devastated areas to the south-east, where there was nothing left to burn or destroy, and had it not been for the cloud of dust which hung over the Firewatch HQ at Berliner Tor the wasted bombs would have gone unnoticed.

# Chapter IX

# Thunder and Lightning

"PURE hell," said Sgt A.P. Bremner of 207 Squadron. "I have no desire to do that again." This was undoubtedly the sentiment of the vast majority of the aircrew who took part in the raid on Hamburg on August 2–3. "A complete fiasco," said F/Lt R.L.L. McCulloch of 101 Squadron, and he echoed the feelings of everyone. These passionate outbursts were not isolated cases, for the group reports were unanimous in their condemnation: "The weather had a crippling effect on the raid" was 5 Group's summary.[1]

At his morning briefing Harris had looked long and hard at the weather chart. There was a possibility that the cumulus cloud forecast to develop over the North Sea during the day would drift towards the enemy coast in the region of the Elbe and Schleswig-Holstein. It might even be 10/10ths. Finally his finger came down on Hamburg.

The port had been left in peace for four days, and Harris rightly thought that one more raid would complete its destruction. There were those in Hamburg who believed the same thing and were fearfully awaiting another raid. Harburg too expected an attack; it had so far escaped serious damage but housed vital industries. August 2–3 was to be the night to put the books straight; the aiming point for the first four waves was to be Hamburg, and then it was to be switched to Harburg for the fifth and sixth waves. The route took the bombers from south to north over the port so that any creepback from the early waves would take the attack south of the river towards the second A/P. The plan was excellent, and when used later at Mannheim on September 5–6, 1943, it brought enormous success, though that night the weather was excellent and gave PFF an opportunity to display their skills. That the Pathfinders possessed the techniques to change aiming points during a raid was amply demonstrated at Peenemünde just 15 days later.

There were 762 crews on the Battle Order on August 2–3, 740 of them on the main target. It was to be marked "by the *Newhaven* method" – and here the first hint of doubt about the weather was shown – "with emergency *Wanganui*". If the cloud was more than 6/10ths, skymarker flares – green with red stars – would be dropped and crews would bomb them on a course of 355° Magnetic. The bets were all on a "scrub"; the weather at the bases was not very good, and although the met men made light of weather conditions both at base and at the target, their briefing had lacked conviction. One factor was omitted from the airmen's calculations: the C-in-C's impatience. Harris' stubbornness was probably a good thing, considering the times and his position, but his impatience sometimes caused him to place his force at risk. Known in Bomber Command as "the Butcher" or "Butch Harris,"[2] he probably merited the title

1. Extracts from ORBs (PRO AIR Nos 27/802; 27/1234; 25/109).
2. In truth I never heard the term used with malice.

# NIGHT OPERATIONS August 2–3

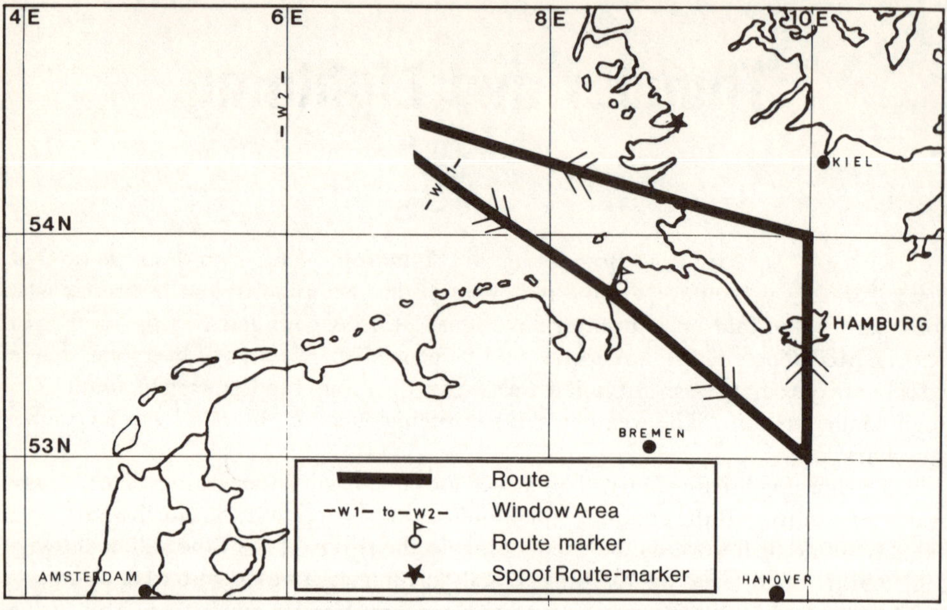


on such a night. It can be argued that it was a calculated risk, but all the signs were there; even the *Pampa*[3] confirmed the danger. Harris' apparent hope that his force would beat the cumulus clouds to the port proved to be wishful thinking; aircrew had enough hazards to combat in completing an operational tour without having to battle with the elements.

A meal with an egg was always a treat in wartime, and so far there were no grumbles. The minutes ticked by and still the cancellation did not come. Around 8 o'clock, with a shrug of the shoulders, the crews made their way down to the flights and went through the motions of getting ready. After another 30 minutes the crew vans were standing by to take them to the aircraft. The humorists were subdued; it was asking too much to go through all this two nights running for nothing. "Why couldn't they make up their minds sooner?" All thoughts were still on a cancellation. To the crews Monday August 2 was turning out to be a repetition of the previous day, when it had taken a series of thunderstorms at bases to force the red Very light out of Flying Control.

To most people's surprise the Very pistol produced a green, and seconds later the noise of engines bursting into life could be heard from North Yorkshire to Suffolk. The lucky ones were the crews who were cancelled or recalled. This time there were no rude names for those who caused the cancellations, like poor Cox on the 29th. At Scampton on the 2nd–3rd the six crews who were cancelled because P/O E.T. Hodgkinson ground-looped on take-off and crashed his Lancaster, which caught fire and obstructed the runway, cheerfully wended their way back to the dispersal pans.

P/O S.M. Hickman of 76 Squadron was soon in trouble; he lost the port engine just after take-off and was the first of the Squadron's boomerangs. Two crews of 100

3. Flown by F/Lt G.H. Hatton at 1845 hours.

Squadron did not even get as far as the coast. F/Sgt P.R. Andrews also had engine failure, losing the starboard outer just after he had retracted his undercarriage, and F/Sgt F.H. Tritton's gunners found that the hydraulics to their turrets were faulty. F/Sgt E. Magnus of 460 Squadron had just taken off from Binbrook when the petrol pump on the starboard outer engine became unserviceable and Magnus abandoned the sortie. Two Wellingtons also had engine trouble and their pilots were forced to make crash landings. F/Lt J. Spychala of 300 Squadron was compelled to feather the starboard engine very soon after take-off, whereupon the Wellington began to lose height. Two miles south of Worksop, with the altimeter registering a mere 300 feet, the bombs were jettisoned and Spychala selected a corn field in which to make a belly landing. The aircraft burst into flames and was burnt out but the crew scrambled clear. Sgt B. Wawrzak suffered superficial burns. W/O J.A.C. Newman, flying one of the six Wellingtons of 166 Squadron and detailed to drop mines in the Elbe estuary, had only been airborne for five minutes when the port engine failed and he had to make a crash landing in a barley field. None of the crew was injured.

There were three principal ways that icing could affect the aircraft of Bomber Command. Icing on the propellers altered the aerofoil section of the blades and so made them less capable of pulling the aircraft through the air. Because the amount of icing on the propellers of multi-engined bombers was not identical, and the rate at which the ice was shed not the same, the constant-speed units could not prevent surging and the problems associated with it. Carburettor icing was fortunately rare, since it stopped the engine through lack of petrol, usually when power was at a premium. However, icing was at its worst when it affected the wings, fuselage and tailplane, for then it brought insurmountable difficulties. On the wings it broke the smooth flow of air over the aerofoil, altering the centre of pressure.[4] The stability of the aircraft being closely related to the centre of pressure, any displacement increased the stalling speed. Ice on the fuselage made the aircraft heavier and also altered the trim. In these circumstances the angle of attack changed and the centre of pressure shifted again, resulting in an increase in stalling speed. Ice on the tailplane made the controls sluggish at a time when quick response was vital. In effect, the pilot was flying an entirely different aircraft with unknown and unpredictable idiosyncrasies. It was impossible to teach pilots in training how to cope with such conditions, and most completed their operational tours without encountering icing. Notes about icing were issued and updated when new information became available. For example, if the aircraft had been flying in very cold but dry air it could become iced-up simply by entering a cloud below the ice level, where the cloud's water vapour would freeze on encountering the cold airframe.

On August 2–3 Hamburg found a new ally, the weather, which threw up two defensive walls between the bombers and the city. From 5°E cloud became a real hazard. Sgt W.D.L. Cameron of 419 Squadron said: "The track was blocked by cumulo-nimbus rising to 25,000 feet; icing and turbulence made it impossible to fly through it."[5] Certainly the Stirlings of 3 Group had no hope of flying above it. Four crews of 90 Squadron found it an impassable barrier; they all attempted to fly through it

4. The wings of each type of aircraft are designed (shaped) to provide the correct amount of lift, which varies with the centre of pressure.
5. ORB (PRO AIR 27/1822).

but had to turn back because the icing was so severe. W/O R.C. Corley went down to 7,000 feet to try to get below the cloud, but without success. News that F/Sgt R.F. Denton had abandoned the sortie came from Catfoss, where he landed. The Flight Sergeant had encountered an electrical storm as well as icing.

There were in all 186 early returns, of which only 12 were from 5 Group; 15 and 49 Squadrons provided most of them, more than half of them turning back before reaching the enemy coast. These early returns certainly ran the gamut of the conditions: W/Cdr P.W. Johnson (49) was caught in an electrical storm and his Lancaster would not maintain height because of severe icing; F/O R. Lown (15), W/O D. Woodruff (15) and Sgt R. Grundy (15) also had to turn back because of severe icing; P/O T. Tomlin (49) had an attack of migraine and was temporarily blinded, but the flight engineer helped his captain to control the Lancaster; Sgt W. Petty (49) jettisoned his cookie to try to get over the cloud. Many crews turned back because of engine failure principally due to icing. F/Sgt L. Watson (49) had to feather both inners, and the ASI and intercom both became unserviceable. After 50 minutes on the return flight the engines started again.

Of the 15 Stirlings of 218 Squadron that had taken off from Downham Market only three crews reached Hamburg and a fourth bombed Last Resort; nine crews jettisoned their bomb loads over the North Sea and two brought them back. At 04°00E F/Sgt W.H. Kruse of 428 Squadron had trouble with the starboard outer, which cut and then caught fire, but fortunately the Graviner fire extinguisher was equal to the occasion. In all 30 bombers were missing; according to ORS, 11 were probably shot down by fighters. There was no definite evidence that any were shot down by flak, but incidents of damage make it likely that the ground defences had some success. However, the weather was undoubtedly the main cause of the comparatively high loss rate.

The end of July 1943 was not a happy time for 76 Squadron, and August opened in the same vein. It has already been recorded how the failure of the port inner just after take-off reduced Hickman's sortie to circuits and bumps. It was no night to be flying even if the bomber had been fully serviceable, and although F/Sgt E.J. Little may have been willing to make the sortie, his Halifax was not in the same frame of mind. As instrument after instrument became unserviceable he was compelled to turn back while he still had control. Capt J.M. Stene's Halifax was struck by lightning, the starboard inner taking the brunt of the flash; it stopped immediately in protest. Stene later coaxed it back to life. Sgt E.N. Wright, not to be outdone, returned early with both of his starboard engines unserviceable. F/Sgt H.R.W. Whittle encountered the same storm and jettisoned his bombs. Sgt L. Falgate made an early return because his compass was all awry. The navigator also had a compass but the difference between them was not constant, varying according to the heading; this was an impossible situation in the best of conditions. Sgt G.C. Dunn battled against the storms and icing as far as 53°17N 09°35E, just south of Hamburg, when the heavens opened up and his Halifax began to ice up again. He gave the elements best, jettisoning his bombs and heading for base.

In addition, three crews had combats. F/Lt J.P.E. Maze was over the Elbe estuary when his Halifax was struck by lightning; he jettisoned the bombs and headed out to sea. He had just settled on course when Sgt C. Ramsden, the rear gunner, saw a Ju88 dead astern 800 yards away, silhouetted against the cloud. The fighter pilot's report probably said: "I saw a Halifax silhouetted against the cloud 800 yards away. I opened fire but the Halifax turned to port and started a corkscrew and my tracer went past the starboard wing. Return fire came from the rear turret. I broke off the attack and lost contact." Twenty minutes later, after they had left the flak far behind, Ramsden's voice came over the intercom: "Turn port, Skipper." Warned by the urgency in the rear gunner's voice, Maze made a steep turn to port and an Fw190 flashed past. Ramsden opened fire but it was more a gesture than a serious attempt to hit the enemy, the violence of the turn having made aiming impossible.

When Sgt Troake was intercepted on July 27–28 his mid-upper, P/O Potter, was dispensing *Window*. Fortunately on this occasion he was in the turret, because it was he who saw the three Ju88s flying in echelon on the Halifax's port beam. He fired four long, discouraging bursts and Troake took evasive action by corkscrewing. When two of the Junkers approached the Halifax Potter concentrated his fire on the nearest. At that instant there was a flash of lightning which temporarily blinded him and probably the fighter pilots too. When he recovered his sight the fighters were nowhere to be seen. Sgt Orr, who had fought off the enemy single-handed on the 28th, did not see the Junkers as a result of their position on the port beam.

F/Lt C.M. Shannon had more excitement in one week than any airman would want in a whole tour. Over Essen on July 26 he lost a propeller and had to land at Holme on Spalding Moor on two engines. The morning of the 30th found him asking for a priority landing again; his port inner had failed near the target. Events on August 2–3 must have made him wonder whether he was ever going to get the gremlins off his back. On the outward journey the bad moments over Essen were relived vividly. The corposant (St Elmo's fire) swirling around the propellers made them look as if they were free of the engines, and he sat mesmerised, wondering which one would go first. The gunners may have been spared their captain's fears, but every now and then there would be a flash from one gun barrel to the other, and though it looked nothing like a tracer shell, anything that broke the darkness spelt "enemy" to them. Then an engine failed and Shannon was forced to feather it, but he felt confident enough to continue on to the target and bomb. North of Hamburg he had just turned onto his course to the coast when Sgt J. Dodgson, his new mid-upper (he had left his previous one, Sgt E.W. Waterman, at Essen),[6] ordered a corkscrew to port. An Me 109 had appeared out of the cloud 150 yards away. *Monica* had warned the gunners to be on the alert, but one could almost feel the fighter pilot's surprise. He broke away to starboard and made for the cloud. Five minutes later he broke cloud some 400 yards astern and Shannon made a steep dive to port; Dodgson opened fire and the Messerschmitt turned to starboard and back into the cloud. The scene was repeated twice more before the German apparently tired of the game, leaving Shannon in peace to thread his way through the cloud. Back at base he did not even bother to ask for a priority landing.

If Shannon's interception seems like some obscure German parlour game, with the enemy at no time making any offensive gesture, then S/Ldr J. Belton's had a strong resemblance to "round and round the mulberry bush". No 466 Squadron was still equipped with Wellingtons in August 1943, and although there were many Halifaxes operating in 4 Group, Air Commodore W.A.D. Brooke (Group SASO) chose to make the sortie with Belton. The Wellington had just crossed the enemy coast when *Monica*

6. Shannon ordered "Abandon aircraft" when he lost the propeller. Though he later rescinded the order Waterman had already jumped.

gave out a warning. Belton made a complete orbit in an unsuccessful attempt to shake off the enemy pilot, so he dived 3,000 feet into cloud and the fighter was lost. Almost immediately the port engine cut and the bombs were jettisoned. In Bomber Command the pilot was in practically all cases the captain of the aircraft, irrespective of rank. This democracy was clearly demonstrated in the Wellington: Belton was outranked by his passenger but there was no attempt on the part of the Air Commodore to take over control. The Squadron Leader was a small man and, with all the power on one side, he found it very difficult to keep the rudder bar straight enough to fly an accurate course. Brooke volunteered to lie on his back in the nose and, putting his feet on the far side of the rudder bar, take some of the strain off Belton. He even stayed in that position during the landing.

Trouble and W/O R.J. Walters were synonymous. His first sortie as captain was to *Nectarine I* to lay mines on July 28. At 53°34N 05°21E he flew across a large enemy convoy of ships in "V" formation. The five or six destroyers accompanying the convoy opened fire on the Stirling, which was thrown on its back.[7] Walters, feeling vindictive after such rough treatment, dropped his mines in front of the convoy. On August 2–3 his was the first of three combats involving two fighters in co-operation.[8] He had negotiated the cloud barrier at 5°E without mishap and reached 07°15E when he was attacked by two fighters simultaneously. They damaged his Stirling, putting the starboard engine out of action. Walters jettisoned his load and returned to base. Three more sorties in August resulted in two early returns and a crash landing at Castle Camps.[9]

When 101 Squadron arrived in the target area the thunderstorm was at its worst. To have battled against the elements for two hours across the North Sea only to find conditions worse at the target would have tempted even the padres to curse the C-in-C, and in those moments it was perhaps fortunate that High Wycombe was so far away. Five crews bombed Wesemünde. Another 10 were more hardy, but with no TIs to help and being above cloud they were forced to bomb blindly, chiefly on ETA. Perhaps McCulloch's "complete fiasco" was the only printable comment.

Just after crossing the enemy coast Sgt M.C. Lowe of 61 Squadron found a huge cloud blocking the track and his Lancaster began to ice up again. First the starboard inner cut and, minutes later, the port inner. Having struggled so far the Sergeant was reluctant to turn back so he tried to restart the engines. The starboard inner remained obdurate but the port inner suddenly responded and the gauges confirmed that it was fit for duty. Icing in the carburettor would appear to have been the reason for its stopping. However, 10 miles short of the target the starboard outer cut. The power was now all on one side, so Lowe jettisoned his cargo and made directly for the coast.

Many other crews who had successfully fought the cloud at 5°E fell foul of the inner wall of cloud between the enemy coast and Hamburg. It also seemed more vicious, and many aircraft seemed to fall out of the sky because of severe icing or because they were caught in the downdraught of this towering cumulo-nimbus. Two crews of 15 Squadron must have thought they were in an express lift to Hell, with the Devil calling out the

7. *Gardeners* usually flew between 500 and 1,000 feet to escape detection by the German GCI; Walters was flying at 630 feet.
8. No combat report.
9. He survived his first tour of operations.

height in thousands of feet. They both started at 14,000 feet. Sgt J. Benny, who had engine trouble, managed to pull out at 4,000 feet, but Bould, having survived a horizontal crash on July 29, seemed certain to perform a vertical encore this time. The Lancaster was a mere 500 feet above the ground when Bould regained control and pulled out of the dive. With Bremerhaven sitting invitingly below he dropped his bombs and turned for the coast. At 500 feet he had two immediate advantages: his Lancaster was a difficult target for the flak and he was unlikely to meet any bombers hedge-hopping their way to Hamburg.

"The higher the Führer (Fewerer)" was a wartime RAF maxim, but conditions were no better at 19,000 feet, which was P/O F.B. Solomon's height when his Lancaster went into a spin due to icing. At that point the bomber was in the downstream of the cumulus, and she hurtled her way down to 8,000 feet before Solomon could pull out.

A special order was sent out to 1 Group under the heading "Maintenance of Height": "Lancasters of 1 Group are not to jettison bombs to get extra height." Even on such a night some captains took the order seriously. Sgt J.A.L. Currie of 12 Squadron was fighting his way through cloud to reach the target when his Lancaster began to ice up and lose height. The aircraft was caught in the downdraught and turned on its back before going into a spin. The engineer, Sgt G. Walker, was knocked unconscious. The Lancaster plummeted down to 8,000 feet before Currie could pull it out of the dive. The ailerons were torn off in the recovery, and control was then maintained by using the engines and the rudder. The bombs were jettisoned and Currie took a direct route to the enemy coast.

1 Group said that the raid must be classified as a failure. Crews reported 10/10ths cloud over the target, though 86 out of the 153 crews from the Group said that they had bombed the main target, chiefly on ETA; 7 Lancasters and 2 Wellington crews claimed to have bombed TIs. F/O J. Mioduchowski of 305 Squadron reported seeing decoy fires and said that he made three runs across the target before dropping his bombs! Most crews reported electrical storms or thunderstorms on the route and many experienced severe icing; 28 made early returns. There were no combats in the Group but 8 crews sustained flak damage.

The ground defences along the whole of the north-western seaboard from Wilhelmshaven to Kiel had a busy night. Although the rain made conditions unpleasant and the cloud almost negated the efforts of the searchlights, because the *Window* was less concentrated the *Würzburgs* were not completely swamped and individual aircraft could be monitored. This gave the FLAK a greater sense of purpose which was quickly felt by the aircrew receiving its attention. Many crews jettisoned their bombs or at best aimed them at the gun batteries. F/Sgt J.P. Hutchinson of 12 Squadron had battled through the elements and, although south of track, he had just settled on his course for Hamburg when he was engaged by accurate predicted flak. One shell burst so close that a piece of shrapnel shattered the Perspex near the bomb-aimer, Sgt C. Walton, who was hit in the face by some of the pieces and temporarily blinded.

W/O J.R. Clark had also crossed the enemy coast south of track when suddenly his Lancaster was engaged by intense predicted flak. On occasions the ground defences were very patient and waited until their victim could be attacked on all sides. It was extremely effective when the searchlights could co-operate. Clark was in this respect fortunate, since the cloud prevented his Lancaster from being coned. He immediately jettisoned his bombs and dived away to safety. From the number of shells bursting at one time he realised it must be a well defended area, most likely Bremen. S/Ldr B. Bell also found himself the centre of attention some 30 miles south-west of the target, and although his Lancaster was hit by flak he pressed on to Hamburg. There, catching a glimpse of the dock area through a break in the cloud, he took the opportunity to drop his cargo. The ground defences had cut their teeth on twin-engined bombers and F/Lt Z. Roter of 300 Squadron was ready to attest that they had lost none of their skill. His Wellington was hit by predicted flak, the damage being chiefly to the starboard mainplane.

Three Halifaxes from 10 Squadron were among the 37 aircraft reported by ORS to have received flak damage, and all three had an engine damaged. P/O A.G. Douglas was over Fintel when the port inner was hit and the artificial horizon became unserviceable. To show his displeasure he dropped his bombs on the village. P/O G.K. Hewlett was over the target when his starboard outer was hit and put out of action. The third victim was S/Ldr A.I.S. Debenham, who had just left the target when two shells burst too near his Halifax for comfort. One burst in front of the nose on the port side, hitting the port outer, the other exploded near the tail unit and the rear gunner had a narrow escape. Then the port inner cut and, to add to the difficulty and strain of flying an aircraft with all the power on one side, the Halifax began to lose height. He jettisoned the ammunition to ease the load, but the Halifax continued to lose height and when Flamborough Head came in sight it was down to 4,000 feet. The port inner suddenly responded to his efforts to restart it and so the problem of making a difficult landing on a strange aerodrome was avoided.

The consensus of opinion was that the enemy had the best of the evening. The ORS said: "There was a slight risk[10] of 10/10ths cumulo-nimbus at the target but this was not considered sufficient to justify cancelling the raid. Unfortunately, weather conditions proved even more severe than had been expected, with solid cloud towering in places to 30,000 feet and heavy thunderstorms. As a result the raid was completely disorganised. . . ." It was 405 Squadron's first big chance to show their marking skills but the conditions made it impossible to mark the target effectively. Green TIs were burning from Z+10 to Z+18 south-east of the Binnen Alster, and again from Z+24 to Z+28, but these were not plotted. There were only 123 photographs which showed anything but cloud; 67 of them showed ground detail, only one was within the three miles and 49 were unplottable. The other 56 showed fire tracks but only one of them was plotted and that was outside three miles. F/Sgt M.P. Callaway was the nearest with 2½ miles at 166° from the aiming point; his closest rival was F/Sgt D.A. Routen, with 3½ miles/149°. 405 Squadron had a disastrous night. They were all keyed up to prove they could compete with the best in PFF, yet of the 16 crews who took off only 5 reached Hamburg; 2 bombed Last Resort, 6 were forced to jettison and 3 were missing.[11]

In fact the conditions made a travesty of all the plans. There was 10/10ths cloud over

10. The *Pampa* report did not rate the risk as slight. In fact, Hatton's money was on a "scrub" (PRO AIR 24/258).

11. This was later reduced to two when Sgt J.A. Phillips and his crew were reported to have baled out over Sweden.

the coast at 53°25N 08°32E, the position for the first set of route markers. Spoof route markers were to be dropped by 139 Squadron 92 miles/333° from Hamburg, but where was Hamburg? The weather also made a mockery of the marking techniques: *Newhaven* was an impossibility and the *Wanganui* flares either disappeared into cloud immediately or, in some instances, burst in the cloud. *Zephyrs* were to be broadcast, but what was the use of a target wind if the aircraft could not reach the target because of the cloud? At the last turning point the cloud towered up to 25,000 feet, with the base at 10,000 feet.

There was scarcely a crew of the 762 on the Battle Order who had a trouble-free sortie. The lucky ones were those who were cancelled. The 83 Squadron historian commiserated with F/Lt W.F.W. Wilmot, who should have been completing his second tour; in fact he was unable to take off due to engine failure. Some 700 crews would gladly have changed places with him had they known beforehand what the next few hours had in store for them: W/Cdr W.H. Shaw of 83 Squadron, for example. Just before starting his bombing run the port inner cut and the other three engines began surging dramatically. The Lancaster lost height rapidly, but 83 Squadron were essentially "press-on types" and the Wing Commander held stoically to his course until the target was bombed. His TIs were later jettisoned well away from Hamburg. The Lancaster continued to lose height and the IAS was a mere 110 knots, which made the North Sea crossing an eternity. Everything that could be jettisoned, except the guns, was fed to the fishes. So determined was the look on their captain's face that the crew would not have been surprised if he had asked for volunteers to bale out. The crew fervently hoped it would not be a recurring nightmare. Chick epitomised 83 Squadron: he came down to 9,000 feet to get below the cloud in order to make a good bombing run. King, who had had a hair-raising crash on his previous sortie, found that the rear turret was unserviceable before reaching the enemy coast – many lesser crews would have turned back with that as an excuse – and both his navigational aids became U/S shortly before crossing it. When the bomb-aimer turned the bombsight on that too was unserviceable, but even then King picked a last-resort target before releasing his cargo.

P/O D.H. Pidding, on his first trip as captain with 83 Squadron, had also caught the "press-on spirit," to quote the ORB. Having bombed the target he was well clear of the enemy coast when Sgt H.D. Lewis saw a single-engined fighter silhouetted against the cloud and identified it as an Fw190. The fighter was making a climbing attack from the port quarter down, so Lewis ordered a diving turn to port. The mid-upper, W/O J.K. Buxton, swung his turret and both gunners opened fire immediately they had the Focke-Wulf in their sights. The enemy fighter did not open fire until he had closed to 200 yards but by then the Lancaster was in the combat manoeuvre. Shells and fighter flashed harmlessly by as good crew co-operation earned its just reward. The mettle of the *Wild Boars* deserves a comment: the pickings over the target on this night were meagre so they foraged over the sea without AI or searchlights to help them.

In common with those of other Groups, some Pathfinder squadrons had trouble-free nights with no combats and little flak damage. No 7 Squadron, apart from losing an experienced crew, P/O A.L. Forbes, on July 29–30, had escaped without serious incident. On the 2nd–3rd only 17 of the 20 on orders took off and of these 10 reached the target; 6 returned early and 2 crews had combats. S/Ldr O.J. Lofthouse was intercepted by two fighters working in conjunction with each other, one with a green identification light and the other a red. F/Sgt A. Davidson, the rear gunner, saw the green 1,000 yards[12] astern and 100 feet below the Lancaster, fine on the starboard quarter. Dead astern the red kept his distance while the green made his attack. Davidson ordered "Dive starboard" and Lofthouse, keyed for the order, made a steep diving turn and continued taking violent evasive action. The fighter pilots doused their identification lights and made eight attacks altogether but never closed to less than 400 yards. They opened fire only on the last pass and missed the Lancaster by a clear 100 yards. The reluctance of the fighter pilots to come in close and the violent evasive action by Lofthouse saved the Lancaster from damage but left Davidson and the mid-upper gunner, F/Sgt A.J. Dart, feeling completely frustrated. On the one hand, the enemy kept out of range most of the time, and on the other, the combat manoeuvres gave them no opportunity to take aim and fire. The fighters must have been *Tame Boars*, because they gave up the chase when Lofthouse's crew began to dispense *Window*, which probably jammed their AI.

For W/O J.F. Robbins (rear gunner) and W/O C.J. Thornhill (mid-upper) it was an entirely different story. F/Lt S. Baker was homeward bound and had reached Wesemünde on the enemy coast when Thornhill ordered his captain to dive to starboard and opened up on an Me210 which was making a climbing attack. Robbins swung his turret to port and fired down the tracer coming from the mid-upper turret even before he spotted the Messerschmitt. The enemy aircraft broke away to port and Baker pulled out from the dive and continued evasive action by corkscrewing, all the time making for the nearby cloud. The Messerschmitt next came in from the starboard quarter and opened fire at 300 yards, but against gunners of Robbins' and Thornhill's class this was courting disaster, for they undoubtedly damaged the fighter. When he reached cloud cover Baker climbed to port, but his adversary must have been a *Tame Boar* because when he broke cover the Messerschmitt was waiting for him, 400 yards away on the starboard quarter fine. Still underestimating the quality of the opposition, the German made a third attack and paid the penalty. At 200 yards he stopped firing and the Messerschmitt fell away to disappear into the cloud as a ball of fire, followed seconds later by a red explosion.

Sgt Bremner was justifiably aggrieved to find that the conditions were impossible. The cloud between the bombers and Hamburg was like an impregnable wall, and at 53°29N 09°19E, south-west of Hamburg, the Sergeant's Lancaster was struck by lightning. There was a blinding flash, followed by complete darkness until the eyes recovered from the shock of being exposed to intense light without warning. The aircraft shuddered as if cuffed by a gigantic hand, and the port inner and starboard outer engines cut. When the pilot's co-ordination returned he feathered the props and hastily assessed the damage. Not liking what he found, he jettisoned the bombs and turned for the coast. The gentle nursing of the Lancaster to maintain height, combined with the strain of keeping the aircraft on course, demanded complete concentration, and the innumerable detours to avoid cloud called for calmness and patience. Finally, Bremner had to shrug off a great weight of tiredness of mind and body to make a safe landing on two engines after being airborne for 6 hours 46 minutes, two hours longer than anticipated. "Pure hell" was a fair assessment.

F/Sgt F. Lawrence of 460 Squadron certainly had a night to remember. Just after

12. When the fighters came closer Davidson identified one as an Me110.

settling on course for the run-up to the target the starboard inner cut, followed by the port inner. It was the Flight Sergeant's last trip of his tour and, having successfully fought his way through the first wall of cloud, he was keen to drop his bombs on Hamburg. When the port outer cut also and the Lancaster began to lose height the prospects began to look bleak, but the track through the target was as direct as any other so he pressed on and dropped his bombs on the port. Once clear of the target and the storm clouds the engines picked up one by one, and Lawrence was able to complete the sortie and his tour without mishap.

The 427 Squadron historian may not have realised he was writing for posterity but he certainly made his narrative colourful, although on July 29 his report is not entirely clear.[13] "We didn't lose any kites but the boch [*sic*] suffered one down and one probable, after having attacked P/O G.P.C. Vandekerckove and crew. Sgt [J.J.] McLean the rear gunner deserves credit for the feat, as Jerry's nightfighter boys are generally not so dumb. On being credited with a probable Sgt [W.A.] Williamson the navigator declared 'Jeez, they never give you anything in this outfit'. McLean replied 'OK Willie, I'll get you another one next time.' "[14] Fortunately, McLean was not called upon to make good his boast because Vandekerckove had plenty to worry about on the 2nd–3rd without having to take evasive action. He bombed the target on ETA and shortly afterwards his Halifax began to lose height. In spite of all Vandekerckove's efforts the altimeter continued to turn anti-clockwise, so while they were still over land and could bale out safely he explained the options to the crew. To quote the squadron historian again: "P/O Vandekerckove and his crew had a 'shaky do' and credit should go to Van for the way he handled his machine. The constant-speed unit on his starboard outer went U/S and on top of that he had heavy icing. Owing to the drag on the starboard side the machine became very hard to control and it came down to 4,000 feet over the Kiel canal. After having a conference the crew without any exception decided to stay with the ship and try to get her home, which after a hard struggle they did. . . ."

No 44 Squadron had an amazing 10 days, experiencing no combats and no serious damage to any of their aircraft. Even on the 2nd–3rd they had only two early returns, one of the best records of the night. In complete contrast, the crews of 467 Squadron seemed to have met with trouble every night and this one was no exception. P/O D. Symonds, with the enemy coast well behind him, could hardly be blamed for thinking that his only battle now was with the elements. Not that the outlook was rosy, since he was hemmed in by cumulo-nimbus. Suddenly *Monica* gave out a warning and turrets began rotating. Eyes searched the sky and as the pips quickened Sgt E.A.B. Sanford, the mid-upper gunner, looked down and saw a Ju88 on the port quarter climbing to attack. He immediately ordered a diving turn to port but the fighter pilot had already opened up at 400 yards and cannon shells were winging their way towards the Lancaster. The Junkers closed to 200 yards, firing all the time, but when Sanford returned his fire the enemy did a tight turn and climbed away to port and into the protection of the nearby cloud. In the flurry and excitement Sanford could not remember whether there was any firing from the rear turret, but in fact Sgt B.N. Pratt, the rear gunner, had been killed during the action. The Lancaster's rudder and

13. There is no combat report.
14. ORB (PRO AIR 27/1845).

starboard outer were hit, but Symonds was equal to the occasion and landed safely at base, Bottesford.

P/O K.A. McIver found himself surrounded by cloud and was reluctant to go through for fear of icing, so he jettisoned two canisters of IBs in the hope that the Lancaster would then climb over the top. It was a vain hope, and the crew were buffeted around as the aircraft was caught first in the strong updraught and then fell away as it got into the downdraught. McIver had battled his way to within 30 miles of the target when the port inner failed. The bombs were jettisoned and he turned for base and patiently threaded his way through the cloud. He also made an excellent landing.

408 Squadron had had an easy ride until the 2nd–3rd. Their crews had slipped in and out of Hamburg without being intercepted and flak damage was minimal, and that included the sorties to the Ruhr. The weather proved to be their worst enemy; 12 crews bombed in the vicinity of Hamburg and there were 4 early returns. While still over the North Sea Sgt M.R. Humphreys' Halifax was struck by lightning and all four engines cut. The bomber fell 5,000 feet before they started again and it was a full 20 minutes before the instruments began to function normally. Having survived that ordeal Humphreys felt somewhat vindictive towards the people who had made the war necessary, so he pressed on to Hamburg. The elements had the last word, however. Just before the target the Halifax iced up and was losing height at the rate of 400 feet per minute, so Humphreys jettisoned his bombs. The same bank of cloud (south of Hamburg) caused Sgt J.D. Harvey to lose control of his Halifax due to icing. The artificial horizon then became unserviceable, followed by the intercom, so the bombs were jettisoned and the sortie was abandoned. The bomber went into an uncontrollable spin and Harvey ordered the crew to abandon aircraft. At 12,000 feet he regained control and rescinded the order, but not before Sgt R. Shire, the Wop, had baled out.

Sgt S.G. Hall was one of the few captains from 207 Squadron who was able to vent some spleen on the enemy, although it was his gunners, Sgts F. Martin and H.J. Bird, who actually had the pleasure of firing the guns and scoring hits on the Fw190 which attacked them. Hall was to the west of Hamburg when the Focke-Wulf appeared on the starboard quarter down, clearly silhouetted against a large bank of cloud. Both gunners opened fire but the fighter came in with guns blazing, closing from 800 to 250 yards before breaking away. Hall made a diving turn to starboard and repeated the manoeuvre when the fighter made a second attack from the same quarter. Again the British gunners opened the firing, and although the enemy braved the hail of lead he was forced to break away at 300 yards with smoke pouring from the starboard wing.

In general, on August 2–3 the German fighters seemed reluctant to engage any bomber showing belligerence. S/Ldr L.H. Eno was at 54°30N 08°00E, homeward bound, when P/O R.W. Lorenzo warned his captain that a Ju88, some 500 yards on the port quarter, was showing some interest in their Halifax. Eno began to corkscrew and Lorenzo fired a short burst in the direction of the Junkers, which immediately moved over to the starboard quarter and closed to 400 yards. A second burst from the rear gunner proved sufficient deterrent, and the enemy aircraft turned away without firing and disappeared into the night. An Me109 intercepted Sgt S.A. Durrant and twice made a pass at his Halifax but kept out of range of his guns. Once again the German flew away without opening fire. Sgt A. Lowe of 90 Squadron was just beginning his run-up to the target when his rear gunner, Sgt C. Sharpe, saw a single-engined fighter

600 yards astern making a climbing attack. A one-second burst from his four 0.303s was sufficient discouragement for the fighter pilot, who broke away without firing.

Although intruders were not regularly operating over England in August 1943, gunners needed to be on the alert for fighters from take-off to touch-down, and as the bomber approached Germany the search became more intense. The enemy coast was a common place for interceptions, so although billowing clouds and electrical storms made it an unsuitable arena, Sgt G. Edy was not too surprised when Sgt E. McDonald, the rear gunner, warned him that there was a twin-engined fighter on the port quarter up. In spite of the fact that the fighter was going away from the bomber, McDonald opened fire. Five minutes later the rear gunner saw a twin-engined fighter, possibly an Me210, flying at right angles to the Lancaster from port to starboard astern. Once again McDonald opened fire and the fighter dived out of range.

It would appear to be poetic justice for one of 5 Group's aircraft to be a victim of "shoot first and say sorry later". F/O A.F. Poore of 106 Squadron was flying along happily when suddenly he saw red tracer in front of the nose of his Lancaster and one shell tore a large hole in the wing. He dived to starboard immediately and Sgts R. Castleman and W.F. Tookey, his gunners, searched the sky and saw a Wellington cross over above the Lancaster. No one actually saw the Wellington fire but neither of the bombers was subsequently attacked by a fighter.

Sgt A.P. Strange was north of Hamburg, homeward bound after dropping his bombs, when P/O J.A. Stephens, the rear gunner, drew his attention to air-to-air firing on the starboard beam. The firing stopped and then Stephens and Sgt E.F. Johnson, his mid-upper gunner, saw an orange light diving towards their Lancaster. They both opened fire and Strange made a diving turn to starboard and into the protection of nearby cloud. The gunners expended some 2,000 rounds, and the fighter broke off the attack without firing and was not seen again.

The third crew to be intercepted by two fighters was captained by F/Sgt H.L. Pattison of 428 Squadron. At 0146 hours, shortly before reaching the target, the rear gunner, Sgt G.A. Bassett, saw two Me109s, one on the starboard quarter above, the other on the port quarter below at 600 yards range. *Monica* was set to operate at 600 yards, so Bassett's estimated range was almost perfect, because *Monica* almost immediately began to give out her warning. The fighter on the starboard quarter had a light in the nose and Bassett rightly assumed it to be the decoy. The rear gunner swung his turret into line with the Messerschmitt on the port quarter and opened fire as it closed in to attack. Pattison made a diving turn to port and the tracer from the enemy's guns went harmlessly by, well to starboard. The fighters were apparently unable to follow the combat manoeuvre, because they were lost to view. Shortly after they had bombed the target *Monica* again gave out a warning and Basset saw a Ju88 dead astern. He advised a corkscrew as the combat manoeuvre, and when the Junkers closed to 400 yards the rear gunner opened fire, forcing the fighter to break away without firing. The combat manoeuvre took the Halifax into cloud and the Junkers was not seen again. Basset believed that he had hit the Me109 during the first encounter but he was not certain enough to claim to have damaged it.

The "Y" Service report was interesting for several reasons. The southerly route to the target should have aroused interest in the controlled night fighter zones but this did not apparently materialise, and only three patrols lasting for more than 20 minutes were heard. This lack of R/T information may have been due to the switch to VHF compelled by the use of *Tinsel*. Patrols were heard in seven areas but there were no *Sieg Heil* claims, although ORS did credit the fighters with 11 of the 30 losses; one unsuccessful attack was recorded. Stade airfield was sending out information of a general nature, giving the height and position of the approaching bombers, but no call signs were used. This may have been because its own fighters were grounded due to weather conditions. The frequent repetition of the messages was a new feature, strengthening the belief that they were not being piped to a particular group of fighters.

A total of 49 interceptions were reported, 7 in the target area, the remainder divided equally between the outward and homeward routes. All combats were serious affairs to the participants, but usually it was possible to sense that one side was in control or had the advantage. In Elder's combat on July 27–28 the fighters were certainly in the driving seat. By their evasive action Lofthouse and Shannon showed that skill was on occasions sufficient to thwart the enemy. Thornhill and Robbins were too good for the opposition, as indeed was Parker's gunner Wharton, and in these cases the combatants were not evenly matched. F/O J.C. Jenkins' combat was a dour life and death struggle which was not settled until Jenkins and his crew escaped unhurt from their crashed Halifax at Melbourne. Jenkins had crossed the enemy coast north-west of Cuxhaven and was weighing up the chances of being able to bomb the target effectively. 3,000 feet below was a solid mass of cloud with an occasional peak towering way above. If the glow of the fires was any criterion, any of a dozen places could be Hamburg. At 0153 hours there were no TIs burning to sway his choice. The absence of searchlights was easily explained – they could not have pierced the cloud – but why was there no flak? Almost as if she was mind-reading, *Monica* sounded a warning and the unspoken questions were thrust to the back of his mind. Sgt R.N. Hurst, knowing the defence was solely in his hands,[15] feverishly searched the sky for anything moving. Fine on the port quarter 500 yards away and slightly below the Halifax a small black object was closing fast. *Monica* was getting hysterical and could not be appeased. Hurst ordered a dive to port and Jenkins jettisoned the bombs and went into the combat manoeuvre immediately. Unscrambling Hurst's voice from the noise of gunfire, Jenkins gathered that the fighter was a Ju88. The enemy opened fire with cannon at 400 yards and had closed to 300 yards before the rear turret had time to rotate into line. Hurst replied with a long burst and saw his tracer hit the Junkers, but the German pilot too had the satisfaction of knowing his shots were striking home. He broke away below and again the frantic search was on. A climbing attack was sound tactics, since the mid-upper was unsighted and the fighter pilot had a clear shot at the petrol tanks and engines; the bomber also presented a larger target from this aspect. Thirty seconds is an eternity in stress conditions. *Monica* was the only one to break the awful silence, and the crew would gladly have thrown her overboard during those tense moments (though when thoughts were rational her value was universally acknowledged). The Junkers reappeared in almost the same position astern, except this time on the starboard quarter fine. Once again the enemy opened fire at 400 yards and shots were exchanged. Hurst had a feeling of exhilaration when he saw that the Junkers was afire in both wings inboard of the engines, yet the enemy came in relentlessly as if realising that he had only seconds left in which to cripple the bomber. Hurst poured more lead into the Junkers, which burst into

15. The mid-upper was dispensing *Window*.

flames and spiralled slowly down into cloud. If the German pilot had to die, a Viking's funeral was a fitting end for a brave warrior. He had left his mark on the bomber, however, and the damage was extensive: both elevators were shot away, the port wheel was punctured, cannon shells had torn holes in both wings and the port bomb door was damaged. There were also two large holes in the nose, the rudder was riddled with bullet holes and there were numerous machine-gun bullet holes in the fuselage. Fortunately none of the crew was injured, and all survived the crash landing at base. Both pilot and gunner were given immediate awards, the officer a DFC and the sergeant a DFM.

So many bombs fell in and round the villages surrounding Hamburg that the inhabitants believed the British were trying to bomb the refugees. The authorities gave no credence to such rumours, realising that the bombs were unaimed. The official German summary of the night's raid ran: "In the night of 3 August 300 enemy aircraft made a heavy attack on Hamburg." Most of the survivors consider this attack the most frightening. The mixture of thunder and lightning, bombs falling everywhere, the sound of gunfire echoing from the cloud and the lack of any pattern in the bombing created intolerable uncertainty. Nerves, strained to the limit by the previous raids, were ill equipped to deal with here a flash from an exploding bomb, there a flash of lightning, and seconds later the roles reversed. The thunderstorm itself was so severe that it would have frightened the timorous, but mixed with bombs it was horrendous. The fires were chiefly in the port area, and here again the thunder and lightning helped the attackers. The Fire Service and ARP could hear the bombers but the sound was diffused by the cloud so that it was impossible to tell when they were overhead. The raid seemed to last an eternity but eventually the All-clear sounded and shortly afterwards the thunderstorm too moved further inland, leaving Hamburg in peace to bury its dead.

The talk in Hamburg was that the British would make one more raid and that it would be on Harburg. As the nights passed there was obvious relief but also some bewilderment. When interviewed Harris said that the number of attacks was not predetermined, the aim being simply to cripple the port. Why then, when the raid of August 2–3 was so poor, was the port not attacked again in force for almost a year? Impatience on the part of the C-in-C seems to be the answer. The whole operation had taken too long. First the weather had held up the initial attack for two days, then the smoke over the city on July 25 had necessitated a switch to Essen. After the second attack came another enforced wait. The raid on July 29–30 almost finished the job, but then smoke, haze and the weather took a hand. The success at Remscheid partly eased Harris's burning impatience, but by Monday August 2, after another two days of inactivity, it must have seemed a case of now or never. The law of diminishing returns had begun to operate in Hamburg, and there were many towns within range which could profitably be destroyed before the nights were long enough to send his force to Berlin. The German capital was the big one, and if it could be destroyed the war would be won. After four days of enforced stand-down because of the weather and two visits to the local, anyone recounting his ordeal of the 2nd–3rd was scoffed at for line-shooting. Harris's men were all set to prove to the Italians that General Eisenhower's threat was no idle boast; the General had warned that if they did not accept President Roosevelt's peace terms their towns would be demolished from the air.

# Chapter X

# The Aftermath

THE effects of the raids on the people of Hamburg lasted for months. The city was without water, gas or electricity, and public transport was at a standstill. Food was in short supply and a state of emergency did little to alleviate the situation. The allocation afforded a bare subsistence, and perhaps only because 43% of the population was missing was it possible to maintain an above-starvation level. "Life continued with ruthless harshness, and where decency, morality and convention had survived the horrors of war, they now broke down under the pressure of hunger and cold."[1]

To try to get some order out of chaos the town was divided into three zones:

The Dead Zone, the area of total devastation, which was off-limits to everyone except those with special passes.

The Evacuated Zone, where all the public utilities were destroyed. Members of the public were allowed into this area but they had to obtain a special permit.

The Live Zone, partially destroyed areas where every effort was made to make life bearable. Bomb damage repair work was initially concentrated in this zone.

From a total of 122,323 houses one third were completely destroyed (35,719) or damaged beyond repair (4,695).[2] Most of Hamburg's population lived in large blocks of flats situated chiefly to the east of the Alster. Before the attacks there were 450,000 such residences; 253,400 (56%) of them were completely destroyed. In retrospect that 43% once again must have been a blessing in disguise, but the situation in general was so appalling that the city officials, who were besieged from all sides, would never have believed that they could have been worse.

The restoration of the water supply was obviously of the greatest priority and with little or no sanitation and hot weather, conditions were ideal for outbreaks of typhus and cholera. Limited drinking water was available from water carts which toured the inhabited areas, but there was no tap water. The chief pumping works at Rothenburgsort was hit during the raid of the 27–28th and two reservoirs were damaged the same night. The works at Billbrook, Billwerder, Curslack and even as far away as Cuxhaven were all affected. Even had they escaped damage the situation would have been little better, for there were 847 breaks in the mains and the special saws for cutting pipes were in very limited supply. It was also essential to isolate the devastated areas in order to eliminate waste and increase pressure. Munition factories had first prority in all the public services, but much of the effort was wasted. It was rather like a prisoner serving concurrent sentences: it mattered little whether the essential services were working or not, since there was no labour.

1. Werner-Silescu, *Hamburg: Phoenix aus der Asche*.
2. Brunswig, *Feuersturm über Hamburg*. These figures do not include dwellings in Harburg.

After three weeks some areas were reconnected to the mains but the pressure was so low that water was available only at ground level. Between 8 p.m. and 10 p.m. each evening the pressure head was raised to 10 metres, which was totally inadequate for the flat dwellers. It was impossible to maintain the pressure for a longer period because, due to the many yet unrepaired breaks, 47% of the supply was lost. To use water for central heating was illegal until mid-September, but by November most of the repairs were completed.

The rise and decline in the domestic use of gas had no connection with *Gomorrah* – the big change from gas to electricity took place after the war – and in 1939 a large number of the poorer homes did not use electricity even for lighting. Although many of the gasworks were hit – the Altona works on July 24–25, Grasbrook, Bahrenfeld (which was gutted), Tiefstack and Wandsbek on the 27–28th, and Barmbek on the 29th – gas was available again in a short space of time. Because of its lethal properties isolation measures were already built in, and so repairs could be carried out selectively. Hamburg had a two-tier gas supply: high-pressure for industry, low-pressure for household use. This proved to be an advantage because the high-pressure pipes, which had to be repaired first, were under the roads, and they had to be cleared of rubble to get the traffic flowing. The low-pressure pipes were under the pavements and work did not begin on them until later.

Tiefstack was very quickly working again and, together with Bergedorf, which was undamaged, was able to supply the armament industry with enough for its needs. "Get it working somehow" seems to have been the maxim, and taking sound parts from damaged machinery became the accepted formula. At Barmbek and Wandsbek the plant was not badly damaged and "borrowing" enabled both works to get back into production. After the raids gas-holders were thin on the ground; they were highly vulnerable and tended to explode when hit. However, the large one (105 metres) at Tiefstack survived a glancing blow from a cookie which dented one side and also bent the framework. It is remarkable that it did not explode, since there were more than 800 shrapnel holes in the storage tank itself. These had all to be welded and other damaged gasholders were cannibalised to get the main one operative.

At first glance it would appear that electricity would have led the field in the services recovery. With the NWK grid system in operation the city should have been able to obtain help from stations outside Hamburg itself, but that was not the case, since damage to the switching stations limited its use. The Neuhof works south of the river – the Americans' prize – was the worst hit of the stations. One of the four direct hits it received destroyed the boiler house and all circuits were rendered unusable. It was three weeks before it was repaired. Tiefstack was working after three and a half days but Barmbek took three months to repair. The shortage of cable to replace that damaged by the bombing and the excessive heat was one of the main causes of the hold-up, but three of the five main transformer stations (Gasstrasse, Barmbek and Karolinenstrasse) also had to be repaired before significant progress could be made. There were 13 other large transformer stations in Hamburg and many received varying degrees of damage. There is no record of how many of the 711 street transformers or the 696 private ones[3] were hit but, taking into account the extensive devastation, it must be counted in hundreds. By

3. Chiefly in factories.

mid-August, 30.4% of the pre-raid electricity supply was available, though it was being consumed chiefly by industry. A fortnight later this had increased to 72.7%, which was probably almost all that was required because after that progress was very slow and output did not get back to its original level until February 1944.

There was no refuse collection for weeks and this gave the swarms of bluebottles, already breeding freely in the Dead Zone, extra places in which to multiply.

If news of the *Katastrophe* had been kept from the rest of Germany, news filtering into the city was similarly restricted. Many of the inhabitants thought that the Russians must have overrun the Reich and that they had been bombed so ruthlessly because they represented a pocket of resistance. There were those in Britain who thought at the time – as some still do today – that this was a good place and a propitious time to open the Second Front. Certainly the area had been softened up and there would have been very little immediate opposition, but even if the resources had been available, the long lines of communication would have made the expedition precarious in the extreme.

Gradually, as conditions began to improve, the people found other things to talk about, but few were ready for the black humorists who surface in any adversity and, with a finger tap to the head, they were dismissed as having "roof damage". The little shops which had escaped the bombing became small emporia as they let space to the less fortunate ones. So the butcher, the baker and the candlestick maker could all be found plying their trade and selling their wares under the same roof. The newspaper *Die Hamburger Fremdenblatt* was on the streets again by August 18, featuring watered-down propaganda accounts which made light of the disaster and bragged about all that was being done to alleviate the plight of the populace.

The fires had been extinguished by the night of August 4 but the smouldering coal and coke required constant watching because, given the slightest opportunity, it burst into flames again.[4] After several nights without an air raid, and as each area became free of fire, the people who had been living a troglodyte existence in the shelters gradually drifted back home, if they still had one, or badgered the authorities to find them accommodation. They were daily augmented by people returning to the stricken city. Although the Police President said that because food and shelter were scarce only workers would be allowed back, women and children defied the ban, much to the embarrassment of the overworked authorities (**Fig 11**). If the issue of ration cards is any criterion, more than 200,000 people had returned by the end of the year. However, the supply of accommodation could not keep pace with demand, and there were still 80,000 unfilled requests on the books.

Limited public transport was resumed after a time as the roads were gradually cleared and repairs to the railways completed. Some 25% of the U-Bahn rolling stock had been destroyed, lines needed repairing, tunnels had to be cleared and three viaducts needed urgent attention. Many stations were damaged, and Schlump, one of the main junctions, had been completely destroyed. A burnt-out train standing on a bridge over the Billhafen still had not been moved ten days after the last raid. Hammerbrook, Rothenburgsort and south Hamm, all parts of the Dead Zone, remained closed to all public traffic and were railed off. The public was told that the whole of eastern Hamburg had, for the time being, ceased to function as a residential

4. A slagheap in Essen, set on fire during an RAF raid, smouldered for four years.

# HAMBURG—THE GOMORRAH ATTACKS

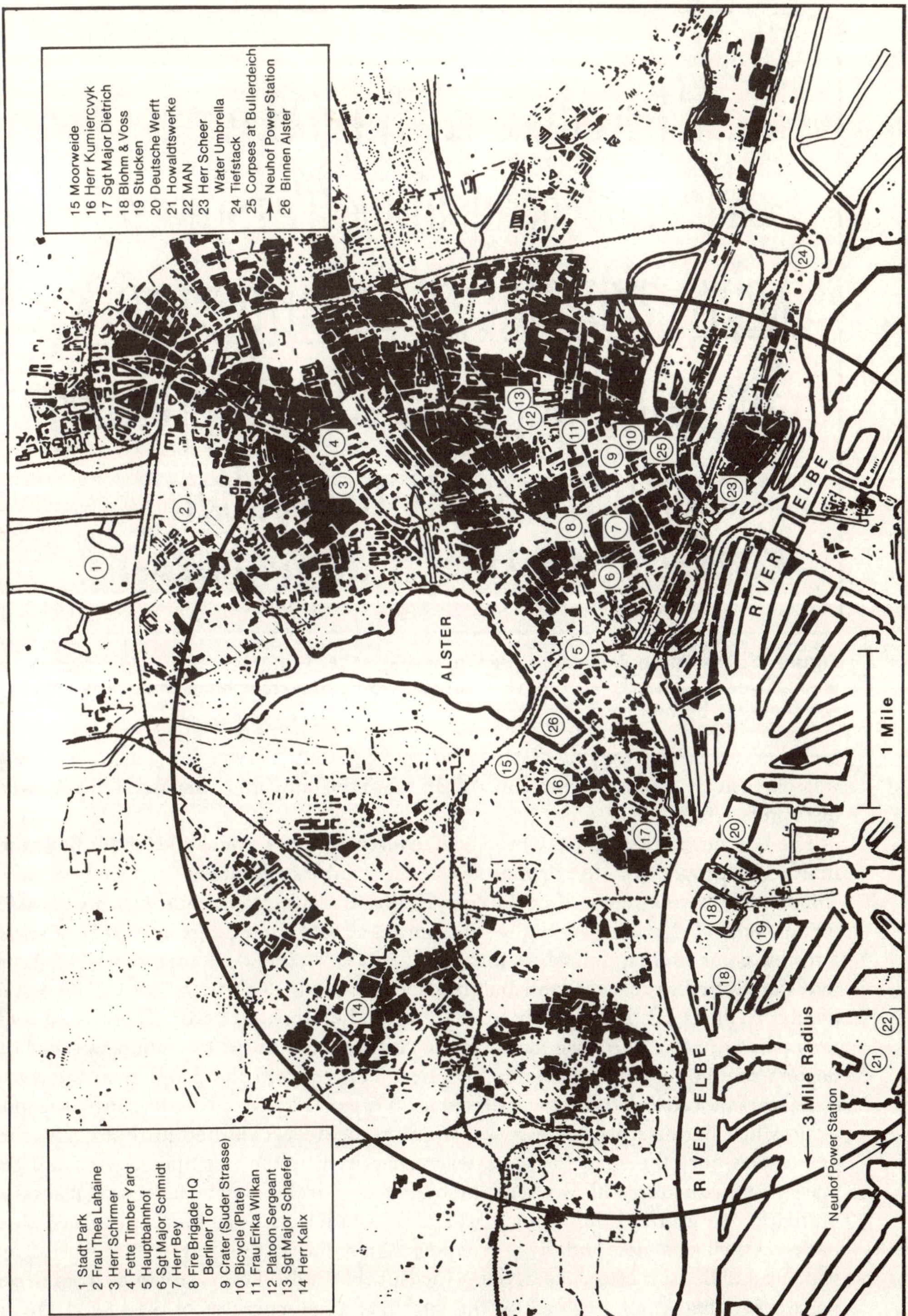

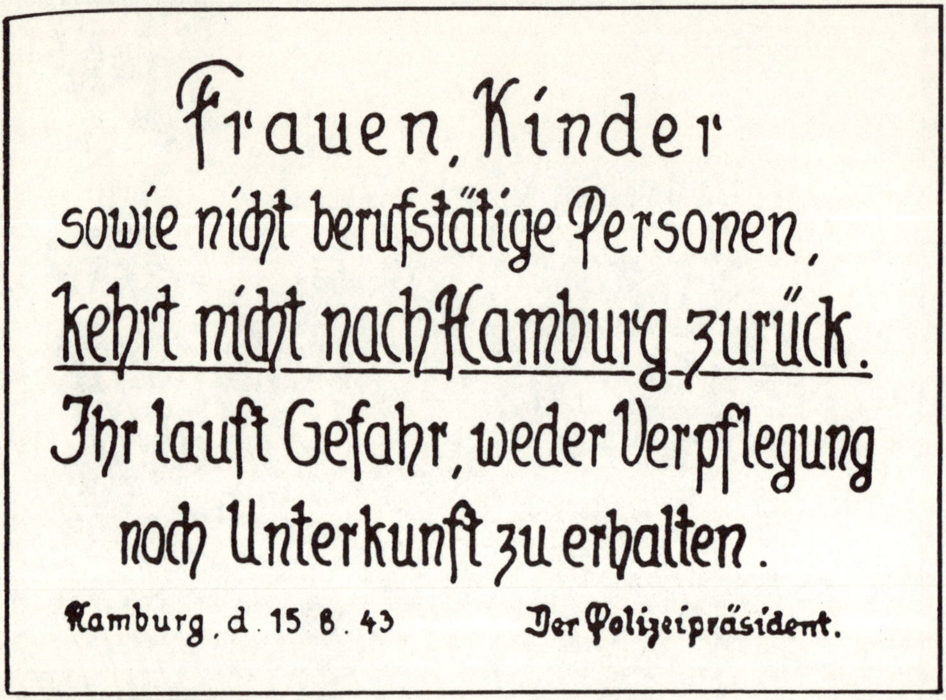


**Figure 11:** The Police President's warning of August 15, 1943: "Women, children, as well as unemployed persons, do not return to Hamburg. You run into danger and there is neither food nor shelter to be had."

area. Services to the outlying districts did not begin until November. The *Hauptbahnhof* was extensively damaged and for a time all main lines from the stricken city were disrupted.

The Rescue and Repair Service, who had already been responsible for guiding more than 6,000 people from the fires and rescuing countless numbers from shelters, were still faced with a mountain of work. With 170 miles of streets to clear they were thankful for any help. Hitler believed in towns helping each other and gangs from as far away as Dresden came to their aid. More than 7,000 houses had to be demolished. The Army too was drafted in to help, and bomb disposal squads dealt with 399 UXBs or DA bombs. In the Dead Zone an estimated 31,000 bodies were recovered. "Estimated" was the operative word, because many of the corpses were burnt to cinders, so that the doctors could only give approximations like "between 200 and 300." That was gruesome work indeed and the hot weather made it essential to get the bodies buried as soon as possible. Because prisoners of war and internees were drafted in to dig the mass graves and bury the dead the work was supervised by the Gestapo. Gloves and gas masks were issued to both workers and overseers, but the stench was so awful and the mutilation so frightful that nausea was almost universal. The Gestapo turned their backs on their prisoners and the horrendous sights; they overindulged their permission to drink and became intoxicated. Some measure of conditions in the camps from which the workers had come is given by the fact that some members of the burial squads actually changed clothes with the dead in order to effect an escape.

No one envied the task of the doctors, who were expected to perform post mortems. Hyperthermia was the most common cause of death on the streets, where people, literally blinded by the blizzard of flying sparks, had stumbled and fallen down, never to rise again. Others, overcome by the heat, had sat down apathetically and perished. There were many instances in which the cause of death was unknown, and puzzling cases of burned corpses lying next to naked ones showing no signs of burns. Others were fully clad, with mouths wide open as they vainly sought for oxygen.

The systematic opening of the shelters could not begin until the middle of August. Even then the interiors were so hot that on numerous occasions when the cellars were opened the inrushing oxygen burst into flames, and the Fire Service had to be standing by. Here suffocation, chiefly through carbon monoxide poisoning, was the main cause of death, but hyperthermia also took its toll. One account tells of cellar floors being covered with fat melted from the victims' bodies.

Even when "just staying alive" had become a thing of the past, all around there was the constant reminder of those terrible ten days. No rebuilding was undertaken before the end of the war, and only unsafe property was demolished or torn down. Ruins dominated the appearance of the city and it was impossible to remain on the streets for any length of time without meeting one of the 37,439 injured, many of whom had lost an arm or a leg, or carried an ugly scar where they had been burned.

An official figure of 31,647 deaths was given on November 30, and of these only 15,802 had been identified: 6,072 men (38.4%) 7,995 women (50.6%) and 1,735 children (11%). The number of dead was officially updated to 41,800 but even this was obviously incorrect, since in many of the cellars a pile of ashes or charred bones was the only evidence that people had been trapped. Again, after the war, when bulldozers levelled the sites before rebuilding began, they unearthed the legs and arms of people whose bodies had been buried under the piles of rubble and had not been found.

"Hamburg was last burnt down in 1842. Had weather conditions at the end of May 1942 been different it would have been a target for the 1,000 bomber attack launched against Cologne on May 30–31. In fact, the centenary conflagration was postponed for a year – but when it was finally celebrated in 1943, it was on a much larger scale than would have been within the scope of Bomber Command in the previous year."[5] Perhaps the Allied air forces took too much credit for the devastation of Hamburg. The weather certainly played its part and undoubtedly was the extra factor that distinguished Hamburg from towns like Hanover, which was later subjected to several raids in a short space of time. Berlin too was attacked as regularly as feasible during the winter, but its size and distance from England saved it from the same degree of destruction.[6] In Hamburg it was not only the weight of bombs but also the concentration that caused the intense heat which set the holocaust in motion. There were two principal differences between the *Katastrophe* and the 29-30th: the firestorm of the *Katastrophe* was atmospheric, and the fires of the 29-30th were more widespread. In Barmbek, the focal point of the 29–30th attack, the destruction was comparable but the heat was being generated over a wider area, the funnel was wider and so not so powerful, and the updraught developed more slowly too. The damage in each of the July attacks was devastating and

5. Bomber Command Quarterly Review.
6. Larger petrol loads meant smaller bomb loads.

blocks of offices were gutted. In addition to its commerce the city had many important factories; few of them escaped damage and many were completely destroyed. It was estimated that Hamburg had 81,000 businesses – shops, stores, banks, commercial establishments, coal and oil depots, warehouses storing foodstuffs and raw materials, chemical and light metal works, and cold storage plants – and almost 40,000 of them were destroyed or severely damaged. The town hall, the law courts and the police headquarters were among the 76 public office buildings rendered uninhabitable. Eighty military installations spread across the town, including the Marienthal, Hindenburg, Lüneburg and Rendsburg barracks, suffered varying degrees of damage from IBs and HE. The gun batteries at Hamm and on the Alster, together with the searchlight battery on Karstadt, were destroyed. In such widespread devastation it was inevitable that schools, churches and hosptials were hit too.

These raids caused the first serious damage in the harbour area, and the port was at a standstill. Some 20% of the harbour installations were destroyed, chiefly in the northern sector, where the quays were extensively cratered and unloading equipment was unserviceable. There were over 750 cranes in the port area, and of these 122 were completely destroyed and more than 250 inoperable. However, absenteeism would have closed the docks in any event. Apart from the large numbers of vessels sunk in the harbour there were others, seriously damaged or burnt out, which were grounded. Sunken barges blocked the canals and, in addition, many of the lock gates had been hit.

Hamburg was (and is) one of the largest *entrepôt* ports of the world, and although much of its international trade was disrupted by the war it was Germany's largest port by far and its extensive dockside warehouses and transport facilities made it a vital sea link. ORS estimated that nearly 500 dockside and railway warehouses were destroyed or damaged. This would seem to have been a conservative claim. An acre of warehouses in Altona was flattened; warehouses and customs sheds in Altstadt were demolished; the warehouses in Hochwasser Bassin, St Georg, were gutted; in Borgfelde 11 acres of miscellaneous warehouses were destroyed by fire; at Baaken Hafen every building was burnt out on one quay stretching for a mile, and another nearby, two-thirds of a mile long, was also gutted. Thousands of tons of food and raw materials went up in flames.

A port's efficiency depends largely on transportation, and before the port could be reopened the many hits on the riverside roads and railways had to be made good. The marshalling yards at Rothenburgsort and the Hanover (Hamburg) goods station suffered severely and both had to be repaired before any volume of transhipment could be undertaken; Rothenburgsort usually handled more than 3,000 wagons a day. Three other dock sidings had lines up, and large quantities of rolling stock were destroyed or derailed. After the war Hamburg officials said that the disruption of transportation did more damage to production figures than any local bombing in the port area.[7]

When the port was reopened on September 7 it was not "business as usual during repairs". There was a lack of manpower, especially skilled workers, and using damaged equipment involved personal risk; the result was a reduction in efficiency of 20–30%.

---

7. In 1943 the Germans dispersed their factories to areas where they were less vulnerable to air attack. When in late 1944 and 1945 the Allied air forces concentrated on disrupting transport, it was not so much the lack of parts but the inability to get them to the assembly points which caused the chaos. The controller at Hamm marshalling yards in the Ruhr said that the bombers kept a better schedule than any of his trains.

Yet because of the decrease in the volume of trade due to the war the port quickly returned to normal.

It would serve no purpose to dwell too long on the sufferings of the inhabitants or to gloat on the success of the raids, but the two following accounts may serve to illustrate the nature of the enemy at whom they were directed.

Each factory was required to keep a record of the damage caused by air attacks and to assess the cost of repairs. Hitler intended to collect the money from the Allies after he had won the war. The figure would have been astronomical; the estimate of the damage at only 121 plants in Hamburg amounted to RM613,993,570 (£49,817,922).

The raids had a unifying influence on the defensive Commanders. After July 28 Hermann Goering instructed Erhard Milch, chief of aircraft production, to concentrate on defensive production. New airborne radar sets like SN2 and *Naxos*, which were immune to jamming by *Window*, were given the highest priority. When the plight of Hamburg was brought up at a meeting in Hitler's HQ the urgent need to strengthen the defences, particularly the Luftwaffe, against day and night bombers was being stressed in the strongest terms when Hitler cut in and shouted , "Rubbish!" He thumped the table to emphasise each word. "Terror can only be broken by terror! Everything else is rubbish!" Hitler was like a gambler who, having nearly broken the bank, suddenly begins to lose. He just cannot believe that the system which has brought him early success can possibly be wrong, and is convinced that he is just suffering a streak of bad luck. He refuses to realise that it could have been a poor system and that good luck had brought about success. In an attempt to make Hitler see the seriousness of the situation his Commanders tried to persuade him to go and see Hamburg for himself. His refusal was a wise decision even though it may have been for the wrong reasons: had he gone to Hamburg he would then have had to go to the Ruhr, Mannheim, Hanover and Schweinfurt, in fact all of the towns devastated by the Allied air forces.

Perhaps the most satisfying result of the raids from the Allied point of view was the dramatic effect they had on the production of submarines. Before the war more than 30,000 men – 1.8% of the city's whole workforce – were employed in Hamburg's shipbuilding yards. At the outbreak of war the naval craft which were being built were completed on high priority. Blohm & Voss, builders of the *Bismarck*, were the largest firm. Of the non-military vessels only those nearing completion were finished, the remainder being launched and the hulls laid up. It was originally intended to use the yards to build destroyers but the scheme was dropped in favour of a large submarine programme. The smaller firms built minesweepers and corvettes and undertook repair work, while Blohm & Voss, Deutsche Werft, Howaldtswerke and Stulcken started building submarines. Apart from a few teething troubles the programme went according to plan until the *Gomorrah* attacks. There were a few "hiccoughs" after RAF raids in 1941 and 1942, when the port was bombed, but the output was maintained. Blohm & Voss alone had completed more than a hundred by the summer of 1943. Even so, in the spring of that year Germany was already losing submarines as fast as she could build them, and after the July raids production was always in arrears. By the end of 1943 there was a leeway of 29 and the backlog increased until the end of the war, when it was estimated to have been between 115 and 150. The attacks also caused delays in the introduction of new types, in particular the prefabricated submarine. An enormous effort was made to keep the production line going and many of the parts were made outside Hamburg and imported, until Blohm & Voss eventually became an assembly plant. 64,000 man-hours was the blueprint figure to build a submarine, but because of the disruption the actual time taken was in the region of 120,000 hours.

Some effort was made post-war to assess the amount of work lost due to raids, but unfortunately the surveys were carried out independently and biases were allowed to cloud the issue. The conclusions proved only something that was already an established fact: that statistics can be made to prove anything. Selective bombing undoutedly had its place in aerial bombardment but Hamburg was not the place to try to prove it. The loss of production in the first four weeks after the raids was due almost entirely to absenteeism, which was caused by area bombing, and 25% of the labour force never returned. Only the larger factories, which were already engaged in war work, were repaired. They did not suffer from the labour shortage because workers were co-opted from the smaller firms, many of which went out of business; even more had been completely destroyed.

The older craftsmen broke down under the strain of working long hours, living in uncomfortable lodgings and making long, slow and tedious journeys to work. Morale did improve in the absence of major attacks, when the men found that it was still possible to live and work in Hamburg. Yet the memory of those fatal days could not be erased, for when the raids started again a sense of hopelessness and increasing apathy became evident and the workers' efficiency fell off alarmingly. The USSBS said: "It is obvious that results of the heavy raids of 1943 were felt up to the moment of the final collapse in May 1945." The city was not attacked again in strength for almost 12 months, but production never again exceeded 89% of the pre-July level, and this figure includes munitions.

For Hamburg there was a long, hard road ahead, but, to paraphrase Herr Brunswig, at the beginning of September a miracle of nature occurred in the desolated areas. Trees and shrubs from which the leaves had been withered by the heat or torn off by the Firestorm winds began to bud and blossom. Between the piles of bricks and rubble and rusted iron railings and even in the wreckage of bombed-out cars young grass and flowers sprouted. Life goes on again. Hope is renewed.

# Appendix I

# Window

*WINDOW* was the code name for the metal strips — 25 × 5cm and tied into bundles of 2,000 weighing about 2lb each — which, when dropped from an aircraft, spread out after 20–30 seconds, each bundle producing a spurious blip similar to that made by an aircraft on the screens of radar equipment. The bundles floated slowly down to earth, and, when dropped in sufficient quantity by a number of aircraft, so flooded the screens that the individual blip made by an aircraft became indistinguishable. A team effort was necessary for success because immunity depended on the screen being completely swamped so that the movement of the aircraft's echo was unobserved. The rate of fall of *Window* was 200–300 feet per minute, and when dropped from height it caused jamming[1] lasting for 15–20 minutes. A concentration at 6,000 feet was the most efficacious.

The German defences relied on three types of radar equipment: *Würzburg*, *Freya* and *Lichtenstein*. The *Würzburg*s and *Freya*s were of two sizes, and each gave distance and bearing; the *Würzburg*s also gave the height. The *Lichtenstein*s were the eyes of the night fighters, but they were "short-sighted" and the range decreased rapidly when the prey was not directly ahead.

The large *Freya*s, situated along the entire length of the enemy coast from Norway to France, had a wide beam and so were able to pick up the British bombers soon after they left the English coast. Their purpose was to give an early warning of an attack and to ascertain the general direction of the force. At this stage most of the bombers were still climbing, so a means of calculating height would have been superfluous. In combination with the *Würzburgs* they enabled a ground controller with a radio-telephone to vector a night fighter towards a bomber until the fighter's crew were able to locate their prey, either visually or on their *Lichtenstein* airborne equipment.

*Window* was designed to jam the *Würzburgs* and, it was hoped, the *Lichtenstein*s. Another countermeasure, *Mandrel*, was used to jam the *Freya*s, while a third, *Tinsel*, jammed the radio-telephone communication.

The *Giant Würzburg* also worked in conjunction with the searchlights and flak batteries, the controllers giving advice on gunlaying. Its large radar screens were difficult to saturate and this is probably why the intensity of the flak was repeatedly reported by bomber crews to be "falling off" later in the raid as the concentration of *Window* built up.

The history of *Window*, like that of many of the aids and countermeasures, was fraught with argument. The idea was put forward but summarily dismissed as early as 1940 because of the danger of the enemy copying it and so putting British GCI out of action. In April 1942, after the German bombing had virtually ground to a halt, the

1. In truth it confused rather than jammed.

subject was raised again by the Chiefs of Staff, but still the defensive voice of Herbert Morrison, backed by Lord Cherwell, held sway. The Americans too were worried lest the enemy use it against them in an attack on the Panama Canal. So the German bombers, although numerically inferior, deprived Bomber Command of its use at this stage.

In October 1942 Air Scientific Intelligence said that it was certain the enemy knew of the *Window* principle. This was true: the Germans had carried out a parallel development, called *Düppel*, and Goebbels was so scared of its potential threat that he forbade any mention of it on pain of death. Consequently, General Wolfgang Martini dutifully locked it away in his safe, where it remained gathering dust. This assertion by the ASI paved the way for some experimental strips to be made and tried.

In November 1942 a further meeting was held. The change in personnel between this meeting and a later one in April 1943 amply illustrates the feelings of the parties involved. Fighter Command sent along their Chief whereas Bomber Command sent their Deputy, Air Marshal Sir Robert Saundby. He said that as *Monica* was to be tried operationally in the immediate future, *Window* provided no advantage en route to and from the target. With a force of 500 bombers over the target area at the same time there was enough confusion already, so he did not wish to press for *Window*.

By April the mood had changed. This time Harris went himself, whereas Fighter Command sent only a deputy. The meeting provided several shocks. The production of *Window* was insufficient to sustain protracted use in quantity. It would be eighteen months before the automatic *Window* launcher reached the squadrons. In the meantime, a crew member would have to undertake the task, which was a full-time job that had to be carried out during the period in the target area, when the aircraft was most vulnerable and when all the crew was already fully occupied. Finally, and even more bizarre, the stocks were of the wrong size.

May 1, 1943, was scheduled as "launching day," but there was further opposition because that date was proposed for the invasion of Sicily. Another meeting was called to select a later date and Herbert Morrison put in an appearance to make a last-ditch stand, saying that he considered this a subject worthy of War Cabinet debate. Fortunately, Churchill was there and, after Portal had pointed out that it was the summer of 1943, not the winter of 1940, he came to the rescue, saying that he thought the matter too technical for the War Cabinet. When the Prime Minister undertook personal responsibility for its introduction, Morrison's objection evaporated. July 23 was fixed as the new introduction date.

Morrison's objection was probably justified in the early days, because he was responsible for the safety of the people, and Harris himself later said that it would have been idiotic to drop metallic strips over Germany in 1940. In this he was almost certainly correct, because by the time Bomber Command had become a real force the Germans would assuredly have found some method of countering *Window*. In fact, the *Wild Boar* tactics were devised within a week of its introduction. Conversely, as Portal pointed out, the situation was entirely changed by 1943 and Morrison's objection was absurd. The lesser lights also tried to find fuel for the opposition. They claimed that it would affect H2S and so interfere with marking and navigation (35 Squadron was involved in disproving this argument). *Monica* too would be affected (other squadrons were detailed to counter this objection). By the spring of 1943 it was obvious to all but a few, who themselves were in no danger of ever being required to fly over Germany, that any aid to cut down losses was a godsend. The Battle of the Ruhr underlined this fact.

The effectiveness of *Window* was clearly demonstrated by the dramatic reduction in the loss and damage rate. **Figure 12** gives the details for each of the four Hamburg raids, and then compares the totals of the first eight raids on Germany subsequent to the introduction of *Window* with those suffered in the Battle of the Ruhr immediately before its use. The figures elicited the following scathing comment from Webster and Frankland: "Its sensational success is a grave verdict on the many decisions to defer its earlier introduction."[2] But is this indictment justified?

Curiously, the delay had its advantages. Perhaps the most significant was the way in which the Mosquitoes, newly introduced into Bomber Command, were able to exploit *Window* by carrying out spoof attacks. A few aircraft dropping *Window* were able to simulate a large attack, drawing the night fighters away from the Main Force. Other aircraft lacked the height, range and speed to do this with impunity.

In addition to *Mandrel* and *Tinsel* (mentioned above), *Grocer*, *ABC*, *Dartboard*, *Drumstick*, *Fidget* and *Carpet*[3] were introduced during the next twelve months and 100 Group was formed to organise and specialise in countermeasures. This could never have happened earlier; it was the result of a process of gradual evolution.

The new freelance methods forced on the German night fighters were to cause many problems and exact a heavy toll, but by the middle of 1944 the countermeasure operations had reached such a high degree of sophistication that, at a time when they could least afford it, the night fighters were using more petrol trying to find the bomber stream than in shooting the bombers down. *Window* was always an integral part of this life-and-death game of hide and seek. Although it was an ever-present threat to stragglers and crews off track, after July 23 GCI never again represented a deadly threat to Bomber Command.

**Figure 12: Bomber Command losses during Operation Gomorrah (% of force)**

| Date | Aircraft detailed | Missing | | Intercepted | Damaged | |
|---|---|---|---|---|---|---|
| | | Total | Known fighter attacks | | Flak | Fighters |
| July 24-25 | 791 | 1.8 | 0.9 | 6.2 | 2.4 | 0.3 |
| July 27-28 | 787 | 2.2 | 1.5 | 9.4 | 4.8 | 0.4 |
| July 29-30 | 782 | 3.6 | 2.0 | 10.0 | 3.2 | 0.5 |
| August 2-3 | 740 | 6.1* | 0.7 | 5.4 | 5.3 | 1.0 |
| Totals for Gomorrah plus Remscheid, Essen, Mannheim and Nuremburg (the four other big raids between July 24-25 and the end of August 1943) (i), compared with the Battle of the Ruhr (ii) | | | | | | |
| (i) | 5184 | 2.9 | 1.4 | 8.4 | 3.5 | 0.5 |
| (ii) | 5054 | 4.5 | 2.6 | 12.2 | 7.8 | 0.6 |

* Distorted by the fact that a number of crews were lost because of the weather conditions.

2. *"The Strategic Air Offensive Against Germany"*.
3. See Glossary for descriptions.

# Appendix II

# Gee

GEE was the brainchild of Mr R.J. Dippy of TRE.[1] He put forward the idea in 1937 and was given the authority to develop it in 1940. The system was based on the fact that the time taken by radio pulses to travel between a transmitter and a receiver can be measured with very high accuracy. When the pulses are transmitted simultaneously from two ground stations, the difference in time taken by them to reach a receiver in an aircraft can be measured; a series of time lags can then be calibrated and displayed on a cathode ray tube. Points having the same difference in range from two fixed positions (A and B in **Fig 13**), known as the constant path difference (c.p.d.), form a parabolic curve round the point with the shortest range. The exception is that when there is no difference in range the points form a straight line: the perpendicular bisector of the line jointing the two points (C and D, **Fig 13**). If A and B are ground stations the time lag series can be married to a corresponding c.p.d. series on a map (the ground) and the navigator can calculate which specific line he is on, a position line.[2]

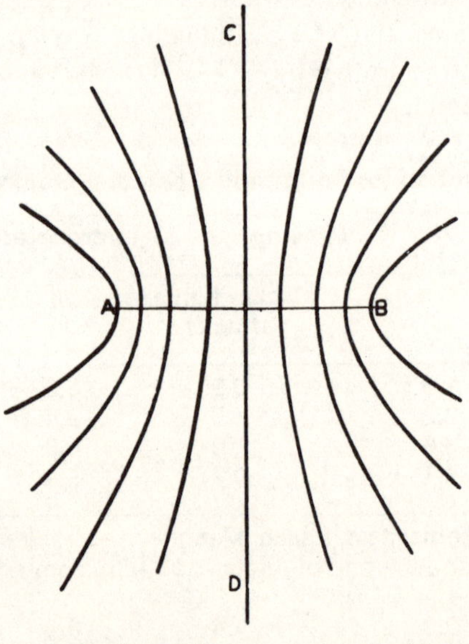


**Figure 13:** A family of hyperbolae formed from curves of constant path difference between two transmitters, A and B. CD is the perpendicular bisector of the two points.

1. Telecommunications Research Establishment.
2. Saward in *The Bomber's Eye* illustrates all c.p.d. as straight; unfortunately this is not true. Unfortunately, because the same degree of accuracy would then be maintained over the whole range, instead of decreasing as the distance from the stations increased.

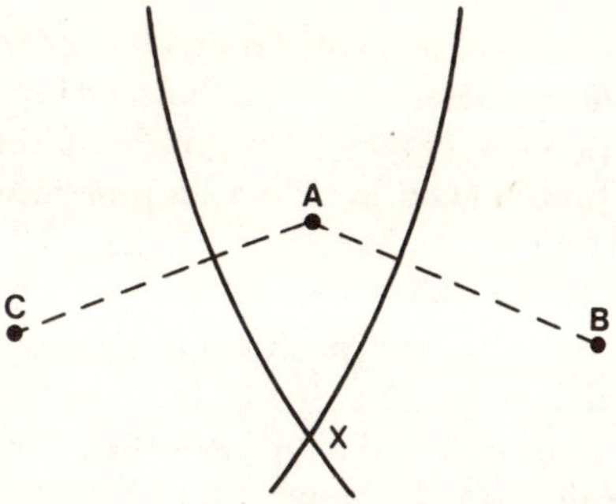


**Figure 14:** A B & C are the stations. × is the position of the observer where the hyperbolae intersect.

Two other stations operating in a similar manner on a similar scale would produce a similar series. If this second series overlapped the first on the map, and both pairs were projected onto a cathode ray tube at the same time, then the navigator could calculate two lines of c.p.d. simultaneously. The aircraft's position would be at the intersection of the two position lines on the map; in navigator's jargon he would have got a "fix" (**Fig 14**).

In practice three not four stations, a master and two slaves, were used. The master transmitted twice as many pulses as the slaves in the sequence ABAC. In order to make identification easy the A pulse preceding the C pulse was made double (**Fig 15**). The slave stations were sited approximately 80 miles from the master at an angle of 120°, with the master at the apex.[3] The two sets of c.p.d. lines then formed a **G**rid, from which the term *Gee* came, or a lattice, as the special maps were called. The angle at which c.p.d. lines intercepted was important because the nearer it was to a right angle the more accurately the co-ordinates could be plotted. The three stations were called a *Gee* chain.

The accuracy of the equipment, and ultimately the fix, depended on the time lag. The timing of the signals was thus of paramount importance, and for this purpose a highly accurate oscillator was fitted into the master. As the signal from the master was used to trigger the slave signals, it follows that, provided the master was "spot on", they would be too. An oscillator with a frequency adjustment was fitted in the aircraft set. If

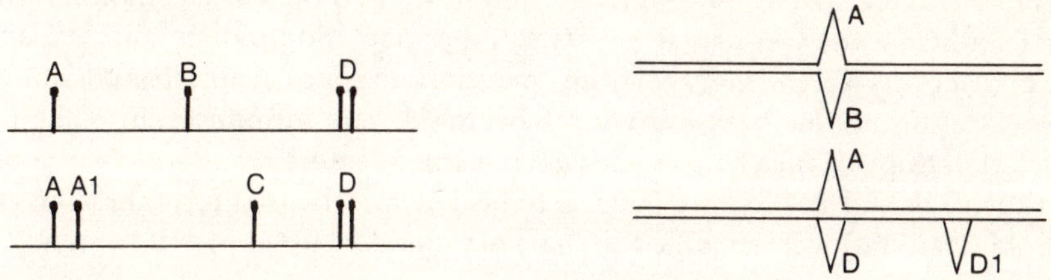


**Figure 15a:** Pulses as seen on *Gee*. **Figure 15b:** Pulses as seen on expanded time scale.

3. Webster and Frankland, in *Strategic Air Offensive Against Germany 1939–1945*, state that the base was approximately 200 miles in length. This would have put the slave stations either in the sea or in enemy territory.

the aircraft receiver was out of phase with the ground the pulses on the cathode ray tube would drift. By adjusting the frequency they could be held for a short time (long enough to take a fix), and so the supreme accuracy of the ground stations was maintained. This above all else turned *Gee* from a good idea to a high-precision actuality.

The operation of *Gee* was so simple that it was nicknamed the "Goon Box," because "any goon" could operate it accurately. Broadly speaking, the box showed three static blips on a cathode ray tube screen, one on the top line and two on the bottom; these were the A pulses. There were two wandering blips, the B and C pulses, which, by twiddling knobs, the navigator had to line up with their corresponding A pulses and persuade them to remain still. Then, by tripping a switch, the pulses were frozen. After noting the exact time the navigator could then read off the co-ordinates at leisure. A skilled operator could get a fix and plot the co-ordinates in less than a minute.

It was possible to home onto a target or base by first setting up the co-ordinates on the set and flying until both sets of pulses came into line. The most accurate method of carrying out this manoeuvre was to make one of the lattice lines the track, and fly along it until the aircraft was home. This system was used over France in 1944 when Bomber Command were attacking enemy positions close to Allied troops.

In wartime *Gee* had three snags: it could be jammed, the range was limited, and distance did not lend enchantment. The last remark needs expanding. Accuracy decreased with distance because the c.p.d. lines became further apart and the angle of cut more acute (**Figs 16 and 17**). As the aircraft travelled away from the stations the pulses shrank until only the heads were visible on the calibrated scale. At the same time they became increasingly emaciated, making them difficult to identify and read. So the maximum range, put at between 350 and 400 miles, was entirely visual and varied enormously from navigator to navigator.

By mid-1941 three transmitting stations had been erected and a few hand-made sets constructed. No 115 Squadron, operating Wellingtons, was selected to try it operationally, and on August 11–12, 1941, two aircraft from the squadron navigated to München Gladbach in the Ruhr, using the equipment successfully. Hanover was the next target chosen, and this seemed to be the limit of the range. The reports of the crews were so enthusiastic that Bomber Command decided to give it the highest priority.

For navigators who had struggled with astro-fixes, radio bearings and dead reckoning on met forecast winds it was the end of a nightmare. The Air Staff were aware that it was possible to jam the signals but estimated that it would be at least six months after capturing a set before the German scientists could design and produce suitable jammers. The existing sets were withdrawn from operations to guard against the possibility of the enemy capturing one prematurely. "J beams"[4] were introduced to make the enemy think that this was the new miracle which had made the navigators smile again, and Air Ministry placed an order for 500 sets to be delivered by the end of the year. All new operational aircraft were modified so that they could be fitted with it as standard equipment.

Despite the priority given to *Gee*, only 150 aircraft had been equipped by the end of February 1942. To guide the less fortunate crews to the target the *Shaker*[5] and *Sampson*[6]

4. See Glossary.
5. See Glossary.
6. See Glossary.

techniques were devised and the general instructions were sent out to Groups on February 21. The *Shaker* plan was for 20 selected Wellington crews equipped with *Gee* to act as Illuminators. The force would be divided into five waves, each with its own Illuminators, 8 for the first wave and 3 each for the following waves. The Illuminators, each carrying 12 bundles of flares, would home onto the target and drop their flares at 10-second intervals on the upwind side. The Target Markers, also selected crews and equipped with *Gee*, would follow at the rate of 2 per minute. They would be carrying an incendiary load and, it was hoped, they would start a concentrated area of fire to give the followers a good aiming point for their HE bombs.

The *Sampson* technique was in many ways similar to Bennett's *Wanganui*:[7] when the target was cloud-covered the bombers dropped their loads by using the flares as an aiming point.

To test the flare technique (not *Sampson* or *Shaker*) 235 aircraft without *Gee* were sent to the Renault works at Billancourt near Paris on March 3–4, 1942, and then twice to the Matford factory at Poissy. True, the targets were only lightly defended and crews were able to attack from heights below 6,000 feet, yet these attacks were so successful that there were high hopes for the 211 heavies, 82 with *Gee*, that were sent to Essen on March 8–9.

If Harris had hoped to put Baron Krupp out of business he must have been a very disappointed man. Krupp's fire service had little to do as only one or two stray sticks of bombs fell within the boundaries of the huge complex. Bomber Command attacked Essen eight times during March and April using the *Shaker* technique, but no worthwhile concentration was achieved. On March 25, for example, most of the followers reported dropping their bombs into a healthy-looking fire, but PRU cover showed hundreds of craters around the decoy fire site at Rheinburg, many miles away from the city centre.

*Gee* did ensure that more aircraft reached the target area, but its accuracy at 300 miles from the ground station was insufficient to locate an aiming point, and pinpointing through the Ruhr's industrial haze had always been a non-starter. Outside the Ruhr its success was more marked: attacks on Cologne (March 13), Lübeck (March 28) and on Rostock on four consecutivie nights from April 23 to 26 caused extensive damage, particularly to the ports. On June 25 the *Sampson* technique had its most notable success when Bremen was attacked through 10/10ths cloud. Crew morale was high, and gone was the nightmare of arriving back over England short of petrol and lost. Command might have been disappointed with results in the Ruhr, but, taking all the attacks into account, the Butt Report was now history.

On August 4 crews returned from Essen with long faces. They had encountered interference on *Gee* from the Dutch coast. The signals were enveloped in what looked like long, wavy grass, which got thicker further inland until it completely blotted them out. Jamming had begun earlier than expected. Besides the wavy grass, a form of cross-hatching or trellis was used, followed later by a combination of the two.

The boffins spent many sleepless nights trying to find some way of filtering out the jamming. Filters were strapped onto existing sets and were incorporated in the Mk II *Gee* sets which made their debut in February 1943. By the end of March 1943 over half

---

7. See Appendix IV.

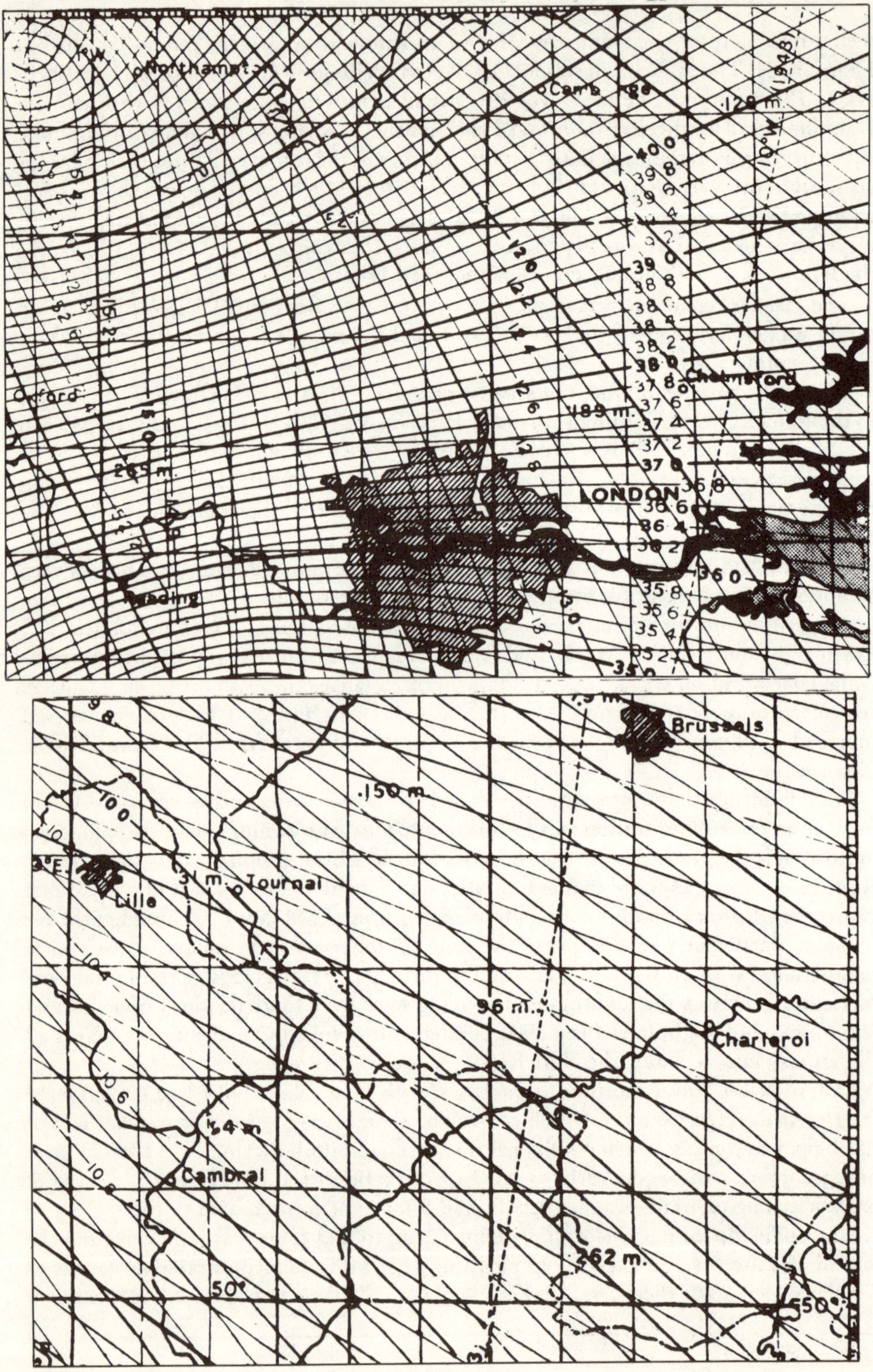
Northampton
Camb
128 m.
Oxford
Chelmsford
189 m.
265 m.
LONDON
Reading
Brussels
.150 m.
Tournai
Lille
31 m.
96 m.
Charleroi
54 m
Cambrai
262 m.
50°

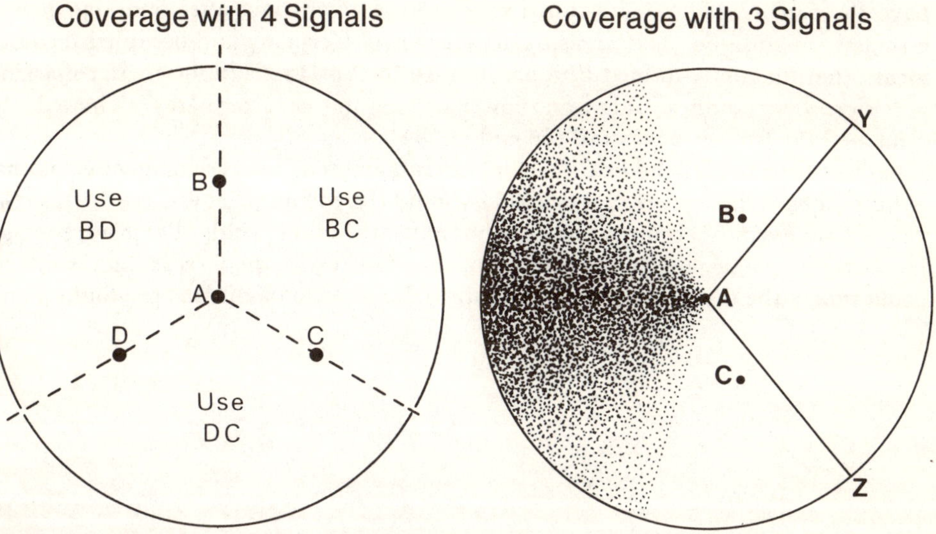


**Figure 18:** The accuracy of a fix depends upon the angle of cut of the hyperbolae. With three stations (ABC) segment YAZ gives the best fixes. The shaded area gives poor fixes. With four stations (ABCD) the coverage is good throughout the 360°.

of the front-line aircraft were fitted with it. The anti-jamming devices worked but had a catastrophic effect on the signals, which just disappeared. The Mk II had three wavelengths but, as with *Knickebein*[8], relief was short-lived. The problem was not overcome until the jamming stations were overrun by the troops. Ground stations were later set up on the Continent, which was indeed fortunate because the night fighters were using H2S to home onto the bombers.

Two more chains, Northern and Southern, were introduced. The Southern chain was useful over France and was used on D-Day by the invasion fleet. Often over Germany one pulse from the Southern chain would be strong enough to use with one from the Eastern chain, and so a "running fix" could be obtained. Eventually five chains were set up in England so that the whole country was accurately covered, and a third slave (a D pulse) was added to cover areas of poor definition (**Fig 18**). The accuracy of this *Gee* combined with the speed and ease with which a simultaneous fix could be obtained, made it a firm favourite with all navigators.

Although *Gee* had the scalps of Lübeck, Rostock and the "1,000" raids on its belt, its indifferent performances in Germany's industrial heart (the Ruhr) more than counter-balanced these successes. Before the German jamming started it was realised that to

8. A German navigational aid which, after it was jammed by the British, was operated on an increased number of channels in an unsuccessful effort to overcome the problem.

**Fig 16** (top): Lattice chart of an area north of London. The angle of cut is excellent and, combined with the closeness of the lattice lines, small errors have a minimal effect on the accuracy of the fixes. **Fig 17** (bottom): A comparable area over Belgium, where the lattice lines are further apart and the angle of cut more acute, so that small errors would result in inaccurate fixes.

have the target positively identified was a great advantage: after jamming it was essential. In addition, its decreasing accuracy over Germany and occupied territory meant that the newly formed PFF had to turn to *Oboe* and H2S for greater marking precision. Because these aids were slower coming into service than anticipated, *Gee* remained the front-runner until the end of 1942.

*Gee* was used in all Bomber Command aircraft and remained the main navigational aid throughout the war. H2S was of no use until the enemy coast was reached, so *Gee* was always the most accurate means of obtaining the initial winds. These were vitally important to a navigator because by comparing them with the forecast met winds he could replan the rest of the flight, using the differences to modify his pre-flight plan.

# Appendix III

# H2S

THE Butt Report[1] highlighted the urgent need for accurate navigational aids to ensure that the bombers reached their targets and identified them. In response the boffins first produced *Gee* and later *Oboe*, but both of these devices had range limitations and could be jammed. *Gee*'s range problem meant that the signals shrank and became emaciated, while the accuracy decreased as the distance from the ground station increased.[2] When jammed, the pulses just disappeared behind the jamming signals, which became stronger the deeper the penetration into enemy territory. *Oboe* signals travelled in straight lines, so the beams had to be angled skywards to counteract the earth's curvature. *Oboe*'s effective range and the aircraft's ceiling were irrevocably linked.

*Oboe* could have been used for navigation but because of its supreme accuracy as a blind bombing device it was used solely for this purpose. Moreover, the limited number of aircraft (one) which could be controlled by a station at any particular time made it unsuitable for a force. So the boffins were asked to produce a navigational aid, preferably unjammable, to operate beyond *Gee* range. It was hoped that the new system's signals would be clear enough to enable the Pathfinder Force to pinpoint within the target area.

As early as 1939 Dr E.G. Bowen had navigated blindly using an AI (air interception) set, but because of the Phoney War only those reports with a "Defence" heading received attention, and the remainder were filed away. A similar report in February 1940 by Professor P.M.S. Blackett pointed out that ASV (Air-to-Surface Vessel) radar picked up coastlines and rivers, but this too was filed away. When the SOS went out from the Air Staff the Telecommunication Research Establishment was able to turn to these reports and use them as a basis for experimentation.

On November 1, 1941, a Blenheim carrying a 9cm AI aerial angled downwards confirmed that objects beneath the aircraft gave reflections of differing intensity on the oscilloscope in the aircraft. Water, being a poor reflector, appeared dark; land appeared lighter; and built-up areas were distinguishable, and even their shape could be made out.

Many of the techniques used in GCI were adapted for H2S – one of the main ones was the rotating beam – and with the development of microwaves it was now possible to make an aerial small enough to be carried in an aircraft. It was also realised that an airborne GCI system would give better results than adaptations of either AI or ASV.

When synchronised with a timebase a rotating scanner sending narrow vertical beams would give a display on a CRT.[3] The echoes would appear on the screen as

1. See Glossary.
2. See Appendix II.
3. Cathode ray tube oscilloscope.

pulses, and, if they were combined with an afterglow to maintain them until the scanner had made a full revolution, a complete picture, called a PPI (Plan Position Indicator), would be built up. Every point on the ground within range would correspond to a unique point in the picture, producing a radar map of the ground. With the aircraft at the centre of the screen, a true relative position (a bearing and distance) could be calculated.

TRE proudly informed Air Staff: "The H2S system offers the likelihood of successful target identification and accurate location with some possibility of selective bombing within the area." Unfortunately the true meaning of "some possibility" was overlooked, much to the discomfort of PFF when H2S came into service.

The British or, if one wished to be generous, the Allies, were far ahead of the Germans in the development of centimetre radar and the Chiefs of Staff were naturally keen to maintain the lead. Two tuneable valves, the klystron and the magnetron, were mainly responsible for this, and although the Germans knew of the former it was believed, correctly, that they had no knowledge of the latter.

A bitter argument[4] began when TRE wanted permission to use the magnetron valve for H2S. The klystron had given disappointing results in trials and it also tended to have a short operational life. The latter was only an inconvenience on the ground, but TRE considered it an unacceptable hazard in the air, where the valve could not be replaced. By contrast the magnetron was more powerful, an so would give better definition. It would be more reliable because it was practically indestructible (even when detonated it retained sufficient form to be reconstructed by the German scientists). This proved to be one of the main arguments for those who opposed its use in the new project: the first H2S aircraft to be shot down over enemy territory would make the Germans aware that the British now had a second valve, and they would soon find out that it was superior. This was the line followed by the Navy members of the Chiefs of Staff. The magnetron was already in use in ASV and its extra power was proving invaluable in spotting U-boats. The Navy members wished to keep it exclusively for ASV sets, reasoning that as soon as the Germans shot down a bomber carrying H2S the valve would no longer be secret and the Germans would be able at least to counter it.[5] They also pointed out that Bomber Command too would suffer if the German fighters were able to home onto the H2S sets.[6] The Americans, who at the time considered H2S frivolous, came out against the use of the magnetron and considered that it would give the enemy the secret " on a platter". Those who favoured its use pointed out that it was useless being ahead if the advantage was not exploited.

Eventually its use was grudgingly approved, but then tragedy struck. On June 7, 1942, when one of the experimental Halifaxes crashed into a mountain in Wales, there were no survivors. Six of the small team assigned to the project were on board. Professor P.I. Dee and Dr A.C.B. Lovell took over the project; all their faith and tireless enthusiasm was needed to overcome the many difficulties encountered in its development. Although Blackett had suggested in his report that a radio altimeter should be

---

4. *Oboe* too was delayed because of this same argument.
5. *Naxos* (see Glossary) was later used to help both the Luftwaffe night fighters and U-boats, and *Korfu* (see Glossary) was used to track the bombers on their way to the target.
6. Similarly, *Window* was another example of the Top Brass being scared to use a powerful weapon for fear the enemy might gain some advantage.

used with ASV, for some reason it had not been realised that H2S did not recognise mountains. The crash certainly brought the point into focus.

In spite of serious production difficulties 23 PFF bombers were equipped by the middle of January 1943, and on the 30th crews using H2S ground-marked Hamburg with red TIs for 130 Main Force crews from 1 and 5 Groups. H2S was not an immediate success: many aircraft arrived over the target with sets unserviceable; new ones were slow to reach the squadrons as, at this stage, it was competing with ASV; and the definition over large towns was unacceptably poor. The "possibility" in TRE's earlier forecast was still only a pipe dream. In addition, navigators found the sets difficult to use, and few fixes were accepted unless strongly corroborated by other facts.

Priority was given to serviceability, and once this was achieved the other problems could be attended to. The Mk IIA was fitted with a new aerial to help fill in the gaps in the PPI picture, and some of the "clutter" in the centre was reduced in the Mk IIB model. However, one of the worst problems was that the PPI went blurred when the aircraft banked or took evasive action. The answer was immediate: "Use a roll stabiliser"; the cure was slower to achieve, this conversion not being begun until March 1944.

In June 1943 the Americans, who less than a year previously had so strongly opposed the project, came forward with an offer to manufacture the sets under licence. They had to be content with ASV production and British firms were at last able to concentrate on H2S without fear of being bludgeoned by the Royal Navy.

The real breakthrough came with the introduction of the Mk III (many PFF navigators would disagree that the sets were a great improvement, for some preferred the old sets), which operated in the 3cm band. The change of radio frequency from 9cm to 3cm gave better definition over large towns and for the first time the "possibility" became a probability. This was however not achieved until after the war, because PFF developed new techniques of marking that made it unnecessary to pinpoint the target on the H2S screen. If emphasis is laid on "widely", it is difficult to disagree with Webster and Frankland's[7] conclusion: "H2S was certainly the most widely useful aid to navigation and bomb-aiming which was ever produced for Bomber Command during the war."

7. *The Strategic Air Offensive Against Germany, 1939–1945.*

# Appendix IV

# Methods of marking

**Figure 19:** Blind groundmarking by H2S or Oboe aircraft. The prefix "Musical" was added when Oboe aircraft were responsible for the marking. For Parramatta and Newhaven, to keep the target marked continuously a secondary force (Backers-up) dropped TIs of a contrasting colour.

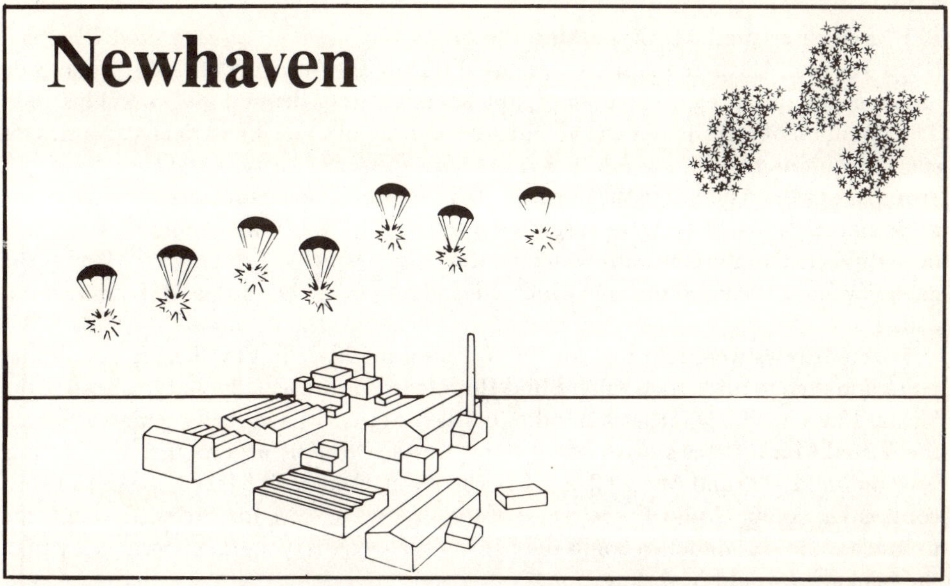


**Figure 20:** Visual marking using Mk XIV bomb-sight, aided at night by a flare force (illuminators).

**Figure 21:** Blind skymarking using TI flares (steady flares emitting contrasting stars) dropped by H2S or Oboe aircraft.

PFF used three methods of marking the target: *Parramatta*, *Newhaven* and *Wanganui* (**Figs 19–21**). All three methods were used during the *Gomorrah* attacks. These code names sound obscure but were simply the home towns of Bennett and two of his staff. The intention of code names was to hide the identity of some secret device. Names for special equipment – *Village Inn*, *Boozer*, *Monica*, *Fishpond*, *Corona*, *Cigar* and *Tinsel*, for example – gave no hint as to the purpose of the devices. Important German towns were given names of fish to keep the target secret. The RAF was full of anomalies: it made little difference to the Germans which method of marking was employed, whereas the enemy would have loved to know which TI colours were to be used, and these were not coded.

Selected crews were required for the *Newhaven* method, first to identify the aiming point and then to mark it visually. Blind Illuminators were usually sent in ahead of the Visual Markers. They released bundles of flares at intervals in the target area to help the Visual Marker crews to see the ground. In the *Gomorrah* attacks this method was used on July 24–25 and August 2–3. The primary markers were backed up with TIs of a contrasting colour. Main Force crews of the first wave were instructed to bomb the primaries, the remainder to bomb the MPI of the secondary markers because by then the primaries would have burnt out.

*Parramatta*, or blind ground-marking, falls into two categories:

(i) When crews using H2S did the initial marking, and

(ii) *Musical*[1] *Parramatta*, when *Oboe* crews were responsible for the primary marking.

In the *Gomorrah* attacks *Parramatta* was used on July 27–28 and 29–30. Blind ground-marking on H2S was never as accurate as visual marking using the Mk XIV bombsight or *Musical* marking using *Oboe*. However, it was efficient enough to lay the foundations for some outstanding attacks beyond *Oboe* range, and certainly enabled targets to be marked when smoke, mist or haze prevented visual identification. "Y" aircraft,[2] providing the H2S equipment was serviceable, dropped their TIs blindly on the target and Backers-up aimed TIs of a contrasting colour[3] at the MPI of all the original markers. Main Force crews were instructed to aim at the centre of the secondary markers and ignore the initial markers unless there were no secondaries burning.

The procedure was different for *Musical* raids. Backers-up aimed visually at the primary markers, which were dropped at intervals throughout the attack. The Main Force was instructed to bomb the primaries and ignore the secondary marking unless no *Oboe* TIs were visible. Highly successful attacks on two Ruhr towns, Essen and Remscheid, were sandwiched between the *Gomorrah* attacks; both these attacks were *Musical Parramatta*s.

Sky-marking or *Wanganui* meant precisely what the name implies: bombing on sky-markers. Flares were dropped blindly by marker crews and fused to burst above the expected height of the cloud in the target area. The Main Force crews were instructed to release their bombs when they had a flare in their bombsights. They were also instructed to make the bombing run on a pre-set course given to them at briefing.

---

1. The adjective *Musical* was used when *Oboe* was employed for primary marking.
2. "Y" aircraft carried H2S.
3. As the colour patterns were changed from time to time for tactical as well as technical reasons the usual colour patterns have been omitted.

*Wanganui* attacks were in the main by far the least accurate of the three because the flares drifted in the wind and it was difficult to aim precisely at a moving target. *Wanganui* did ensure that the bombs fell in the target area and enabled Bomber Command to carry out attacks when targets were cloud-covered. On August 2–3, because there was a possibility of cloud in the area, marker crews were instructed to drop flares if there was more than 6/10ths cloud.

# Appendix V

# PFF crew duties

THERE were eight PFF duties[1], and because the Force acted as a team the success of a raid depended on how well each group performed its allotted task. All crews were expected to be able to execute the various duties, so much so that the duty names were applied to the aircraft and not the crews.[2] However, it is true to say that a certain amount of specialisation did take place during 1944–5, and also that experienced crews were selected to perform certain duties which called for particular skills.

The first role undertaken by crews joining 8 Group was Supporter. Bennett blooded inexperienced crews by sending them to the target with the first group of the marker force to increase the number of aircraft in the target area at the beginning of the raid. Before *Window* the AA defences could engage a small number of aircraft with predicted flak. Even after *Window* it took time and a number of aircraft to swamp the *Würzburg* screens. To be effective crews had to be over the target on time. When so ordered and armed they attacked the ground defences, often with AP (anti-personnel) bombs.

*Windowers*, as the name clearly defines, dropped *Window*, going in ahead of the marker crews. Even a small amount of *Window* made it more difficult for the enemy radar to pick out individual aircraft. The idea was to buy a little peace for the marker crews, who could then make more accurate runs to the aiming point. The Light Night Striking Force (LNSF) was primarily responsible for carrying out this task. Because the Mosquitoes were less susceptible to damage from both flak and fighters they were able, by making spoof attacks on a town in small numbers and by dropping *Window*, to make the Germans believe it was the main target. The prime example of this was on December 3, 1943, when 10 Mosquitoes *Windowed* a false track to Berlin and dropped TIs, making the Germans believe that the capital was the target for the large force of bombers then over the Reich territory. The night fighters were sent to defend the Big City but the bombers turned south to Leipzig and carried out a devastating raid with a loss rate of only 4.4%, an astonishingly low percentage for a deep penetration at that time.[3]

Backers-up, later also called Visual Centerers, had to estimate the MPI of all the primary markers and then, using a Mk XIV bombsight, aim their TIs at this point.[4] Often they were instructed to overshoot the estimated position by one or two seconds in order to counteract the tendency of the Main Force to undershoot. They usually

---

1. Three more – Master Bomber, Deputy Master Bomber and Long Stop – were introduced later.
2. The B Forms, for example, called for 8 Blind Markers, not Blind Marker crews.
3. The previous night on Berlin it had been 9.1%.
4. The exception was when *Oboe* Mosquitoes were dropping the primary markers. The Mosquitoes marked at intervals throughout the attacks. Backers-up aimed at their markers, which were considered to be very accurate.

dropped TIs of a colour contrasting with those of the primary markers. Route markers too were backed up, but in this instance with the same colour.

Route markers dropped TIs at important turning points to enable the Main Force to maintain a stream and keep individual aircraft within the protection afforded by *Window*. Unfortunately the night fighters used them to filter into the stream. Later, as navigation improved, these markers became of more use to the enemy and so were used only sparingly. Land markers were a special type of route marker: if crews made a timed run from these TIs they could never bomb "dummies", because the time factor would be wrong.

Blind Illuminators navigated to the target by H2S and dropped flares blindly to aid the Visual Markers in *Newhaven* attacks. They arrived over the target before the marker crews and dropped bundles of flares at intervals over the target area. Bomb-aimers in the Visual Marker crews would, with the aid of this extra illumination, be able to identify the aiming point, or at least pick up a feature which would give them a bearing to the aiming point.

Primary Visual Markers aimed their TIs visually using the Mk XIV bombsight. They did not release unless the pilot and bomb-aimer made a positive identification. As this was the most exacting of all the duties only selected crews were assigned to the task.

Blind Markers dropped TIs and sky-markers using only their special equipment; if it was unserviceable they retained their markers. H2S was not as accurate as *Oboe*. Moreover, the *Oboe* crews obeyed signals sent out from the peace and quiet of the English countryside, whereas blind bombing using H2S depended on calculations made by an individual while under stress caused by the dangers of being one of only a few aircraft over a well defended target. The defenders gave these few aircraft special attention because they knew that the success or failure of a raid depended on how accurately they marked the target.

Recenterers marked the target blindly using H2S, and usually with a two-second overshoot. They arrived over the target midway through the raid, the idea being that as the Main Force tended to undershoot, if they saw the TIs some distance away they might be encouraged to wait a few seconds longer before they released their cargoes. Recenterers usually carried the same colour of TI as the Backers-up, and if their special equipment was unserviceable they acted in this role, bombing visually. PFF crews were often required to perform more than one role. They also carried bombs and were expected to make a separate run to drop them.

# Index

**V**



**W**



**Z**